Questions and Answers: Countries

Guatemala

A Question and Answer Book

by Mary Englar

Consultant:
Colin M. MacLachlan
John Christy Barr Distinguished Professor of History
Tulane University
New Orleans, Louisiana

Capstone press
Mankato, Minnesota

Fact Finders is published by Capstone Press,
151 Good Counsel Drive, P.O. Box 669, Mankato, Minnesota 56002.
www.capstonepress.com

Library of Congress Cataloging-in-Publication Data
Englar, Mary.
    Guatemala : a question and answer book / by Mary Englar.
    p. cm.—(Fact finders. Questions and answers. Countries)
Summary: "Describes the geography, history, economy, and culture of Guatemala in a
    question-and-answer format"–Provided by publisher.
    Includes bibliographical references and index.
    ISBN 0–7368–4356–6 (hardcover)
    1. Guatemala—Juvenile literature. I. Title. II. Series.
F1463.2.E54 2006
972.81—dc22   2005001169

Editorial Credits

Silver Editions, editorial, design, and production; Kia Adams, set designer; Ortelius Design, Inc., cartographer; Wanda Winch, photo researcher; Scott Thoms, photo editor

Photo Credits

AP Photo/Carlos Lopez, 9

Beryl Goldberg, 21

Brand X Pictures/Philip Coblentz, 1

Corbis/Enzo & Paolo Ragazzini, 12–13; Reuters, 19, 22–23; Sergio Pitamitz, 27

Craig Lovell, 20

Doranne Jacobson, cover (foreground), 18

One Mile Up, Inc. 29 (flag)

Peter Arnold, Inc./Jorgen Schytte 16–17; Martha Cooper, cover (background);
    Sean Sprague, 25

Photo Courtesy of Paul Baker, 29 (coin)

Photo Courtesy of Richard Sutherland, 29 (bill)

South American Pictures/Chris Sharp, 15; Robert Francis, 4; Tony Morrison, 11

The Granger Collection, New York, 7

Artistic Effects:

Photodisc/Siede Preis, 16, 24

1 2 3 4 5 6 10 09 08 07 06 05

Table of Contents

Features

Where is Guatemala?

Guatemala is in Central America. It is a little smaller than Tennessee.

Mountains cover southwest Guatemala. A few mountains are active **volcanoes.** The rich mountain soil is good for farming. Many lakes lie in mountain valleys. Lake Atitlán is a large mountain lake. It covers nearly 50 square miles (130 square kilometers).

A volcano rises along the shore of Lake Atitlán.

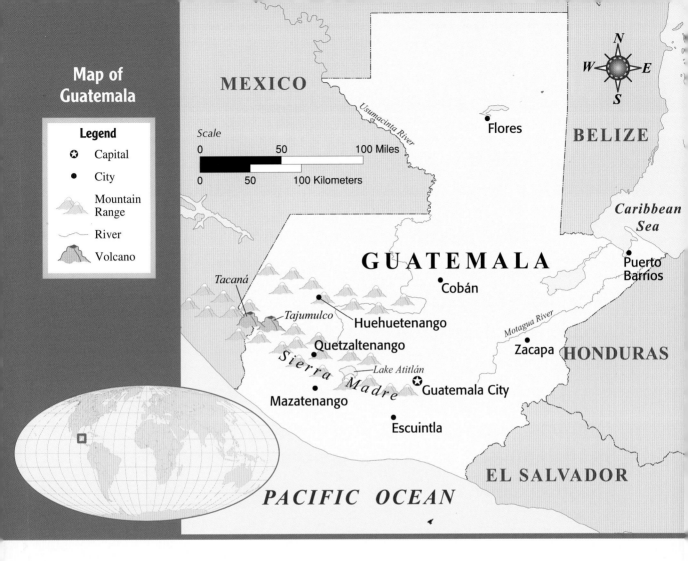

Map of Guatemala

Legend

- ✪ Capital
- ● City
- Mountain Range
- River
- Volcano

Scale

| 0 | 50 | 100 Miles |
| 0 | 50 | 100 Kilometers |

MEXICO

Usumacinta River

● Flores

BELIZE

GUATEMALA

Caribbean Sea

● Cobán

● Puerto Barrios

Tacaná

Tajumulco

● Huehuetenango

Motagua River

● Quetzaltenango

● Zacapa

HONDURAS

Sierra Madre

Lake Atitlán

✪ Guatemala City

● Mazatenango

● Escuintla

EL SALVADOR

PACIFIC OCEAN

The rest of Guatemala is lowlands and coastal plains. The hot Pacific coast has large coffee, sugarcane, and cotton **plantations.** Rain forests cover much of the north.

5

When did Guatemala become a country?

Guatemala became a country in 1821. Before that, Guatemala was a **colony** of Spain. Spanish soldiers came to Guatemala in the early 1500s. They were hoping to find gold.

The Spanish fought the Maya Indians for the land. The Maya had lived in Guatemala for hundreds of years. The Spanish won because they had guns and horses.

Fact!

Guatemala's longest civil war lasted for 36 years. The different sides finally made peace in December 1996.

Spanish soldiers take control of Guatemala in 1523.

In 1821, Mexico declared independence from Spain. At this time, Guatemala decided to join the Mexican Empire. The Mexican Empire broke up in 1823. Guatemala then became an independent country again.

What type of government does Guatemala have?

Guatemala's government is a **constitutional republic**. A national government runs the country. Every four years, the people vote for new leaders. All Guatemalans age 18 and older vote.

The people vote for a president and a vice president. The president is the head of the government. He or she cannot serve for more than four years.

Fact!

Guatemalan soldiers are not allowed to vote. In the past, the army often took over the government.

Some Maya Indians are members of the National Congress.

The people also vote for 158 members of the National Congress. The Congress makes laws. Guatemala's National Congress is similar to the U.S. Congress. The National Congress meets in Guatemala City, the capital of Guatemala.

What kind of housing does Guatemala have?

In large cities, people live in houses or apartment buildings. Some large houses have outdoor gardens.

Many people move to the cities to find good jobs. They build houses with old wood and tin. Their homes do not have water or electricity. These people are very poor.

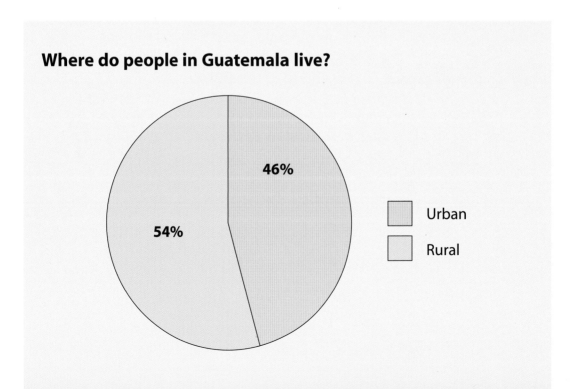

Where do people in Guatemala live?

46%

54%

Urban

Rural

Some Guatemalans live in houses made of wood and thatch.

Most Guatemalans live in small houses. Rural houses have one or two rooms. Houses usually have mud or concrete walls and tin roofs. Some are made from wood and have thatched roofs. Farmers grow vegetables on the land around their houses.

What are Guatemala's forms of transportation?

Guatemala's transportation takes many forms. Cars, taxis, motorcycles, and buses crowd the city streets. Guatemala City has a large airport.

Buses run in the cities and between villages. Rural buses carry people and animals to outdoor markets. The people are used to sharing buses with chickens, goats, and sheep.

Fact!

Guatemala buys old school buses from the United States and Canada. The buses are painted bright colors.

Buses sometimes cause traffic jams in Guatemala City.

Roads connect many places in Guatemala. Paved roads connect the big cities. Most rural roads are dirt. Some small villages do not have roads. People ride horses or walk to their villages.

What are Guatemala's major industries?

Most Guatemalans work in farming. They pick bananas or coffee beans. Farmers also grow corn and beans for their families.

People in cities often work in **service industries.** They work as teachers, government workers, and salespeople.

Tourism also brings many jobs. Tourists come to see the old Mayan cities and to buy **textiles.** Guatemalans work in restaurants and hotels in tourist areas.

What does Guatemala import and export?

Imports	Exports
construction materials	bananas
electricity	clothing
fuel	coffee

Coffee beans, one of Guatemala's exports, are picked when ripe.

Guatemalans also work in factories. Factory workers make furniture and clothing. Others pack sugar, bananas, and coffee to be shipped to other countries.

What is school like in Guatemala?

School is free for all children from grade school through high school. The school year lasts from January to October.

Children ages 7 through 14 should go to school, but many of them cannot. Some families need their children to work in the fields. Many small towns have no schools.

Fact!

More than half of Guatemalan children speak Mayan languages at home. When they go to school, they must learn Spanish to understand the lessons.

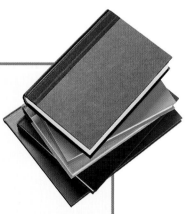

At a village school, children crowd around a table to study.

Guatemala has worked hard to build schools and train new teachers in big cities. Now, most children go to school for at least three years. Only half of the children complete six years of school.

What are Guatemala's favorite sports and games?

Soccer is Guatemala's favorite sport. Soccer is called *fútbol* in Spanish. Guatemala has a national soccer team. It plays against other Central American teams for a chance to play in the World Cup.

Guatemalan boys enjoy playing soccer on a local field.

Martin Machon (right) of the Guatemalan national team fights a Costa Rican player for the ball during a game.

Other popular sports are basketball, baseball, and bicycling. The Tour of Guatemala bicycle race takes place every October. It lasts 12 days. Teams from Guatemala and other countries race for 1,020 miles (1,642 kilometers).

What are the traditional art forms in Guatemala?

Guatemala is known for its traditional clothing. American Indian women make clothes by **weaving** cotton or wool. Each woman makes special blouses for herself and her daughters. No two blouses are exactly the same.

A Guatemalan woman uses a loom to weave traditional cloth.

A marimba band plays at a hotel in Antigua.

Marimba band music is popular in Guatemala. The marimba is a musical instrument that is like a xylophone. The players hit a wooden keyboard with small hammers called mallets. A marimba band may also include other instruments.

What major holidays do Guatemalans celebrate?

Guatemalans celebrate the Day of the Dead on November 1. On this day, people honor family members who have died. They take food to the **cemetery.** They leave food on their family graves. In the town of Santiago, boys build huge kites. They fly the kites over the cemetery. Some kites are 20 feet (6 meters) long.

What other holidays do people in Guatemala celebrate?

Christmas Day
Independence Day
Labor Day
New Year's Day

Maya Indians celebrate the Day of the Dead by flying a giant kite.

Most Guatemalans also celebrate Christian holidays. The week before Easter is called Holy Week. On Good Friday, people use flowers to decorate the street. The colorful flowers look like a carpet.

What are the traditional foods of Guatemala?

Most Guatemalans eat black beans and **tortillas** every day. Beans are mashed, fried, or cooked in soups. Tortillas are made from corn flour and water. Most women bake tortillas before every meal. In the cities, people buy tortillas at a bakery.

Fact!

Hot peppers are called chilies. The longer some chilies are cooked, the hotter they taste.

A Guatemalan woman prepares tortillas for her family.

In rural areas, farmers grow corn and other vegetables for their families. People in the cities like to eat more meat. Along the coast, fish is often cooked with coconut milk.

What is family life like in Guatemala?

More than half of Guatemala's families live in rural areas. Most of these families are American Indian. Everyone in the family must work. Parents work their own land. They may also work on large plantations. After school, children help with the family garden and animals.

What are the ethnic backgrounds of people in Guatemala?

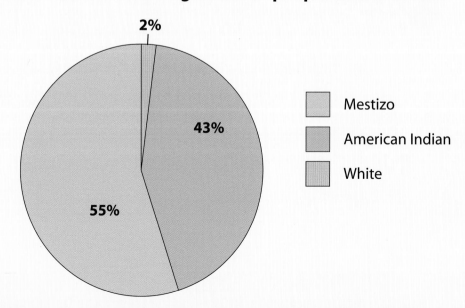

Members of a Guatemalan family gather outside their city home.

In the cities, family life is different for the rich and the poor. Families that have enough money send their children to school. After school, these children play with their friends. But most Guatemalans are poor. Poor children must work to help their parents.

Guatemala Fast Facts

Official name:

Republic of Guatemala

Land area:

41,865 square miles
(108,430 square kilometers)

Average annual precipitation:

52 inches (132 centimeters)

Average January temperature:

62 degrees Fahrenheit
(17 degrees Celsius)

Average July temperature:

66 degrees Fahrenheit
(19 degrees Celsius)

Population:

14,280,596 people

Capital city:

Guatemala City

Languages:

Spanish, about 20 American
Indian languages

Natural resources:

chicle (used in chewing gum),
fish oil, hydropower, nickel, timber

Religions:

Roman Catholic	59%
Protestant	40%
Traditional Mayan	1%

Money and Flag

Money:

Guatemalan money is the quetzal. One quetzal equals 100 centavos. In 2005, one U.S. dollar equaled 7.66 quetzals. One Canadian dollar equaled 6.18 quetzals.

Flag:

The Guatemalan flag has blue and white stripes once used by the United Provinces of Central America. In the center is the quetzal, the national bird of Guatemala. It stands for liberty.

Learn to Speak Spanish

Most people in Guatemala speak Spanish. It is Guatemala's official language. Learn to speak some Spanish words using the chart below.

English	Spanish	Pronunciation
good morning	buenos días	(BWAY-nohs DEE-ahs)
good-bye	adiós	(ah-dee-OHS)
please	por favor	(POR fah-VOR)
thank you	gracias	(GRAH-see-us)
yes	sí	(SEE)
no	no	(NO)
How are you?	¿Cómo estás?	(KOH-moh ay-STAHS)
I'm fine	Bien	(BEE-en)

Glossary

cemetery (SEM-uh-ter-ee)—a place where dead people are buried

colony (KOL-uh-nee)—an area that is settled by people from another country and that is ruled by that country

constitutional republic (kon-sti-TOO-shuhn-uhl ree-PUHB-lik)—a government in which the people elect their leaders and have a written system of laws

plantation (plan-TAY-shuhn)—large farm where coffee, cotton, or bananas are grown

service industries (SUR-viss IN-duh-streez)—businesses that help and take care of customers

textile (TEK-stile)—fabric or cloth that has been woven

tortilla (tor-TEE-yuh)—round, flat bread made from corn or flour

volcano (vol-KAY-noh)—a mountain that sometimes sends out hot lava, steam, and ash

weaving (WEEV-ing)—to make cloth by passing threads over and under each other

Internet Sites

FactHound offers a safe, fun way to find Internet sites related to this book. All of the sites on FactHound have been researched by our staff.

Here's how:
1. Visit *www.facthound.com*
2. Type in this special code **0736843566** for age-appropriate sites. Or enter a search word related to this book for a more general search.
3. Click on the **Fetch It** button.

FactHound will fetch the best sites for you!

Read More

Delgado, Kevin. *Guatemala.* Modern Nations of the World. Farmington Hills, Mich.: Lucent Books, 2005.

Dendinger, Roger E. *Guatemala.* Modern World Nations. Philadelphia: Chelsea House, 2004.

Morris, Neil. *Everyday Life of the Aztecs, Incas & Maya.* Uncovering History. North Mankato, Minn.: Smart Apple Media, 2003.

Shields, Charles J. *Guatemala.* Discovering Central America. Philadelphia: Mason Crest, 2003.

Index

OUT OF HARM'S WAY

Out of Harm's Way tells of Jack Thompson's courageous battle against those who will stop at nothing to poison our children's minds. As a David among Goliaths, he is an example of someone who sees evil for what it is and is not afraid to fight it. It details his spiritual journey and warfare against those who will use any means to profit by degrading and destroying lives.

JAY LOVE
Alabama state representative

Out of Harm's Way tells an incredible story that every American needs to read. Jack Thompson reveals his own journey from skepticism to faith as one of God's chief operatives in the culture wars of our time. Don't miss this fascinating book.

DR. JERRY FALWELL,
Founder and Chancellor
Liberty University

Jack Thompson has written a fascinating account of his experience as a Christian activist challenging the media. He demonstrates beyond a doubt that individuals can make a difference in influencing social policy. Even those who don't agree with all of his beliefs will be impressed by his courage and insight.

EUGENE F. PROVENZO, JR.
Author, Video Kids

American parents who are frustrated by the broadcast filth and dangers of violent video games that their children are exposed to can sleep better at night knowing Jack Thompson is in the trenches fighting for us. He's a crusader in the truest form and *Out of Harm's Way* chronicles his impressive and increasingly-successful battle to return decency and morality to our great nation's households.

MIKE GALLAGHER
Syndicated radio host
Author, Surrounded by Idiots: Fighting Liberal Lunacy in America

Wow! This is a riveting book and, as you read it, you will be thinking that you're glad you're not Jack Thompson. Then, if you're like me, you'll think that maybe you ought to, at least, be like him. Perhaps we have let Jack do the fighting for us for too long. He doesn't shilly-shally about very important matters. Because of this book, I've decided not to shilly-shally either. This is a very important and challenging book. For your sake and the sake of your children and the nation's children, you can't afford not to read it.

STEVE BROWN
Professor, Reformed Theological Seminary

OUT OF HARM'S WAY

JACK THOMPSON

TYNDALE HOUSE PUBLISHERS, INC. CAROL STREAM, ILLINOIS

TYNDALE is a registered trademark of Tyndale House Publishers, Inc.

Tyndale's quill logo is a trademark of Tyndale House Publishers, Inc.

Visit Tyndale's exciting Web site at www.tyndale.com

Out of Harm's Way

Copyright © 2005 by Jack Thompson. All rights reserved.

Cover photo and author photo copyright © 2005 by Brian MacDonald. All rights reserved.

Designed by Luke Daab

Unless otherwise indicated, all Scripture quotations are taken from the *Holy Bible*, New International Version®. NIV®. Copyright © 1973, 1978, 1984 by International Bible Society. Used by permission of Zondervan Publishing House. All rights reserved.

Scripture quotations marked NLT are taken from the *Holy Bible*, New Living Translation, copyright © 1996, 2004. Used by permission of Tyndale House Publishers, Inc., Carol Stream, Illinois 60188. All rights reserved.

Scripture quotations marked NASB are taken from the *New American Standard Bible*, © 1960, 1962, 1963, 1968, 1971, 1972, 1973, 1975, 1977 by The Lockman Foundation. Used by permission.

Library of Congress Cataloging-in-Publication Data

Thompson, Jack, date.

  Out of harm's way / Jack Thompson

    p. cm.

  Includes bibliographical references

  ISBN-13: 978-1-4143-0442-7 (hardcover)

  ISBN-10: 1-4143-0442-0 (hardcover)

  ISBN-13: 978-1-4143-0443-4 (pbk.)

  ISBN-10: 1-4143-0443-9 (pbk.)

    1. Christianity and culture—United States. 2. Mass media—Religious aspects—Christianity. 3. Popular culture—Religious aspects—Christianity. I. Title.

  BR11.C8T477 2006

  261'.0973—dc22

  2005021257

Printed in the United States of America

09 08 07 06 05

5   4   3   2   1

DEDICATION

*To Kayce Steger, Jessica James, and Nicole Hadley, killed on
December 1, 1997, in Paducah, Kentucky, by a video gamer in what
was supposed to be a safe place, your school.*

*When I die, I shall read this book to you in heaven.
It was written for you.*

1/24/10

TABLE OF CONTENTS

David replied to the Philistine [Goliath], "You come to me with sword, spear, and javelin, but I come to you in the name of the LORD of Heaven's Armies—the God of the armies of Israel, whom you have defied. Today the LORD will conquer you, . . . and the whole world will know that there is a God in Israel! And everyone assembled here will know that the LORD rescues his people, but not with sword and spear. This is the LORD's battle, and he will give you to us!"
1 Samuel 17:45-47 (NLT)

INTRODUCTION
GOD LETS GO

Years ago our son, John, reached the age when it was time for him to stop riding his bike with training wheels on it. He had progressed from a tricycle to a two-wheeler, and then to the notion that "Daddy, I want to ride my bike with no training wheels on it, like all the other big boys do."

I have bad knees, resulting from the combination of injuring them in a skiing accident when I was young, running four marathons, and inheriting bad genes, all of which have necessitated three surgeries. How was I going to run alongside Johnny's bike, holding on, gimpy knees and all, as he pedaled and developed his sense of balance? My job would be to catch him or the bike before the inevitable crashes. I knew my knees would scream out—reminding me that the doctors had told me never to run again—but there was no other choice. Daddy would have to gulp ibuprofen to get Johnny into the two-wheel world.

To facilitate my role as human safety net, I created a makeshift handle fashioned from a golf club shaft and grip that I was able to clamp to the frame at the back of the bike. I held on to that handle as Johnny pedaled, and I could grab it if the bike started to go over.

My knees still ached, but at least I had a handle to grab. Still, I hoped the goal would be reached in a matter of days rather than weeks.

So off we went around the block, Johnny with his helmet on, Mommy waving and shouting encouragement from the front door, Daddy's knees aching after only ten steps. *How in the name of heaven am I going to make it around the half-mile block?* I wondered. I'd do it because my son needed me to—that's how.

My right hand held tight to the Golf Pride antidisaster contraption every moment of every pedaled inch. Johnny kept looking over his left shoulder to see if I was there doing just that. He could feel I was there because the bike would not tip over even when he did something that should have made it tip over. But he wanted visual confirmation and assurance of my presence, and Johnny would slow down in order to get it. Once he was satisfied, he would speed up again. *Oh, joy. We're going faster now! Ouch.*

With each day came more journeys around the block using the same system. It wasn't long before I began to take my hand off the grip for a few moments at a time. There was a catch, though. When the hand came off, I needed to keep up my speed to make Johnny think I was still holding on. I didn't want him to become fearful, start overcorrecting, and invariably crash. I wanted him to think I was perfectly and totally in control.

After he had gone a considerable distance with my hand off the saving golf grip, I would say to him, "Johnny, you just went the last hundred feet without my holding on!"

"Really?" he would shriek in a combination of delight and suppressed terror, whereupon he would oversteer and almost crash. He had lost focus and concentration. He had gone, in a moment, from enjoying the ride to fearing the worst; his fear unraveled his confidence. But the longer we practiced, the greater his confidence grew. He was learning to ride a two-wheeler with Daddy there to help him. The moment of truth was coming.

One day the two of us set out on what proved to be the last two-wheeler training day, although I wasn't aware of it at the time. Midway through our half-mile trek, I saw that Johnny was pedaling smoothly, without any wobbles and without checking over his left shoulder to see if Daddy was there. He was immersed in the ride and not on who was with him.

I let go. I didn't give him a push because I didn't want him to know I was no longer right there at his side physically. But my heart was there pounding in his chest. I didn't want him to fall and scrape any square inch of that precious, priceless little body. But I had to give him the opportunity to fall—or to ride.

Once Johnny was a hundred yards away or so, I shouted, "Johnny, you're doing great!" As soon as he heard me the bike wobbled, because he could tell from the sound of my voice that I wasn't a golf-club's distance behind him. The bike wobbled but Johnny did not fall. He made it the rest of the way around the block on his own. I backtracked around the block and hurried to meet him at our home. "Daddy, I can ride my bike on my own!" he squealed.

"You're a big boy now, Johnny. I'm proud of you." I had to turn away so he would not see my tears. I wanted nothing but joy for him in this moment.

A popular saying among many Christians, certainly for as long as I have been one, is "Let go and let God." Although some people might consider it a cliché, it reinforces the truth that human beings should not worry—about anything. The saying, in a way, embodies in shortened form the meaning of this beautiful passage from the Gospel according to Matthew:

> *Look at the birds of the air; they do not sow or reap or store away in barns, and yet your heavenly Father feeds them. Are you not much more valuable than they? Who of you by worrying can add a single hour to his life?*
>
> *And why do you worry about clothes? See how the lilies of the field grow. They do not labor or spin. Yet I tell you that not even Solomon in all his splendor was dressed like one of these. If that is how God clothes the grass of the*

field, which is here today and tomorrow is thrown into the fire, will he not much more clothe you, O you of little faith? So do not worry, saying, "What shall we eat?" or "What shall we drink?" or "What shall we wear?" For the pagans run after all these things, and your heavenly Father knows that you need them. But seek first his kingdom and his righteousness, and all these things will be given to you as well. Therefore do not worry about tomorrow, for tomorrow will worry about itself. Each day has enough trouble of its own. Matthew 6:26-34

I have been a "culture warrior," fighting the entertainment industry for more than seventeen years now. The seemingly most apt, and thus the most searing and hurtful criticism of me, has come from my fellow Christians who have said to me in one form or another, "If you believe in God and His sovereignty and His power, then why have you taken it upon yourself to confront the culture when He, in fact, is in control?" The question also is posed to me this way: "Shouldn't you just concentrate on sharing the gospel, and let the gospel take care of the world?"

Those are good questions, hard questions, questions I have asked myself on more than one sleepless night after more than one battle-filled day. But the answer that the questioners want—that I should "let go and let God"—is not the right answer.

The fact is, God makes it very clear that we are to be "salt and light" in the world. The body of Christ is made up of different members, each of us having different talents and different spiritual gifts, and each of us called to act upon them, even if they seem odd to others in the body. I had a pastor once who told me that it was inappropriate for me to inject Christ into social issues. It would have never occurred to me to say to that pastor that God had made a mistake when He called *him* to his preaching ministry. God, I could see, was using him as salt and light in a way that was unique to him.

At some point in my early days as a Christian, I said to God, "I want You to use me to change the world." It was not a prayerful expression of grandiosity, self-conceit, or megalomania. It was a humble prayer, at least that's how it felt to me. I wanted God to use me. I didn't tell Him how I wanted to be used. I just said, in effect, it might be time for me to do something with my faith. It was a precursor of what I would one day hear from my own son: "Daddy, I want to ride my bike with no training wheels on it, like all the other big boys do."

Did I "let go and let God," or did God let go of me, in a sense, so I could pursue what today feels like a ministry? Something happened to me in the middle of the block of my life that God was taking me around. He let go and gave me exactly what I had begged Him to do—to let me, one day, be a "big boy." I wanted to do something exciting. He heard my prayer and answered it.

God did this with His precious Son, Jesus. God the Father let go of God the Son and sent Him around the block on His own. That was not easy for God. It was probably the hardest thing God had ever done. God the Father did not want one square inch of that precious boy's skin cut, but He knew it would be terribly cut.

God's faith was so much more than mine has ever been when it comes to my son's safety, or anything else for that matter. God "let go." I'm sure God the Father felt great pain as He allowed the incarnation of the Son, but I think there was joy and pride as well, just as I felt when my son sailed off on that bike on his own. Would I have wanted to keep my son safe if it meant I would never have felt the joy that comes from knowing I had prepared my son, in this little thing, to try it on his own? No, and neither would God, in whose image we are created, have been fully God without knowing this sorrow, while at the same time feeling the pride of a Father as His Son traveled away from safety.

In the Academy Award–winning movie *Chariots of Fire*, there is a memorable scene where the main character, Eric Liddell, is shown standing on the heath of his native Scotland. His sister, Jenny, has just seen him outrun his competitors in a race. Jenny is troubled by what she has seen, because she realizes that Eric is a talented runner. But Eric, she believes, has been called to be a missionary. She thinks that competitive running is a worldly distraction that is getting in the way of the mission field and that Eric is ignoring God's call. So Jenny asks her brother, "Eric, why do you run?" It's a simple question, albeit a loving rebuke. Eric Liddell, with a wry smile on his face, responds the only way he can: "God made me fast, and when I run, I feel His pleasure."

Many Christians in America do not understand and are troubled by the fact that some of us fight with the world, with its entertainment, with its assault upon our children. To them, it would seem better and more loving for us culture warriors to just preach the gospel and let God take care of everything else. To those who counsel me "to let go and let God," I have an answer that has inconvenienced me far more than you'll ever know: God gave me this mission, and when I act upon it, I feel His pleasure.

Eric Liddell, of course, went on to witness the power of God's grace when he ran and took a gold medal at the 1924 Olympics in Paris.

I couldn't run an athletic race such as Liddell ran in Paris because of my knees. But when I use the skills and talents God has given me to fight in this culture war, I feel His pleasure. Please come along to hear about the course He planned for me. And as you do, may you, too, feel His pleasure.

1

TO THE GATES OF HELL

On October 6, 2004, shock jock Howard Stern threw in the towel. He sat before his microphone in his New York studio at WXRK 92.3 FM and told the millions listening to his syndicated show via Viacom's Infinity Broadcasting that he was done with broadcasting on the public airwaves.

"I'm going to satellite radio because the FCC has made it impossible for me to continue doing what I do, a pornographic radio show. They have tied my hands. I can't give you, my fans, what you want and deserve," he said. "Starting January 1, 2006, I'll be on Sirius, and the FCC won't be able to touch me. Broadcast radio is dead."

Howard Stern then turned his wrath on me. "There's this lunatic lawyer in Miami who got me off the air in South Florida, off all Clear Channel stations across the country. One man did that. That's how insane this has gotten."

I knew I was the "lunatic lawyer" to whom Stern was referring. I had been the one who convinced Clear Channel to dump him from all of its stations. I had been the one to secure a $495,000 FCC fine against *The Howard Stern Show*, all in the months leading up to this moment.

Seventeen years of battling with other shock jocks over the same issues—the portrayal of women as objects to be humiliated, the distribution of pornography to children, all in violation of state and federal laws—had culminated in the self-proclaimed "King of All Media" declaring victory in order to hide his defeat.

His new name should be Coward Stern. Although he claimed this fight was all about his freedom of speech as an American, here he was fleeing the public airwaves, unwilling to fight for his version of the First Amendment. Howard Stern was blaming everyone but Howard Stern. This moment had been worth the seventeen years of effort and pain I had gone through to get here. It didn't get much better than this, but at times, it had been much worse.

⚠

Life hadn't always been this complicated. In fact, it had started out rather simply. I first met Patricia Halvorson when we were fellow classmates at Vanderbilt Law School in Nashville, Tennessee. On May 15, 1976, we missed our graduation ceremony to get married in her hometown of Hudson, Wisconsin. I'm certain we had more fun at our ceremony than our classmates did at theirs. Our honeymoon was spent pulling a U-Haul, which was attached to the bumper of our Pontiac, to Miami, Florida, a distance of 1,800 miles.

We rented a little concrete block home on Key Biscayne, with the rent reduced thirty dollars to $220 per month because I agreed to mow the grass. Few people in Miami mowed their own yards then, even fewer now. But on the west side of Cleveland, Ohio, where I grew up in the 1950s and 1960s, everyone mowed his own yard. Midwestern habits are hard to shake.

That first Miami summer, Patricia and I studied for the Florida bar exam, which we had to pass in order to practice law. My wife had a job lined up, having served the summer before as a clerk in an old, respected Miami firm. The partners liked her so much they offered her a position as an associate when she graduated the next year. Patricia had worked her way through college as a waitress, taking out student loans when she had to. She would eventually become the first woman partner in that firm.

I hadn't found a job yet, but I wasn't concerned. I knew that once I passed the bar, I would be sure to find something.

It's not as if I hadn't already had opportunities. In my final year of law school I had flown from Nashville to Miami during Thanksgiving break to interview for a job I hoped to begin upon graduation. Florida has eleven judicial circuits, each one with its own local prosecutor called a state attorney. I wanted to begin my law career as a prosecutor, so I arranged an interview with the office of Dade County State Attorney Richard Gerstein.

When I arrived I was told I would be interviewed by Gerstein's first assistant, a woman by the name of Janet Reno.

I walked into Janet Reno's office and immediately noticed how tall she was. I'm six feet, or at least I was then, and I had to look up pretty steeply to make eye contact. I extended my hand and said, "Nice to meet you, Ms. Reno."

"Nice to meet you, too, Mr. Thompson. Have a seat."

Ms. Reno, wearing a blue, flower-print dress, pushed her chair backwards, sat down, and put one foot and then the other on her desktop blotter. Her feet were apart, pointed at me, toes up, without either the ankles or legs crossed. The only thing crossed at that moment in that office were my fingers, hoping that Janet Reno would not do the whole interview in this, shall we say, posture.

Then it got worse. The interview lasted about ten minutes, roughly half of which were consumed by a lawyer named Hank Adorno (who became Reno's first assistant when she was appointed Dade County State Attorney upon Richard Gerstein's resignation in 1978) repeatedly running in and out of her office, asking her questions about cases.

I was confused. I was a student with next to no spending money. I had bought a ticket to fly down to Miami to interview for this job, but

Janet Reno couldn't give me ten uninterrupted minutes of discourse—and even that had to take place between her shoes as if they were conversational goalposts. I felt that I was being intimidated rather than interviewed. But why?

I became even more confused by Ms. Reno's line of questioning. She didn't ask me anything about my academic or professional background. She didn't seem to care whether or not I was prepared to be a prosecutor. Instead, Janet Reno posed three hypothetical crime investigations to me in which the police had acted improperly. She wanted to know if I agreed that the cases should be thrown out. I think she was fishing to find out if I shared her *ideology* about how to run a criminal justice system. I considered each scenario, and told her that in all three of these hypothetical cases, the police had acted in ways that were defensible and that the prosecutions could be salvaged.

"Are you ever skeptical of the police version of a case, Mr. Thompson?"

"Not generally," I said. "Seems to me that's the criminal defense lawyer's job."

Wrong answer.

Years later I would read one account of Janet Reno's life that helped me to understand what I couldn't have known then. Sandy D'Alemberte, Reno's mentor at the powerful law firm of Steel, Hector & Davis, tells how he had lined up a job for her as a prosecutor in Gerstein's office. When D'Alemberte suggested to Reno that she should go work in the state attorney's office, she shouted, "Why would I want to do that? I hate the police!" I believe that she wound up taking the job for that very reason, since prosecutors who hate the police can frustrate them in their jobs far more effectively than a defense lawyer can. The Trojans had used that horse for a reason.

Janet Reno's parents had been reporters for the two newspapers in town, the *Miami Herald* and the *Miami News*, the latter now out of business. Her father, Robert Reno, was the police beat reporter for the *Herald*. Maybe she got her enmity for the "thin blue line" from that parental vocation.

Indeed, years later, in a *Miami Herald* profile of Kathy Fernandez Rundle, Assistant Dade County State Attorney, her boss, State Attorney Reno is described as a "frustrated social worker."[1]

Boy, did I learn that on that November morning in 1975 in Janet Reno's office.

I was relieved, after my ten minutes of pain were up, to get out of Reno's "garment district," but I was more than a little dismayed that a gung-ho, lock-up-the-bad-guys fellow like me couldn't work in the prosecutor's office in Miami. I liked the police. But I think that's why Janet didn't like me.

Oh well, I thought. *I won't have to fool with her again.*

Wrong again.

⚠

I went into the July 1976 Florida bar exam more confident than my wife. I've always been confident about everything, even when I have no reason to be. But fear is an appropriate thing to feel for anyone taking a bar exam because, as Yogi Berra once said, "Your whole future is ahead of you." My wife studied harder than I did. She did not want to fail the exam. I *knew* I would not fail it.

We got our bar results in September. My wife passed; I failed.

I was crushed, embarrassed, and angry at myself. What a great way to start a marriage! Your wife can capitalize on three years of law school and practice law, and you can't. Nice going.

My parents had always told me that I was special, that I was bright, that there was nothing I could not do. And they always selflessly gave me the means by which to prove them right.

Now I had let them down. I had let my wife down too. It was worse than a bad dream—it was a really bad reality.

This was the first time in my life that something had felt like failure. It certainly was the first time *I* felt like a failure in anything significant. What was I going to do? Once the shock wore off, I began to rationalize.

I blamed others, of course, as well as other "things"—certainly not myself.

I told my wife that I didn't want to live in Florida anymore, certainly not Miami. I hated Miami—the people weren't friendly, and it was too hot. I accused her: "You're the one who wanted to come to Miami. You're the reason I'm in this horrible state whose bar exam is unfair." Fully half of the people who took the exam that year had failed it, which convinced me that the exam itself must have been unfair. Anything to hang my hat on other than my own mistake.

I wanted out of Florida, out of a lot of things, maybe even out of the marriage that had brought me here. I loved my wife, but I loved the feeling of invincibility even more.

Things continued on this downhill course until Patricia said to me, "Jack, you're understandably depressed and frustrated. Why don't we go to church this Sunday for a little bit of encouragement? I miss church, and you promised me when we were engaged that you and I would go when we got married."

"Fine. We'll go to church." *It will be stupid,* I thought, *and that will be the end of that obligation.*

We had been married in the Presbyterian church right on my in-laws' street in Wisconsin, so it was natural to walk to Key Biscayne Presbyterian Church, a mere two hundred yards away from our rented home. I felt better about it when I realized that this was the church Richard Nixon attended when he was president. The "Southern White House" had been right there on the same street as the church. The helipad at which Navy One had landed was one of the first things I went to see when we arrived there in the spring. Looking at it, I remembered holding a sign for Nixon on my elementary school playground on Election Day, November 8, 1960. Nine years old and already part of what Hillary Clinton later called a "vast right-wing conspiracy."

That Sunday we went to church, all dressed up the way folks at that time looked when they went to church in the Midwest. I wore a coat and tie, despite it being a typical 90/90 Miami day: 90-degree heat and 90 percent humidity.

When we arrived, I took note of three remarkable things. First it was a church in the round. The minister's pulpit was located in the middle of the sanctuary with the choir behind him and the congregation wrapped around him on the other three sides. *Wow*, I thought. *This looks like the summer theater in Canal Fulton, Ohio, that my parents used to take my sister and me to.* More importantly, there was no place to hide in the back of the church. Rats.

The next remarkable thing was that, as far as I could tell, I was the only person under forty with a tie on, let alone a coat. The older worshippers were in what I, and obviously they, thought of as their traditional Sunday best, but nobody else was.

The majority of the younger attendees were dressed casually—in golf shirts, beach sandals, and even shorts. *Shorts!* I had never seen such a thing in a church during a Sunday worship service anywhere. But this was Miami, which at the time was running a national tourism ad that said: "Come to Miami. The rules are different here." I'll say.

But even though this was Miami, I wondered if I had wandered into a hippie commune. No, I told myself, this is a Presbyterian church. Presbyterians aren't hippies. Richard Nixon, although raised a Quaker, went here, for heaven's sake! Nixon wouldn't go to a hippie church. He fought with the hippies over the Vietnam War. No, it must just be "casual Sunday" this week. Maybe there is a beachside picnic after church.

And then the third remarkable thing struck me, after I had soaked in the first two visually disconcerting elements of Key Biscayne Presbyterian: the noise. This didn't sound like a sanctuary just before a worship service. This sounded like a restaurant on a busy Saturday night.

People weren't seated in pews whispering to one another in hushed tones. They were standing up to wave and shout greetings at one another across the sanctuary. People were laughing loudly; kids were scurrying; folks were smiling. People were, well, raucous. *What is going on here?* I thought. I didn't like this. Church was supposed to be solemn, like a funeral. Church had always been a place I didn't want to be. Doing something you didn't want to do seemed to be a better way to fulfill a duty.

But there was something intangible in the air—in this place that didn't feel like a church. There was not just noise. There was an immeasurable, mysterious electricity, the kind that is in the air at the very beginning of a football game as the kicker positions the ball on the tee. You can't describe it. It isn't a sound, really, but it's there. You can feel it more than hear it. It is an anticipation that something exciting is about to happen.

So, amid the din and the anticipation, my wife and I sat down a ways from where the preacher would be standing, just in case what felt to me like an impending building explosion might disintegrate the altar. I didn't want to be at ground zero.

We sat down next to a couple who seemed to be about fifteen years older than we were. He had on a coat and tie, so I felt like he possibly represented a little sanity in what seemed like a holy nuthouse.

We smiled at them, but the last thing I wanted to do was *talk* with anyone. Frankly, despite the fact that I had agreed to come to church, I didn't want to give Patricia the opportunity to say, "See, there *are* friendly people in Miami."

Too late for that, however, as this couple, Jim and Marcia Youngblood, asked us if we were visiting the church for the first time. I smiled again wanly, as my wife told them that yes, we had just gotten married in the spring and had come down to Miami to live, having graduated from Vanderbilt.

"Vanderbilt!" they both exclaimed. "Our son Doug goes there. He just loves Nashville. Oh, we're so glad you are here. . . ." The talking continued, I going through appropriate facial expressions, and my wife carrying nearly all of our side of the conversation. I was uneasy with the creeping notion that this couple was genuinely pleasant, genuinely funny, and genuinely pleased we were there. This did not seem like an act to get us to attend and then join the church.

I remember thinking these were the first people I had met in Miami that I might want to see again. I didn't like that feeling; in fact, I hated it.

The service began as the minister, a man by the name of Steve Brown, walked in to take his seat at what one would have to call, in this place, "center stage." Pastor Brown was tall, lanky, balding, his friendly face punctuated by brown eyes.

It proved to be a traditional, fully Presbyterian service. A wonderful choir, wonderful hymns, but a very unusual pastoral prayer just before the sermon. "Father, forgive the preacher his sins, for You know they are many. Let those here see not him, but rather only Your Son, crucified, in whose name we pray. Amen."

A pastor publicly speaking of his sins? That was a new one for me. Maybe this guy, Steve Brown, would have something else strange to say.

I listened as best I could, distracted by my growing confusion. I remember hearing things that rang true but also things that didn't make sense. Grace—what was that?

Pastor Brown's voice was both distracting and appealing at the same time. Part of me was resisting what I was hearing, thinking that maybe I was being hoodwinked into believing his message because he was such an effective communicator. It was the same feeling I had had years before whenever I saw a Billy Graham Crusade on television: I was always struck by the theater of it all, but distrustful of the message.

Steve Brown's voice was the deep voice of a man who could have had a future in broadcasting. What I didn't know at the time was that he had a *past* in broadcasting.

His speaking was nonrepetitive, always to the point. I could not fully grasp his message, but I knew he was getting it across to somebody, because heads were nodding. People were laughing at jokes that were actually funny. Not "pastor joke" funny. I mean *really* funny. Golf course-buddy funny.

He wasn't preaching to fill the hour. He was preaching like a sprinter runs. This was a preacher in a rush to get us somewhere. *That's a switch*, I thought.

He concluded by saying, "You think about that. Amen." I would have liked to, but I wasn't sure what I had heard.

The service was over, and Patricia and I and the Youngbloods stood up. I shook Jim's hand, and Marcia hugged my wife. I believe they said something like "Have a wonderful week. It was so nice to see you two here." I knew I was in trouble. This, although confusing, had been sort of fun. I felt off balance, as if I had stood up too quickly.

We went to church the next Sunday, and it was even more fun. I didn't wear a coat, but I still wore a tie. *After all, I'm from the Midwest*, I thought.

Before the third Sunday rolled around, I called the church to set up an appointment with Steve Brown. I had some questions. I was surprised when his secretary, Cathy, said he would be able to see me the next day.

When I arrived that next day at the door of his study, Steve greeted me with an outstretched hand and a smile that made me feel at home. There was a familiarity here, but not a suffocating embrace that would have made me feel trapped. On a side table was a rendering of Sisyphus endlessly pushing a boulder up the hill. Maybe this pastor knew that's how I was feeling.

I started this way: "Mr. Brown, I—"

"Please, that's my dad's name. Call me Steve."

"Okay, Steve. My wife and I started coming here two weeks ago. I have been struck by your wonderful sermons." I didn't tell him that although I enjoyed hearing them, I didn't understand them. So I told him what I could truthfully say: "You seem like a very wise man. I have come to ask your advice because I have a bit of a vocational problem. My wife and I just got married and moved to Miami. I failed the Florida bar exam and I don't know what to do. I would appreciate your advice on my vocational problem."

"Jack, you don't have a vocational problem. You have a sin problem. You are a sinner, and you need to accept a gift that Jesus Christ offers you to solve that problem with sin." I was unable to speak, not fully sure of what he was saying, although I knew I didn't expect to hear that.

But this didn't seem like a distant sermon. This pastor was talking directly to me, and I was listening. I knew there was something he had that I needed to understand as well.

He didn't explain it all to me. He simply said this: "Jack, if you have been less than loving, less than what you want to be to your wife, go to her right away, today, and tell her, 'Sweetheart, I am sorry for all the pain I may have caused you. Forgive me.'"

At that I began to sob. My heart had been pierced. I had been making my wife miserable for weeks. Since failing the bar exam, I had been impossible to live with. The slightest annoyance at home made me angry. I took anything and everything Patricia said the wrong way. Because of this, her work at the office became a place where she could find refuge from me since our home was anything but a refuge from work. In short, I had made our marriage a battlefield for no reason other than that I was unhappy. Misery loves company, and I was making sure that the one I loved would keep me company in that. I was not loving my wife. In fact, I was hurting her—on purpose. But it felt as if I could not stop.

Crying in front of a complete stranger. Great. But I couldn't help it. Eventually the Kleenex helped, and when the tears stopped, Steve said this: "I have a book here I would like you to read. In fact, you're going to come back here in a week and tell me what you think about it. But don't worry, there won't be an exam." I winced. I wasn't doing well on exams. "It's called *Mere Christianity*, and its author is C. S. Lewis. I think you'll like it."

I went home, and that night I apologized to my wife for being such a pain. More tears. Patricia, being who she is and what she is, accepted my apology. We had seen the movie version of Erich Segal's *Love Story* when we were in college. I remembered the famous line "Love means never having to say you're sorry." What nonsense. Because I loved my wife, I knew I needed to say I was sorry. Because she loved someone even more than she loved me, she was able to forgive me. I did not know yet who that person was, but I knew her forgiveness felt good. I felt as if we were finally headed somewhere, but I still started reading the book the pastor gave me the next day. I finished it the same day, which is saying something because I was and am mildly dyslexic. Reading even a small book is a chore. It takes me about an hour to read twenty paperback pages, but reading this book was no chore.

This book stripped away all the "stuff" that I and others had stuck onto Christianity to make it seem just another hocus-pocus religion. Lewis wanted the reader to see who Jesus Christ really is, what Christianity—mere Christianity—devoid of the extraneous religious trappings, is. Lewis confronted me with the simple Cross, and he asked me for a decision on what it meant.

Lewis's little book appealed to my head, not just to my heart. I was midway through it, when I said to myself: *This makes sense. This is true. I believe this!*

At that moment, I became a Christian. "In the twinkling of an eye," I felt different. I mean, completely different—physically, head to toe. This was more than just an emotional feeling. A huge weight was lifted off my shoulders. I am not using a metaphor. I literally felt as if a real weight was gone, a weight that had been growing heavier for years. As I had grown older, I had felt a grinding hate building inside me. I had found reasons to despise whatever and whomever I didn't like. Halfway through this book, that hate was gone.

The truth in this book that appealed to my head and not my emotions made my heart soar and took me on a giddy, joyous ride that lasted for months. Yes, I was "high on Jesus," but I also knew He was who He said He was—someone who left heaven, died for my sins, and offered me eternal life. Who wouldn't be giddy in realizing there was a way out of what twenty-five years of life had taught me was a trap with no escape?

The next day I called Steve Brown. I needed to see him again, soon. His secretary checked and said, "Come over at ten."

When I sat down in Steve's office, I now felt he was not just my pastor, but also my friend who had given me something. "Steve," I said, "I think I've become a Christian." Steve said, "I think you have too."

I told him I *felt* different. Steve said, "Some people feel that way when they believe; some people don't. But regardless of how you *feel*, what you believe is true. Let's pray."

I have always remembered one thing that Steve Brown prayed for me that day: "Lord, remind Jack daily that it is not going to be easy to be a Christian. Let him know that You will always be there with him, even if You take him to the gates of hell."

For a reason I did not understand, I began to smile and my heart jumped when I heard that I might go to "the gates of hell." That was strange. Why would I want to go there? Little did I know that ten years later not only would I stand at the gates of hell, but I would also pass through and stay there awhile.

2

TRIAL RUN

Three months after becoming a Christian, I took the Florida bar exam again. This time I studied for it more earnestly, and I passed. To me, that was a miracle. I felt that the only reason I was a lawyer and a Christian was because God had broken me with an unexpected failure. He had a special claim on my professional life. I got "two for one" in the deal—an eternal life in heaven and a better life right here and now on earth.

The next ten years passed quickly. Ten years of happy marriage. Ten years of being a lawyer and living in what now seemed to be exciting, not just hot, Miami.

Although I was a lawyer, I was not sure exactly what kind of lawyer I wanted to be. Frankly, I wasn't sure what I was supposed to do with this vocational gift that I felt extremely indebted to repay somebody for. So I tried some different avenues.

I went to work for a local computer company whose president, Henry Myer, sold Honeywell computers to local businesses. I did the company's in-house legal work as well as tried my hand at selling computers. One day shortly after I had joined the company, Henry gave me a huge stack of computer printouts listing the names of local companies with their phone numbers. "What are these for, Henry?" I asked.

"You're going to make 'cold calls' to these companies to try and sell our computers."

"But, Henry," I said, "what if they have a computer?"

"Convince them they need a new one," he replied.

This task, calling companies out of the blue and trying to convince them they needed a Honeywell computer (which cost thousands and sometimes tens of thousands of dollars), made me appreciate for the first time what my dad had done for a living for thirty-eight years: sell paint to industrial customers for Sherwin-Williams. I also had renewed respect for my father-in-law who for decades, made cold calls as an insurance salesman for Monarch Life in the upper Midwest.

Boy, I thought, *being a lawyer has got to be easier than this. This is scary.* I was rejected one hundred times before I even got a nibble. But I finally got a nibble, and then a sale, of a very large system to Lillie Rubin, the upscale women's dress retailer located in Miami. The sale gave me something to put in a savings account. Finally, I felt like I was contributing financially to this two-person family.

I eventually told Henry that I did not think selling computers was my calling, and he understood. In 1980, I went to work for the Babcock Company, an old Miami company that built affordable housing and had become a subsidiary of the corporate giant Weyerhaeuser. I did the company's local in-house legal work, all the while learning about the construction industry. It was fascinating to meet talented people who were able to turn raw concrete and lumber into beautiful homes.

Patricia and I bought a Babcock home in a large, middle-income development called Bent Tree. I thought I would work for this company for a long time. But when a former Dade County politician became the head of the company, he started filling the employee roster with former county workers. It was clear that these political friends had the inside track for promotions, and I knew it was time to move on.

I then landed my first "real lawyer" job as a new associate at one of the oldest and largest firms in Florida: Blackwell, Walker, Gray, Powers,

Flick & Hoehl. The "Powers" in that long name was Samuel J. Powers Jr., one of the most respected and feared trial lawyers in South Florida.

Mr. Powers was general counsel to North Shore Medical Center, South Miami Hospital, and what was then called the South Florida Blood Bank, now the Red Cross.

People knew they could count on Sam Powers both ethically and within the rules of his profession to do all that he could to beat the dickens out of any opponent in a courtroom.

As an enlisted man in the navy during World War II, Sam Powers was stationed for a while in Miami before deciding to make it his home. He was a close personal friend of Alexander Haig, former chairman of NATO and eventually Richard Nixon's secretary of state.

When Nixon faced impeachment for Watergate, Alexander Haig recommended Sam Powers to represent President Nixon. Nixon asked Sam, and he accepted but later stepped down from the assignment. When I asked Mr. Powers how James St. Clair ended up as President Nixon's impeachment counsel, he said this, "Jack, that was simple. I read the file, concluded he was guilty, and fired the president as my client. I wasn't going to be a part of that disaster."

So this was my boss from 1981 to 1985: a man who had fired the president of the United States.

Sam Powers and I had a special bond for a lot of reasons. He represented health-care providers, not just because it was a living but because he loved what they did. Sam liked the fact that my grandfather, who was a doctor, had died in a southern Ohio snowstorm on his way to care for a patient.

Sam assigned me to represent the South Miami Hospital in all of its medical malpractice work; most of those cases were obstetrical cases— baby delivery cases—that somehow went wrong. I learned so much from these cases, but one in particular taught me more about human nature than medicine or law. I learned just how far some people are willing to go to hurt a child, and how far others will go to protect that child.

The case involved a woman who was the patient of one of the most popular obstetricians at the hospital—the sheer number of deliveries he handled was impressive. But in this case, the baby was stillborn—blue and not breathing—apparently dead on arrival into this world.

The nurses in the operating room tried to resuscitate the baby but were unsuccessful. Then things got worse. This doctor, who had failed to do an ultrasound during the pregnancy, suddenly realized the woman was carrying twins. The second baby was still in the mother's womb.

The doctor ordered the nurses to stop trying to resuscitate the first baby and to turn their attention to the second baby. When the nurses hesitated, the doctor said, "Put a blanket over the dead baby and put it on the shelf. We have to save this one!" The nurses did as they were instructed and turned their attention back to the mother.

The second baby was healthy and "perfect." The delivery team left the delivery room, except for one nurse who saw the blanket on top of the "dead" baby move. The baby was not dead but was gasping for air. Immediately, the remaining nurse began resuscitative efforts and the baby, although struggling, began to breathe.

Alerted to what was happening, the doctor was stunned and afraid. He told the parents that although the first baby was breathing, she had been deprived of oxygen for so long that she would not survive the night. He also said that if she did somehow survive, she would be in a vegetative state her entire life.

In this way he convinced the parents that standard medical care should be withheld. He insisted that both extra oxygen and heat not be administered to the first baby in the incubator. In other words, he ordered that the incubator not be used to do what it was designed to do: help a struggling newborn.

In the operating room, the doctor knew that he had committed malpractice by not diagnosing twins. It seemed he now wanted to kill the most damning evidence of his malpractice—a brain-damaged baby. He also probably realized that in the dollars and cents of malpractice, a dead baby adds up to far lower monetary damages than a brain-damaged baby.

"They came in here wanting a healthy baby, and they got one," the doctor told the nurses on duty. "I don't want anything done to keep this first baby alive."

Although nurses are trained to abide by a doctor's order whether they agree with it or not, these nurses chose to risk their jobs and defy the doctor's orders.

The baby in the incubator made it through the night. One nurse recounted in her deposition that she was a Christian and that she laid her hands on the baby repeatedly through that first night, praying over her tiny body. She and God, she said, pulled that baby through that initial crisis.

The doctor was furious. The parents sued the doctor, and it became my case to defend. For those who mattered most—the children—the case had a happy ending. Six years later, both girls were healthy. Amazingly, the first twin who came back to life has an IQ of 130—higher than the second twin!

As I worked on this case, I learned just how far people within corporate structures will go to cover their tracks. More important, I learned that it takes just one person of faith to save a child, to do something courageous in the face of threats. This nurse, and those who worked with her, had acted on faith. She was willing to pay any price to save just one little girl. The case shook me, and it changed me.

I managed to get myself fired from Blackwell, Walker, Gray, Powers, Flick & Hoehl after Sam Powers retired. You see, I had this very bad habit of speaking the truth, even when I knew it would get me into trouble. Without Sam Powers there to protect me from the internal politics of this large firm, I found myself speaking the truth and, shortly afterward, looking for new work.

I joined a smaller firm in Miami that also did medical malpractice defense work. I entered this new job feeling hopeful. Within weeks I was desperate. It was a terrible place to work, and I felt trapped. Had I become a lawyer and then a litigator just to wind up in a firm where I felt ensnared in office politics with no sense that what I was doing would help someone?

For the first time in my adult life, I fell into a deep valley of depression. *Has God made me a believer and a lawyer to wind up here?* I wondered. *Does God know what He is doing?*

I was angry at God. I felt like He had sent me down a dead end, that He had made a mistake. This time I really did need the vocational advice I had first sought from Steve Brown. I turned to a friend my wife and I had known for ten years at Key Biscayne Presbyterian Church for that advice.

Lottie Hillard was a Christian counselor who helped people with all sorts of problems. Lottie did not give me any kind of psychological test to determine my interests and reasonable vocational choices. That would have been the traditional approach, to help me narrow down what I wanted to do and what I was trained or equipped to do. Instead, Lottie asked me a simple question, phrased three different ways: "Jack, what do you want to do with your life? What is your passion? What is it you think God is calling you to do?"

The question surprised me. It was so direct, and it required me to explore myself rather than my external options. I paused, and then I blurted out, "Lottie, I don't want to do what I have been doing, working in an office, making no difference as far as I can tell in anyone's life. There's nothing wrong with that, but that's not for me. I want to make a difference. I don't want to be bored. Frankly, I'd rather be in harm's way if I have to be. I want to use the fact that I am a lawyer to help people in a radical way, in a way that might even change the world. That may sound egomaniacal, but that's my honest answer."

Lottie didn't bat an eye. "Then you need to go for it," she said. "Don't please others with your job choice. Please yourself. Otherwise, you'll be miserable. I believe God made us with our hopes and our desires, and we need to try to fulfill those so that we please Him and ourselves. What you need to do, in earnest, is pray that God brings your way exactly what He would have you do. He will be faithful in showing you what to do and enabling you to do it. That's the vocational advice, and the only advice, I would give you, except for one more thing."

"What's that?" I asked.

"Be careful what you pray for, Jack," she said. "You might get it."

I took Lottie's advice, and I prayed: God, let me be used by You in a way that helps others and satisfies my desire to be used. Show me what to do.

After praying for a number of days and talking with Christian friends and mentors, I felt that God was telling me to start my own law practice. Rather than seek a job with someone else, I would be my own boss. I wanted to dedicate that law practice to helping people not just as a lawyer, but also as a Christian. In other words, I wanted to be both a Christian and a lawyer on God's terms, and I wanted to see if that would work in the midst of a law practice.

It did. People I knew began to recommend me to their friends, and before long, I had a number of clients on my books. I did house closings, given my real estate background from my Babcock Company days. I handled some criminal cases as well as simple estate-planning cases. Slowly, my practice was growing, and I was having fun. I was actually making money. While I was enjoying this new chapter in my career, I grew to appreciate Patricia even more. She was working hard in an established firm and without the security of her steady, reliable paycheck, I knew this experiment could not work. I was fortunate, and I knew it. My wife was enabling what felt very much to me like a ministry. Without her, there would be no ministry.

Then one day, I made a fateful decision. I decided to listen to the radio. What I heard changed my life.

3

RADIO ACTIVE

In my youth, I had been keenly interested in politics, along with the ideas and ideologies that drive it. Entering law school as a conservative Republican, I was also libertarian in my conservative Republicanism, meaning that I was convinced that "victimless crimes"—crimes like prostitution, drug use, and obscenity distribution—were just that: victimless. All of that was part of my bedrock Republican conservative belief that government should be limited and small. I still believe government should be small. As to whether citizens should be allowed to engage in certain behaviors or sins, I felt that was their business. I was convinced at that time that absolutely no one was harmed by such behaviors except the person acting that way.

Having become a Christian had not changed my view. Indeed, ten years into my Christian walk, my faith actually seemed to confirm the idea that sins involving drugs, illicit sex, or consumption of degrading material such as obscenity were problems that affected only one's own relationship with God—and nobody else's. It was and is a naive view, born of ignorance but nourished in my own generation, the "Me Generation," whose mantra has been "If it feels good, do it." Nobody but you is hurt by that. At least that is what I thought in 1987.

Woodstock occurred the summer before I began college in 1969. When I got to college, free love and recreational drug use had been in full flower. These were the fruits of libertarianism. But eighteen years after that, I still had not registered that all this "freedom" might have some unintended consequences.

When I accepted Christ, my libertarianism found a home in the strain of American evangelical Christianity that stressed God's grace and minimized the judgment that stems from His holiness. Some have called this cheap grace. It is certainly a convenient grace that encourages one to look away from the sins that give grace meaning.

My smug Christian confidence that "I'm okay and you're okay" was about to change. It was not a change I was looking for. It was a change that came looking for me.

In the autumn of 1987, as a libertarian, conservative Republican, Christian American, I discovered that some very wayward adults were doing some very bad things to children in my hometown. I was driving in my car in Miami in the middle of the morning rush hour when I turned my radio dial to one of our local stations. What I heard coming through my speakers was horrible, enough to make even a Howard Stern fan blush. Okay, not most of them, but some of them.

This radio station was running a contest encouraging young male listeners to send in pictures of themselves, along with the type of sexual activity they enjoyed. The homosexual male host of the morning show would then choose one entrant to join him on an all-expenses-paid vacation.

I had never heard anything like this on the radio in my life. I was naive and uninformed, it turns out, because what I heard was emblematic of a new, but not brand-new, genre of radio "entertainment" whose purpose was to shock listeners with its over-the-top sexual, racist, gross content in order to draw attention, boost ratings, and thus make money.

The appeal of shock radio was and is akin to the urge one feels to rubberneck at the scene of an auto accident. It is an interest or a fascination with the ugly or the hurtful or the perverse that feeds what is dark in us.

Germans have a word for this rubbernecking response. They call it *schadenfreude*. Shock radio feeds that darkness and makes money on it at the same time.

The appropriate, healthy response to such material is shock and revulsion. It had better be the immediate response; otherwise, the unwitting—even people of faith who should know better—can easily find themselves sucked in by it.

Shock is what I felt in my bones when I heard what I heard. I knew that what I heard was harmful to others, but that thought challenged my libertarian views profoundly. I thought of the schoolhouse rhyme "Sticks and stones may break my bones, but words will never hurt me." But I knew that these words were indeed hurting someone. The young boys who heard an adult male soliciting them for sex were certainly being hurt, whether they realized it or not. The radio host made these listeners believe that this was an acceptable behavior by an adult.

I felt unnerved. I couldn't stop thinking about what I had just heard. I wondered what, if anything, could be done. Even though I was a lawyer, I did not know if the law said anything regarding whether or not such material could be broadcast legally.

Let me correct that. It was *because* I was a lawyer that I did not know the law regarding all this. American law professors, and Vanderbilt's were no exception, are almost universally committed to the notion that the First Amendment to the United States Constitution is an absolute guarantee to publish, broadcast, and otherwise disseminate any entertainment of any kind to anybody. My law professors had been very keen to impart this near-religious commitment to First Amendment absolutism to their students.

So here I was, a lawyer who knew he had heard something very wrong, but who did not know if there was a way to right this wrong. I thought back to something Steve Brown had repeatedly said in his sermons: "Thirst presupposes that there is water somewhere." What I had heard gave me a thirst, and I was out to quench it.

I went immediately to the University of Miami Law School's library. I needed to find out what could and could not be broadcast on the public airwaves, but I didn't even know where to begin. In 1987, we did not have the Internet, so I could not Google "FCC obscenity" or some other string of words. At the time, I did not even know what that string of words would be.

With the help of a kind law librarian, I found the reference materials that led me quickly to what I was looking for.

In 1934, Congress had passed a law creating the Federal Communications Commission (FCC) in order to regulate the public airwaves. The public airwaves are those frequencies on which AM and FM radio is broadcast and television broadcasts are transmitted. Of course, in 1934, the latter two did not even exist, but the FCC's regulatory mandate from Congress has logically and necessarily expanded to include not only FM and television broadcasts, but also more issues, including technologically driven ones pertaining to cable television and even the Internet.

Decades earlier, Congress had given the FCC the mandate to regulate not just the technologies of broadcasts on the public airwaves, but also the *content*. Why? I found the answer to that question in the United States Supreme Court case of *FCC v. Pacifica Foundation*, also known as the "George Carlin seven dirty words" case.

That case had been filed after a California commercial radio station aired a recording of comedian George Carlin's routine in which he related the "seven dirty words" that one could not say on the radio or on television. Of course, in the routine, Carlin said them all repeatedly.

This station, which aired the routine in the early evening when children would be in the listening audience, was cited by the Federal Communications Commission not for airing obscenity, which is pornographic material so explicit and so grotesque that it is contraband even for sale to adults, but rather for broadcasting what is called "indecent material." The station challenged the authority of the FCC to regulate broadcast content along these lines, claiming, among other things, that the First Amendment to the U.S. Constitution protects the right of a broadcaster to air indecent material.

The Supreme Court disagreed, and the recitation of the law on this constitutional issue was made very clear. As I read through the files, I realized that it was still the law. I found that the FCC could punish the airing of any material that met a three-prong test: (1) It must deal with sexual or excretory activity, (2) in a way that is patently offensive and harmful to children, and (3) violates a local community's standard as to what is appropriate for broadcast.

Since *Pacifica*, the courts and the FCC had made it clear that there is a "safe harbor" between 10 p.m. and 6 a.m. in which indecent material can be aired. Therefore, if a station wanted to air pornographic material, it could do so in those eight hours when very few children, theoretically, would be in the audience.

The more I researched the matter, the more I learned that shock radio had become a phenomenon that was reaching countless kids. What I had heard on this Miami radio station *shocked me*. What I heard seemed not only totally inappropriate for children, but also harmful to them, for what I heard that day was a description of certain sexual behaviors that the host was portraying to children as appropriate, normal, and healthy. I wasn't even a father yet, but I knew in my bones this was wrong. And I knew it was harmful. Having spent the day in the University of Miami Law School's library, I also knew it was illegal. I decided to act.

That day I wrote and sent a one-page letter that would change my life. I had no idea it would change my life. If I had known that, I would not have written it. God knows that. He knows me better than I know myself. With the writing of that letter I was about to tangle with people far more clever than I, but not nearly as clever as the God who was about to use me despite my libertarianism, despite my own sins, despite my shortcomings. I was about to be tested. I had no idea what I was in for.

4

INTO THE BREACH

As soon as I got to my office, I sat down and wrote a letter to the Federal Communications Commission, relating, as a lawyer should, what I heard, when I heard it (at eight o'clock in the morning, when kids were listening *and calling* the show), and why what I heard violated the law passed by Congress, enforced by the FCC, and held constitutional by the United States Supreme Court. I sent a copy of the letter to the offending station's general manager, hoping that he might do the right thing and tell the host to knock it off. Boy, was I naive.

What happened? Nothing—for days. It was well into September, and this radio host of the most-listened-to show in South Florida was still airing his indecent material. In addition to the "trolling" for boys, the host continued to air other sexually-charged material that was clearly over the line drawn by the FCC and Congress. In spite of my attempts to stop it, this was continuing unabated.

I wasn't in shock anymore; I was furious. The FCC hadn't even acknowledged my letter. Obviously nobody else was complaining because it was business as usual at the station. I felt caught in some sort of nebulous zone between what should be and what was. I got so angry I picked up the phone and called the show.

"Jack, go ahead."

"This is Jack Thompson. Did you get the copy of the letter I sent the FCC explaining that you are breaking the law on a daily basis with your show?"

"Oh, this is Jack Thompson in Coral Gables! *You're* the one. If the show is so awful, why don't you turn it off or change the dial?"

"I don't want to turn it off. Somebody with some sense has to have it on."

"Jack, you can't turn it off because you love the show, which is why you listen to it, Jack."

"I don't listen to your show. I *monitor* your show."

That was the end of our broadcast conversation. He hung up.

Well, at least I told him and his audience that somebody didn't care for what he was doing on the air in my community. I figured I had made my point, in his face no less.

Within minutes, my phone rang. I was told, by a person who didn't identify himself, "We know who you are, and we know where you live. You're a dead man." Then the caller hung up.

As soon as I hung up, the phone rang again. A different voice said, "You had better check your car each morning, because one morning there will be a bomb under it."

Another caller, seconds later: "You won't know where, and you won't know when, but we will kill you."

My hands were shaking as I turned on the radio. The host had retrieved my letter to the station's general manager and was reading my formal name—John B. Thompson, as it appeared on my letterhead, spelling it slowly, along with my middle initial—and giving out my phone number, so that listeners could call me and threaten me. He wanted to make sure they had the right John Thompson, so they could find my house as well.

I must have received twenty death threats that day, some of which I recorded on my answering machine. Pizzas were delivered, calls came from realtors saying they had been informed that I wanted to sell our house since I'd be moving shortly (how clever), and a number of local

30

urologists' offices called to confirm the appointments a Mr. John Thompson had made just that morning for the doctor to examine his penis. Talk about one-track minds.

I found myself at what felt like the gates of hell. I knew these people, who were unbalanced enough to be fans of this radio host, were out to get me, at least with threats. I was now a target.

I contacted the police. There was nothing they could do about the death threats because they didn't know who was threatening me. They said they couldn't do anything about the station's inciting these threats, since the method was cleverly indirect, although very effective. I disagreed with them about whether this was soliciting death threats, but I couldn't make them arrest anyone.

If local police officers would not act, I thought maybe their boss would. It was someone I had met before. Janet Reno had become the Dade County state attorney two years after I interviewed for a job with her.

Despite my off-putting job interview thirteen years earlier with Ms. Reno, I had read accounts that she was an advocate for the protection of children from anyone who would harm them. I didn't know whether she was or not, but since she was in charge of law enforcement in Dade County, I thought it made sense to approach her about what was going on at the station. I had discovered that I was not alone in becoming a target of this particular radio host. A Dade County Commission meeting had been cancelled just before it voted on a bilingualism ordinance because of bomb threats called into the Commission chambers. We learned that the bomb threat had been made just *minutes after this same radio host had broadcast the phone number to the office.* I wish I had known that before I wrote my letter. I might not have written and called the show if I had known. I thought that Reno would be interested in the fact that mine was not an isolated incident.

Reno had successfully prosecuted the Country Walk day care child molestation case; later, ABC aired a made-for-TV movie called *Unspeakable Acts* based on the news event. Reno had become more than a blip on the national political radar screen of those concerned with sexual abuse of children. So I wrote a letter to Janet Reno, informing her of what, in my legal opinion, were illegal activities going on at the radio station, including the incitement of death threats against me.

She wrote me back and agreed that she would open an investigation on both counts.

Buoyed by that news, I felt that perhaps good *would* triumph in this seeming battle between good and evil. I was scheduled to deliver a speech several days later before the downtown Miami Kiwanis Club. I had been invited to explain how the local "radio war" was going. My fight had become a bit of a local news story, and that was gratifying. I figured evil would not appreciate the publicity.

During that speech, I told the audience that State Attorney Janet Reno had promised an investigation of the station in question. Buddy Nevins, a reporter for Fort Lauderdale's *Sun-Sentinel*, was in the audience that Friday and reported the story in the next day's paper. I was pleased to see that when Nevins had called Reno, she confirmed that she had, in fact, opened the investigation of the station.

On Monday, the next broadcast day, I tuned in to hear how the station would react to Saturday's news report. The radio host went on the air and said in no uncertain terms that if Reno persisted with her investigation of him, he would come forward with their evidence of her closeted lesbianism. He spoke of Reno's alleged relationship with Ann Bishop, a local ABC-TV affiliate news anchor, widely rumored to be a lesbian. I couldn't believe it. With this threat, the host may well have committed yet another crime—extortion.

Unfortunately, the apparent blackmail worked. Janet Reno dropped the investigation. I was getting a crash course in how few friends I would have in all of this.

I knew then that I was on my own, at least unassisted by Dade County's top cop. So I tried a little self-help. I filed a lawsuit in Dade County seeking a temporary restraining order prohibiting the airing of my name and phone number, since the purpose of doing so was to encourage people to harass me with, among other things, death threats.

I then called the corporate owner of the radio station and told the company's executive vice president that his employee was inciting people to threaten to kill me by giving out my name and phone number on the air. As we talked, this executive vice president agreed with me that this had to stop and subsequently agreed to the injunction prohibiting any further airing of my name, address, and phone number.

Within two days, however, the host gave out my name and number once again, violating the injunction and increasing the number of death threats I received. I went to court, representing myself, to enforce the injunction. The station was held in violation of the injunction, but no fine was assessed. The judge sternly warned the station's attorney to make sure this didn't happen again.

Days later, the judge and I ran into each other as I was going into the Dade County Courthouse on another matter and he was leaving for lunch. I didn't bring up the radio station matter because I knew that would be an unethical *ex parte* communication with the court about a pending matter. He had retained jurisdiction over the case if there were any more violations of the agreed-to injunction.

The judge looked at me and said, "Mr. Thompson, you made a mistake in getting that injunction." I smiled and didn't say a word. "Instead of getting an injunction, you should have shot him." He wasn't smiling.

Upcoming events would prove, if not the legality of that advice, at least that the judge knew what I didn't: You can't win a fight in a legal setting with people who acknowledge no laws.

The short version of the story is this: The station kept broadcasting my name, address, and phone number, despite the injunction and despite the court's ruling that the station had already violated it once. I went back to court, back to the same judge.

But this judge wanted no more of this case. He took himself off the case because he felt "so strongly about this matter that the court cannot be fair and impartial." *Oh great,* I thought. *I've been so successful in showing the court that these people are outlaws, so successful that the judge thinks that I should have killed the host. And even if he was speaking euphemistically, now he says he can't be fair.*

My sole practitioner law practice, which was successful when all this started, had collapsed. People did not want their lawyer to be someone who had taken on the media, especially the local media, in this way. It was just as well. I had a full-time job dealing with the death threats and the other fallout. Patricia, my incredibly understanding lawyer wife, was earning a paycheck, so we could survive on that. She knew that I was in a war that was taking all my time, all my energy, and all of the prayer I could muster.

The case was bogged down with a new judge, while the solicitations of death threats broadcast over the airwaves continued. I felt like we were getting nowhere. So I went to the station and I said, "Look, I don't really want your money. I want to be left alone. I've made my point to the FCC. You've made your point that your on-air 'talent' is a popular sociopath with a microphone. Let's enter into an agreement—a contract—whereby I give up my legal efforts against you all, and you agree to leave me alone. No more broadcasting of my name, address, and phone number. And you have to agree to stop violating FCC laws prohibiting the broadcast of indecent material. After all, it's in your interest, from the standpoint of holding on to your license. If you will agree to that, I will forgo my remedies before the FCC and in court. For each breach of this agreement, as determined by an arbiter, the violating party will pay five thousand dollars for each violation. Deal?"

Word came back through the station's attorney. It was a deal. I signed it and the station's parent company signed it. The sanction of five thousand dollars per violation was agreed to. My nightmare of being a lone voice, at least in Miami, against "shock radio" was over.

⚠

Wrong. The host violated the agreement, by my count, more than one hundred times on the first day the agreement was enacted. So much for contracts.

I was beginning to think the judge might have been right. But short of murder, what was I to do? Well, to start with, I knew I needed to enforce the contract. I told the station's lawyer that I planned to use the enforcement mechanisms set forth in the agreement.

I suppose I could have walked away from the fight at this point and maybe at some earlier points, but I couldn't shake the thought that I got into this because of the show's content—and that content remained unchanged. *What's the point of giving up now,* I thought, *having accomplished nothing?*

Besides, by this time in my life I had already run four marathons. In a marathon, at about the twenty-mile mark, you hit "the wall," the point at which the body starts to shut down from fatigue. The body says no. But the mind must say yes. It becomes an internal battle with practical consequences. Only an act of will can pull you through that wall. When I thought about my battle with this Miami radio station, I thought a great deal about winning, but I wondered if it was possible—and at what cost? It began to feel as if I had hit the wall, as if there were no end in sight.

But rather than my will pulling me forward, I had the distinct sense that I was being led by God, for my body had certainly had enough. I knew there was something else going on, and it was spiritual. Like the apostle Paul's motivational words to the people of Corinth, "Do you not know that those who run in a race all run, but only one receives the prize? Run in such a way that you may win" (1 Corinthians 9:24, NASB). I had reason to keep pushing. Although I was making mistakes, or what felt like mistakes (such as calling the show), I was literally "feeling" God's presence and approval. That feeling of God's support was really what was keeping me going.

This was a war, and what I was learning was that short of total surrender, it is much harder to get out of a war than it is to get into one. Since I didn't seem to be making progress in the courtroom, I decided to wage this war on a different kind of battlefield. I would confront the show's advertisers.

Every day I had been cataloguing the sometimes hundreds of violations of our agreement and FCC decency standards, and by monitoring and chronicling the content of the show, I was augmenting my filings with the FCC that began with my letter months earlier. Since the station broke the agreement, I was not legally bound by my promise not to go to the FCC for relief.

So I used these written catalogs in my new strategy of contacting the station's advertisers and telling them, both in writing and in phone calls, what the content of the show (broadcast to children) was.

My one-man campaign of informing the advertisers met with some success. Most local advertisers stayed on the show because they already knew its content and its shock value had so increased listenership that they were getting increased business. Some of these businesses were not exactly high-end, ethical operations to begin with, so there was a certain logic in their thinking that tasteless products would appeal to tasteless listeners. I couldn't fault their business acumen, just their nonexistent moral quotient.

But the national advertisers, the ones who bought ad spots on local stations through national ad agencies, had no idea what was on the show they were supporting financially, because they didn't bother to find out. Using the Arbitron ratings, the ad agencies simply found stations with large listening audiences and bought time in those markets.

I became the fly in the "see no evil" advertising agency ointment, faxing letters to the CEOs of these Fortune 500 companies, telling them they were advertising their products on a station that was violating the law. I explained that this might make anyone who happened upon the station to boycott buying their nationally known products. In other words, why would you want to sully your product's reputation with shock radio?

Upon the receipt of these letters, many of the large corporations told their national ad agencies to pull their spots. Whenever I became aware of such action, I asked representatives of the companies if they would write me a letter explaining what they had done and why. Those letters became an excellent "sales tool" for me to use in convincing other companies to do the same thing.

I had no idea what I was doing or how to do it. There was no preparation for this war. I was learning how to do an advertiser boycott of a show as I went. Truth be told, I really wasn't smart enough to think of some of this stuff. The Holy Spirit, the third person in God's Trinity, was instructing me what to do. I didn't hear voices. I was acting on "hunches" beyond my acumen. I was feeling God's pleasure, and with small successes building up, I felt that maybe, just maybe, this nightmare might end.

My spiritual life, ignited by the white-hot aspect of this battle, had become one with my physical life. I felt like I was in constant prayer. *God, should I do this? Should I not do that? Please make these people stop. Please, God, give me strength to get through one more day. God, why have You taken my faithfulness and used it to destroy my law practice? God, let my wife understand. Thank You for a wife who does understand and puts up with this nonsense I have brought upon both of us. God, deliver me from this evil.*

I was rapidly losing my naïveté about what kind of world I was living in. Early on in this mess I often had to pinch myself to be sure I wasn't in a nightmare. I was daily running up against abject depravity, depravity that was being sold publicly with no general public outcry. Is this really what America had become? I wasn't sure, but I was certainly being stripped of the notion that there was some sort of residual decency in the public arena that would make this nonsense stop. I felt very alone in my fight.

Then I got a real break. It came in the form of a letter from the organization founded by John Walsh. Americans now know John Walsh as the host of *America's Most Wanted*. Mr. Walsh and his wife had lost their son, Adam, in nearby Hollywood, Florida, when a pedophile kidnapped, beheaded, and buried him. John Walsh had turned his unspeakable loss—which eclipsed by a factor of a million or more what I was going through—into a force for good.

John Walsh's television show was the outgrowth of an organization he and his wife created—the Adam Walsh Foundation—to prevent, as best they could, harm being visited upon other children. I had written a letter to the Adam Walsh Foundation, explaining what this station was doing to harm children in our community.

I got a call from the foundation's executive director. "Can you send us tapes of the show?" Yes, I could. I had devised a system over the last few months whereby I taped the shows and played them back at hyperspeed, skipping over all commercials, news updates, and other extraneous material. The radio station was aware I was cataloging the violations of the agreement, because on a daily basis I was sending their new lawyer the violations, as I was required by the agreement to do, and I told them these violations were being sent to the FCC as well.

The station's host was telling his listeners that I was "obsessed" because I was spending more than four hours a day listening to and cataloging the violations. "Jack Thompson needs to get a life," he said. What he didn't say was that his station had taken some, but not all, of my life away.

In fact, using my recording method, I was able to listen to and catalog the content of the show in one hour each day, typing the catalogs as I simultaneously listened to them, which I felt was a small price to pay to get back my safety and my life and my law practice.

I wondered if this fight had become an effort to protect myself and to seek vengeance, replacing my first motive to stop indecent broadcasting. In other words, had this become a fight for Jack Thompson rather than for children?

I had to keep reviewing my motives and my methods, and make sure, as best I could, that nothing got out of line.

I didn't realize it then, but today I can look back and better answer those questions. When a soldier finds himself in a foxhole in a distant land, as some of our fathers did in World War II, were they fighting for themselves, for their own safety, or were they fighting for some greater cause? Did their day-to-day struggles to preserve their lives obliterate the greater cause?

I think they would say that by staying alive they were serving the cause. Battling the enemy successfully both protected them and served the cause. I felt then and I feel now that in keeping my head above water,

I was somehow serving others as well. So I sent copies of the audio tapes to the Adam Walsh Foundation.

What I got back was well worth the effort. It was a letter written on Adam Walsh Foundation stationery, which featured the unforgettably haunting image of little Adam Walsh, alive and smiling at his daddy, with a baseball cap pushed back to reveal his happy face—a face now in a grave. The letter, written to the Federal Communications Commission with an indication at the bottom that I had been sent a copy, was short and to the point and said, in effect:

> We have listened to tapes [provided] of [the] broadcasts. . . .
> We conclude that on the public airwaves, in the middle of the day, the host is soliciting sex from teenage boys in violation of FCC laws and other laws as well.
>
> We encourage the FCC to act with all diligence to punish this illegal activity.

I had in my hands the equivalent of a public relations nuclear bomb. Now, all of a sudden, this was not Jack Thompson saying this. It was a foundation, known and respected across the country because of the determination of John Walsh not to allow his loss to be in vain. People could ignore Jack Thompson. They could not as easily ignore the Adam Walsh Foundation.

My enemies—and make no mistake, that's what they were—now had a problem. The battlefield had shifted. I felt like the cavalry had just arrived. To prove to my enemies that I knew what I had, I began sending the Adam Walsh Foundation letter to national advertisers on the show. They began to flee in droves.

Desperate to staunch the flow of ad dollars, the station filed a lawsuit against me in Dade County Circuit Court, alleging that I was engaging in extortion by telling advertisers that the public's perception of the quality of their product might suffer from their financial support of a pornographic radio show. They argued that I was "threatening" the advertisers in pointing out this obvious fact to them, so obvious that once they became aware of the show's content, they were fleeing from it.

This lawsuit was what I would label a "SLAPP" suit—strategic litigation against public participation. Its purpose is not to bring a legitimate claim but rather, by the weight of litigation, to deter a citizen from exercising his rights under the Constitution. This broadcast entity was claiming that what it was doing was protected by the First Amendment and then it turned around and filed a lawsuit to deter a citizen—me—from exercising his First Amendment rights!

The problem for the station, though, is that in the midst of the 1960s civil rights movement, the United States Supreme Court decided the case of *NAACP v. Claiborne Hardware*, which I learned about during yet another trip to the law library at the University of Miami. I was getting to be such a regular there that the librarians called me by name.

In the NAACP case, the High Court said that the First Amendment protected the NAACP when it threatened a customer boycott of a certain local hardware store for engaging in racist hiring practices. Thus, according to this case, such threats are not extortion in any sense of the word. Economic boycotts, the Supreme Court said, constitute political action, which enjoys the highest rung of protection by the First Amendment. Go at it, the Court seemed to be saying.

"Political speech," which is discourse about public issues, is First Amendment speech, unlike "obscenity" and "indecent material" trafficked to children, neither of which enjoys any First Amendment protection.

It was clear to me that an advertiser boycott was akin to a customer boycott. I cited that Supreme Court case at the Dade trial court and secured a summary judgment against the host and the radio station. They, of course, appealed, again trying to wear me down, but Florida's Third District Court of Appeal, the court just one rung below the Florida Supreme Court, affirmed the trial court's ruling in my favor. I had beaten these scoundrels in court, thereby protecting the financial weapon—an economic boycott—I had fashioned against them.

I had handled the summary judgment hearing as well as the appeal and the appellate argument before the Third District myself. It almost felt good to be back in court, especially since I now didn't have any clients to represent there. Well, I did have one client, but he wasn't paying me anything, and I had plenty of people in my hometown willing to swear that I had a fool for a client.

Thus, with the appellate ruling going in my favor, the First Amendment, according to Florida law, protected me in what I was doing regarding the station's advertisers.

Having won that important court case—important to me, anyway—I really began to cost the radio station big money. So what did the host do? He jumped to another station, a crosstown talk-station rival, in what appeared to be an attempt to get away from me.

I think the host took his shock radio shtick to this station hoping that his problems with Jack Thompson would not follow him there. At the news conference announcing the host's arrival at the new station, their general manager made it clear, however, that there would be absolutely no constraints on the content of this host's show.

And indeed, as I listened to his new program, it was clear that there were absolutely no constraints; in fact, the broadcast had to be the filthiest one in American history, in my opinion.

I knew the host was throwing down the gauntlet. So I dug in to continue the battle. He continued to spout his indecency on a daily basis, often directed specifically at children. He also still referred to me by name on his program and encouraged his listeners to contact and harass me. I felt I had to chase him if I wanted to stop him. I had tried injunctions, agreements, court victories—nothing worked. Someone was going to have to win this thing for it to stop. I wanted the law to be obeyed, but I also wanted these people to leave me alone. I didn't want them destroyed; I simply wanted them to stop violating the law. Period.

My goals were twofold: (1) stopping the filth that had first stunned me, and (2) stopping the merchants of it who kept inciting people to threaten to kill me. My very public fight with the radio station had worked its way into the local papers. Reading about the situation,

Tommy Watson, the pastor of First Baptist Church of Perrine in Miami, was convinced by the nature of my stance that I must be a Christian. The papers and other media were portraying me as just some puritanical nut. Tommy Watson knew better. He asked me to come to their Sunday night church service and tell my story.

Despite some of my successes, I felt beaten down. Going into that church service I felt like a lone and very weary ranger. For months, I had been handling death threats, dealing with litigation, and monitoring daily radio shows, all part of doing daily hand-to-hand combat with people who wanted to destroy me.

Patricia and I had a brilliant professor in law school by the name of John Wade. Professor Wade was world famous not only for his treatise on torts, but also for the fact that he had endured and survived, with other American GIs, the Bataan Death March in World War II. I felt as if I had been on a discouraging march for many, many months. I knew I was not engaged in a war with guns and armor, but it surely felt like I was fighting a treacherous battle against evil.

I told Tommy Watson's congregation that although I was a Presbyterian, I was not one of the "frozen chosen." I was Baptist in my attitude: I was acting out my faith, outside the four walls of the church, out in society, out in the public square, where persecution as well as tangible blessings were coming my way, especially that evening.

For about thirty minutes, I shared my story and encouraged my brothers and sisters to join in the fight. I told them what was being aired on these radio shows and how that could affect our community. I asked for prayer and any other help they felt led to give me. When the service was over, I felt buoyant, almost jubilant, as people came to me to tell me they would pray for me for as long as it took for this battle to end. They seemed to understand me.

After that, I didn't feel so alone. God's people were going to be warriors with me through prayer, they said. *Those prayers will be heard,* I thought. *They need to be heard, because sometimes I feel too besieged, too discouraged to pray. I need these others to do it for me.*

One congregant approached me after the service and told me something I particularly needed to hear, something that gave me special comfort: "Don't worry, Jack. In the moments when you feel alone, remember that God and you make a majority." I liked that. I would need that.

For little did I know that my personal war against radio pornography was going to get a whole lot worse before it would get better.

5

PROTRACTED CONFLICT

After the holidays, 1989 began with my hope that the new year would bring new challenges and a passing of old ones. This war with the radio stations had gone on for sixteen months. I was still monitoring and cataloging the FCC violations on the new station in order to apprise advertisers as well as the FCC, and I was also litigating with the first station in an effort to enforce the agreement that we both had signed. This station had targeted children; then it targeted me. It was crucial that somehow these wrongs be made known so they could be stopped.

As I continued to fight this seemingly uphill battle, God continued to speak to me: "Hang in there," He seemed to be saying. Patricia was enduring the protracted conflict as best she could. We had a sense that no matter how much the other side threw at me, we had angels protecting us. I had read Frank Peretti's book *This Present Darkness*, which imaginatively details the spirit world that envelops us. This book helped me to better understand what I was going through.

Another book that helped me deal with the continuing fight was C. S. Lewis's *The Screwtape Letters*. As I read the book, I realized that ultimately evil cannot prevail against those who follow God. This gave me great comfort. But to be honest, there were days when it felt like all I could do was put one foot in front of the other and hope that I was going somewhere.

About that time I got a phone call from someone who wanted to be my client. A client! That would be refreshing. This client, or more precisely clients, was a group of parents of children in the Dade County public school system, the nation's fourth largest school district. They wanted me to represent them precisely because I was "radioactive," in both senses of that word. They had heard about my battle against the local radio stations, and they said they wanted a David who was willing to take on yet another Goliath.

These South Dade parents had formed a group called POPS—Parents Opposing Pornography in Schools. They had found that certain audiotapes dealing with sex and other topics were being used in their elementary kids' classes in a rather remarkable way.

The tapes were part of a telephone teenage counseling service called Switchboard of Miami, whose ostensible purpose was to provide crisis counseling and help prevent teen suicide. The tape series, called the LINK Line, could be accessed by dialing a certain local phone number, and in doing so, a student—or anyone—would hear a voice menu offering tapes on different subjects, including drugs, sex, suicide, and other "hot button" issues.

LINK Line was heavily promoted on the local ABC television affiliate, WPLG, owned by the famous South Florida Graham family which includes U.S. senator Bob Graham. The voice used to introduce the menu was longtime WPLG news anchor Ann Bishop, a legend of South Florida news.

BellSouth was a key promoter of LINK Line. At the time, BellSouth was the provider of telephone service throughout Florida and much of the southeastern United States, which not only listed the LINK Line number in its phone books but also had numerous ads for the service in those same books.

United Way underwrote the whole project with donations provided to Switchboard of Miami and the LINK Line project.

One of the POPS parents told me that posters promoting these tapes were placed on the walls of their children's elementary schools. In addition to that, speakerphones were set up in classrooms to air the audiotapes to kids from elementary through high school grades as part of the sex education and other classes. This parent gave me the number to call and told me to listen especially to four of the tapes by punching in the respective menu number. I couldn't believe what I heard.

A tape called "Homosexuality" stated that sexual orientation is not a choice, it's a given, determined in the womb like left-handedness. According to the tapes, as you grow older, it is normal to feel urges to go one way or the other in your sexual choice. Children should not be afraid to experiment, because in doing so they would discover their true sexual orientation.

A tape called "Drugs" said something like this: "Kids are known to experiment with drugs. Try to stay away from the more dangerous, addictive ones, and whatever you do, don't drive a car while impaired." Not exactly a "Just Say No" to drugs message.

A tape dealing with "Religion" said in effect: "Religion, like other myths, can be the source of much confusion in life, including bigotry. Don't let anyone tell you what to believe."

Finally, a tape about "Parents" told listeners that parents often don't understand their children. It encouraged kids to seek out others they could talk to, like counselors and other friends at school, including Switchboard of Miami.

After hearing these tapes, I did some legal research, then met with the parents. They wanted to know what, if anything, could be done about these tapes that they felt were undercutting what they were trying to teach their kids about sex, drugs, religion, and the role of parents in their children's lives.

I was looking forward to talking with people about something other than local radio, although I couldn't help but see the connection: This was simply another case of misguided adults foisting upon some other parents' children their opinion of what constitutes appropriate behavior.

Here's what I told them: "Look, I'm a Christian. As a Christian, I am shocked by what I have heard on these tapes. More importantly, however, as a lawyer I know we have to move beyond our indignation and build a case on the facts. We can't fight this thing citing our outrage as Christians. You can't even win it by saying it is making your job as parents more difficult. The people responsible for this will ignore us.

"We have to make a *legal* case that these tapes, some of them at least, are illegal. And I believe we can do that. In other words, we must not make this a battle of our values against their values, but rather their values against the law." I explained that in researching the subject, I had learned some very interesting things. A Florida statute pertaining to sex education in the public schools had been passed in 1978—so it wasn't some relic from the 1800s—that makes it illegal for any public school to teach anything other than abstinence prior to marriage to its students. The statute states also that it is illegal to portray as normal any sex other than heterosexual sex in a marriage.[1]

I told them that the tape on drug use violated federal law because the Department of Education requires that any public school system receiving federal education funds must only teach a "zero tolerance" for drug use, with the message loud and clear that the use of any illegal drugs under any circumstances should not occur. The remedy under federal law is a total cutoff of federal funds, which for a huge school system like Dade would be a huge hit. As to the swipes against parents and religion, there was no law, per se, on those topics, but I told them that if we proved our point on the other two issues of drugs and sex, we could consider it a victory.

I explained that although my public fight with the radio stations had begun because my sense of decency had been offended, I had worked hard to build my case against the stations on the laws that were being violated. My first rule of engagement on these things was to try to secure the enforcement of laws rather than build a case on feelings. I was a lawyer, and that would be my strategy and my weapon. But as a Christian, I told them, my faith was the gasoline in my tank. They understood perfectly.

"So what do we do?" they asked. I told them that I would write a letter to all the folks in the loop on these LINK Line tapes and inform them that certain tapes were violating state and federal laws. Then we would wait to see what the response was. "And what if they don't respond by changing the tapes?" the parents wanted to know.

"Then we take it up a notch," I told them.

"What does 'up a notch' mean?"

"I'm not sure," I said, "but I'll think of something." We prayed, and I left to write that letter.

When I left my meeting with these parents, I was struck by how betrayed they all felt by a system that had targeted their flesh and blood with messages and teachings that countered what they wanted to teach their children. They had complained to the school administrators about the LINK Line tapes but the school turned a deaf ear. My wife and I had no children, but I could feel their parental anguish. There was an edge of anger to their pain. I believe if they had not been angry they never would have contacted me. I felt like I could not let them down. If I did, I would also be letting their kids down.

⚠

I sent the letter to United Way's local president, to Switchboard of Miami, to WPLG's Ann Bishop, to Senator Bob Graham, to the CEO of BellSouth in Atlanta, and to the Dade County school board superintendent. My strategy has always been to give the folks who are doing something objectionable the chance, once they are confronted with it, to come to their senses and turn away from what they are doing.

I believe this methodology is set forth in the Bible, and I have found that the Bible really is both a good guide for personal behavior and a warrior's guide to spiritual warfare, even when—*especially when*—fighting with others who are made of flesh and blood.

Matthew 18:15-17 says that if your brother within the church is sinning, you are to go to him, trying to get him to repent. If he refuses, you are to take one or two others with you. If he still won't repent, you are to tell it to the church so that discipline, for his sake, might begin. This template suggests that if an out-of-control organization won't come to its senses, you are to go to the public to begin the "disciplinary" process.

When I sent out the letter, I was trying to do that. The fact that this approach is set forth in Scripture for believers does not mean that it won't work for nonbelievers as well. Truth is truth—for example, gravity "works" for believers and nonbelievers alike.

Two weeks after sending out the letters, there was no response. In the meantime, I was doing some research, trying to figure out where in the world these LINK Line tapes had come from. I found that, except for the local introductory voice of Ann Bishop, they had been recorded at the University of Wisconsin–Madison, long known as Berkeley East because of its proud status as a beehive of liberal thought and action. The tapes were called the HealthLine tapes at UW–Madison, and they were distributed by the school throughout the country to public schools and other organizations, like Switchboard of Miami.

The UW–Madison chancellor at the time was Donna Shalala, who four years later would be chosen by President Bill Clinton to be his secretary of health and human services. Shalala was well-known nationally among conservatives as the "High Priestess of Political Correctness," for upon her initiative and insistence, certain forms of "hate speech" had been outlawed on campus. Shalala did not simply say that illegal speech should be prosecuted, but rather that any speech that might be considered hurtful to others would not be tolerated. This was a far cry from my insistence that democratically enacted broadcast standards must be enforced. It was an attempt by Shalala, on her campus, to make certain speech illegal simply because some professors found it offensive. Having heard nothing from any of the people and organizations I had written to, I decided it was time to "take it up a notch."

I called the University of Wisconsin–Madison and found the department that produced the tapes. I asked to speak with the person heading the effort to produce and distribute the HealthLine tapes. Her name was

Anne Whittaker, and she was a nurse. "Is Nurse Whittaker available to talk with me?" I asked.

In a cheery upper-midwestern voice, lilting with a Scandinavian accent, the secretary said, "You betcha!" I was transferred to Nurse Whittaker, and I began the conversation with this: "Nurse Whittaker, this is Jim Anderson from Miami. I am thrilled to find your HealthLine tapes down here, made available to kids as the LINK Line tapes. I just wanted to call and thank you, especially since I am a gay man appreciative of the clear messages you are giving the kids about the gay lifestyle."

Anne Whittaker was apparently excited to get this call. I seemed to have hit her play button. "Oh, we worked especially hard on the homosexuality tape. We got some progressive Quakers to help us on that, so that kids would understand that it is okay to be gay or lesbian or bisexual."

We talked about some of the other tapes, how useful they were to pointing kids in directions other than where their parents might want them to go. I asked her, "As much as I like the tapes, aren't some of these kind of controversial?"

"Oh, absolutely. But here is what we do. We get the program started in a community with the noncontroversial tapes so that the intolerant, noisy, religious minority doesn't get upset. Then, when the coast is clear, we put in place the more controversial tapes."

"Under cover of darkness," I offered.

"Exactly," she said.

"Well, thanks so much for doing what you're doing. You'll be hearing more from me, I think, as I try to get the word out on what you are doing." That was a promise I meant.

"You call anytime. It's good to hear from people who appreciate what we're doing."

I knew that if I could prove that this conversation had occurred, I could potentially blow LINK Line clean out of the water. But I had no way to corroborate what she had just told me—yet. I needed a witness.

I had lied to this woman. Is anyone, particularly a Christian, allowed to do such a thing? In my mind, in a situation such as this, absolutely.

You may, upon reading this, disagree with me. You may have a reasonable argument to support your view that I sinned in doing this. I do not think I did. I believe I used a subterfuge, as a spy would use to hide his identity, in order to prove the dangerous activities of others. Can Christians use deception in order to get at the truth? Yes, I think we can, just as those who engage daily in espionage on our behalf use deceit to serve a higher good. We now know that a breakdown, through governmental neglect, of our intelligence network—our espionage—helped lead to September 11.

I felt back in 1989, as I do now, that the scriptural admonition to Christians to be "shrewd as serpents and innocent as doves" (Matthew 10:16, NASB) allowed a culture warrior to use stealth means in order to get at the truth and thereby prevent harm.

But this is dangerous stuff, especially to culture warriors. I knew I constantly had to check my motives, which I thought, frankly, were in good order in this deception. I didn't pause before using the deception. I felt it was right then and still do. But I respect the reader who might think otherwise.

⚠

I took the results of my reconnaissance up the road to Fort Lauderdale, to Coral Ridge Ministries, the outreach arm of Coral Ridge Presbyterian Church, whose senior pastor and founder is Dr. D. James Kennedy. Before I even knew such battles were being waged, Dr. Kennedy had been fighting the fights I now found myself in.

Coral Ridge happened to be in the broadcast zone of the radio stations I was presently fighting, and Coral Ridge Ministries had reported about my local war on shock radio. Dr. Kennedy had himself been targeted by this shock radio host, so I felt that we were kindred spirits on that and many other things.

Coral Ridge had been at the national forefront of expressing concern that public school sex education had become a means of proselytizing the notion that "if it feels good, do it." I took the results of my research of LINK Line to Coral Ridge to let them know about the LINK Line tapes in their own backyard in Miami. I thought they might be interested in it as a story for their broadcast, *Truths That Transform*.

They were more than interested. I spoke with a writer for *Truths That Transform*, and she told me she felt a clear call to expose the true agenda of certain sex-ed proponents: to undermine the influence of family and church on matters of sex.

I asked her if she would care to listen in on a subsequent conversation with the good nurse Whittaker. "Sure," she said.

So through the magic of BellSouth's own three-way calling function, with this Coral Ridge reporter in Fort Lauderdale, me in Miami, and Anne Whittaker in Madison, I did a reprise of my earlier call and I got her to talk with me again, this time by expressing my interest in getting the tapes into more communities. Anne Whittaker repeated everything she had told me in our first conversation.

Dr. Kennedy recorded and aired a *Truths That Transform* radio program about the LINK Line case, telling the nation about the deception and the harm emanating from the University of Wisconsin–Madison.

The conservative Rockford Institute in Rockford, Illinois, heard Dr. Kennedy's broadcast about the LINK Line case. They asked me to write an article about the issue for their monthly publication called *Chronicles*. I wrote the piece and sent it to everyone connected with LINK Line, including Anne Whittaker and her boss, Donna Shalala.

My strategy then, as it has been since, is to the let the other side know as much as I could about what I was doing, so that they knew I was calling them out into the open battlefield, just as David confronted Goliath.

I had also learned along the way that it's best to go right to the top with these battles so that nobody in the target organization can claim, plausibly, that they did not know what was going on.

Light was not only shining on evil, but the authors of the evil knew it, and they were concerned. What they did not know was that I had a witness to my second conversation with Anne Whittaker, which I had not mentioned in the article. I didn't want to use that safety net yet.

Next, I called Tony Burns, honorary chairman of Dade's United Way. Burns was also chairman and CEO of Miami-headquartered Ryder Systems. He agreed to meet with me, so I asked my friend, Mike Thompson, to join me, since I was learning the value of having a witness. Mr. Burns, a Mormon, said he was deeply concerned about the content of the tapes and the fact that United Way was supporting such things. Clearly, the content of these tapes was at odds with some of the religious and moral beliefs of many of the United Way's supporters. I had given Mr. Burns and United Way a public relations problem. He said he would sincerely look into and try to resolve this matter. We thanked him, encouraged that we had pierced the veil of indifference by means of the *Chronicles* article. The truth was hitting the fan.

Then the fan hit me.

6

LOVE YOUR ENEMIES

In the summer of 1989, I received a letter from the Florida Bar informing me that a formal complaint had been filed against me by the University of Wisconsin–Madison through Anne Whittaker. The basis of the complaint was that I had grossly mischaracterized and even fabricated both what was on the tapes and what she had said to me. I had made it all up, thereby acting unprofessionally.

If the Florida Bar were to come after me, this would be a problem. The Florida Bar, like all state bars, is not known for its kindness toward conservative activists like me.

In my formal written response to the bar, I pointed out that the appropriate remedy for defamation—lying about someone—is a libel action, and that there was a very good reason that even if the school filed such an action, it would not be successful. The tapes themselves proved that my characterization of them was accurate. Shalala and her troops knew that.

As to what I alleged Anne Whittaker had said regarding UW–Madison's deceptions, I told the bar that I could prove what I wrote was true. This was something they did not yet know. I had a witness, an "ear witness," who had heard everything. It would not be my word against Anne

Whittaker's. It would be my word and that of a journalist—albeit a Christian-ministry journalist—against Anne Whittaker's word. I submitted an affidavit from the journalist.

A few days after I filed that response with the Florida Bar, I got an amendment to the formal complaint: I was now being investigated by both the bar and by Janet Reno's Dade County State Attorney's Office for allegedly violating state and federal felony statutes prohibiting unauthorized interception of electronic communications. In other words, by having a third party listen in on my call with Anne Whittaker, I had supposedly engaged in an illegal wiretap.

Talk about being stuck between a rock and a hard place. If I hadn't had a witness, I wouldn't be able to prove what Anne Whittaker had said. Could I have had the conversation with Whittaker and told her that someone else was on the line? Yes, I could have, but a hunch told me she would not have been as forthcoming. She might have sensed something was up. Besides, the journalist didn't want to do it that way. I had specifically asked her, and she had said no.

I was glad I had done it the way I did, but nobody likes being investigated for an alleged felony. I was fortunate that the law at both the state and federal levels was clear. There is no "interception" of a wire communication unless it is recorded on one end of the call or unless it is with a wiretap—that is, by a listening device other than the phone itself. That's why they're called "wiretap laws."

What I didn't know right away, but I found out later, was that Dade County State Attorney Janet Reno had been behind the bar complaint against me as well as her office's own investigation. In studying the documentary evidence against me in the files of the Florida Bar, I discovered a letter from the bar showing that the Switchboard of Miami had directly encouraged Anne Whittaker to bring a bar complaint against me. Who was a trustee on the board of Switchboard of Miami? Janet Reno. Who served as Switchboard of Miami's in-house legal adviser? Janet Reno. Who turned out to be a friend of Chancellor Donna Shalala? Janet Reno. In fact, now more than a decade later, Janet Reno is a close friend and a neighbor of Donna Shalala, who is now president of the University of Miami. The time the two of them spent together in the Clinton cabinet helped sell Shalala on taking that post after her Clinton years. Who also turned out to be a personal friend of WPLG's Ann Bishop, the one whose voice introduced the various tapes to kids on the phone? Janet Reno.

The "Sisterhood," as it came to be called by those who have sought to explain the interactions and orchestrated efforts of radical feminists, was gunning for Jack Thompson.

Not only did Reno apparently suggest the bar complaint, it was clear that she had been a very personal part of the conduit that funneled the HealthLine tapes to the Switchboard of Miami. I think Janet Reno and Donna Shalala were doing all they could to stop me from raining on this politically correct parade.

Fortunately, when the bar looked at the wiretap statutes, which clearly do not prohibit someone silently listening in on a third line, it could not prove I had violated any state or federal statutes. Further, Reno's fingerprints were all over this bar grievance. When I submitted notarized transcripts of the LINK Line tapes, it was clear, too, that my characterization of what was on the tapes was accurate. This was too much even for the bar to pursue in an attempt to whack Jack Thompson. The bar complaint was dismissed. No criminal charges were brought. No defamation action was ever filed by Anne Whittaker. I was relieved that, in this case at least, the truth prevailed.

In addition, Ryder chairman Tony Burns convinced United Way to persuade Switchboard of Miami to modify the LINK Line tapes so that they complied with the law, since they were being used in the schools. This was done.

It was a huge victory, and we were thrilled.

The school system skirmish was worth the trouble because it helped show me that even the protracted radio war might one day end. If I could beat back a phony criminal investigation and a bogus bar complaint, then I might eventually extricate myself from my radio wars.

But apparently not yet.

⚠

Within days of the LINK Line victory, I was served with multiple lawsuits separately filed by the shock jock's new station, by the shock jock personally, and by another host at the new station. The complaints each alleged that I was fabricating the content of the indecent shows both to advertisers and to the Federal Communications Commission.

The station had previously tried to prove to a court that I had no legal right to contact advertisers, but the court had said otherwise. Now, they changed their strategy: I might have the right to contact the advertisers, they said, but I did not have the right to lie about the content. *Here we go again*, I thought.

The station and its parent company, it seemed, had had enough of Jack Thompson. It seemed they were trying to take me out—with multiple lawsuits, filed with different judges, making me run from one courtroom to the next. I wondered if they hoped to either exhaust me to the point of saying "I can't take this anymore" or win these cases and bankrupt me with sizable verdicts. They had sued me in these cases for millions of dollars.

It was clear that my efforts were already costing my opponents. The general manager of the new station was telling the newspapers that "Jack Thompson has cost us $500,000 in advertising revenue."

Wow, I thought. *I didn't know I was doing that well.*

As gratifying as that admission was, this new litigation was a multifaceted nightmare. I had to win every case in order to win at all; the other side only had to win one. They had a team of lawyers; I was the only one on the other side. *You and God are a majority*, I remembered. We were about to find out if that was true.

This felt dangerous. As sure as I was of the rightness of the principles for which this fight began, I wondered nearly every minute whether I'd made a terrible mistake in taking all this on. I had felt myself being pulled along to do this by some force, but I now had an in-my-bones doubt about this next stage. This team of lawyers planned to squish me like a bug. This would be fun for them. It did not feel like fun to me.

On more than one occasion, in the midst of this new danger, I felt as if my insides were melting—melting from fear. When I prayed, I felt like the *Wizard of Oz*'s Wicked Witch of the West when she was splashed with water. My prayers to God were a lot like her shrieks: "I'm melting! Give me strength! Deliver me!"

When I got myself into this radio war I was confident—overly confident—that I knew what I was doing, just as I was overconfident when I took the bar exam and then failed. I was no longer confident. I was scared to death.

Sometimes when Patricia and I talked about our situation, I would find myself dissolving into tears. "I'm so afraid," I'd say to her. Patricia was always brave for me, telling me that I must win and that I would win. She had courage when I lacked it. Nevertheless, I knew I had better get some spiritual counseling from somebody who could understand how scared I was and could help me decide what to do.

I called a man named Larry Poland one night at his home in California. Although I had never met Larry, a friend had suggested that I call him. Larry Poland had founded Mastermedia International, a Los Angeles–based organization whose mission was and is to bring the gospel of Christ to those within the secular entertainment industry. Mastermedia prays for leaders in the American entertainment media and also organizes and facilitates Bible studies and prayer groups of believers within the industry.

If I had been acting like an operative of the Defense Department in this culture war, Larry Poland and the prayer warriors of Mastermedia had been waging that war like operatives in the State Department. Larry Poland was using diplomatic love to reach those in the secular entertainment industry. My love, if it had been that, had been expressed via confrontation. It was a good time for me to talk with a Christian diplomat, because my bomb dropping had gotten me into the target's own crosshairs.

Holding the phone and waiting for Larry to pick up, I felt I was trapped inside an inner compartment in the *Titanic*. I felt—no, I *knew*—that all was lost. I knew I was not a good enough lawyer to beat these clever lawyers. I was in a panic induced by the just-filed lawsuits. Larry Poland told me he had begun as a culture warrior of sorts when he had complained about astronauts' profanity broadcast live from space on prime-time television. He later became instrumental in organizing a boycott of Martin Scorsese's blasphemous *The Last Temptation of Christ,* and he wrote a book about the experience called *The Last Temptation of Hollywood.* The boycott was a huge success. In part because of the efforts of Larry and the American Family Association, the movie was a commercial disaster.

As we talked that night on the phone, I apologized to Larry for intruding on his evening. I explained who I was and told him that someone had suggested that I call him for advice. But Larry knew exactly where I was in all this without ever having met me. "Jack, you are doing and have done the right thing. You are doing God's work in battling these forces of darkness. Satan is behind them, and God is behind you. It is absolutely terrifying to be in the place you are in, but God chooses some of us to be there.

"But, Jack, my dear brother, what I hear in your voice and in your words and in the tone of both is that your heart is not right. You cannot do this work, you cannot fight this fight, unless you love these people with whom you battle. Jack, you must see yourself as a sinner no better and no worse than they are. You cannot let the bitterness that grows from what they have done to you eat you up, because not only will it destroy you, but it will harm your relationship with the Lord. You must pray for these people. They must see Christ in you, not just Jack Thompson in you. Not only is that just and right, but it will also unnerve them. I hear too much vinegar in what you are about, not enough of the sweetness of the Lord. You can't love the Lord and hate these people at the same time, no matter how just your cause."

This man who had never met me had pierced me to the heart, just as Steve Brown had done thirteen years earlier when he told me I had to love my wife. I now had to love my enemies as well, and to make that be real, not just words on a page.

Yes, I was a new creature in Christ, and yes, I was doing God's work by taking on these evil deeds. But fighting for what is good did not make *me* good. I was simply a fallen, sin-prone creature doing battle. The battle was righteous. I was not. Only Christ is righteous. Larry reminded me of that.

I remembered a line from *The Untouchables* that seemed to reflect the danger Larry was warning me about. Near the end of the movie, federal agent Eliot Ness says, "I have broken every law I have swor[n] to uphold. I have become what I beheld, and I am content that I have done right."[1]

I knew that I could never get to the point where I thought that the end I was seeking justified any means to get there. Larry Poland told me I must love these people in word and in deed and in heart, while at the same time still fight against them. This was to be a difficult task, but I had to "love my enemies." It was the only way.

Realizing the truth of what Larry had so gently told me, I sobbed on the phone for several minutes. I was afraid of what this truth might mean. I did hate these people and what they had done to me and to children. "Larry, do I let all this go, stop fighting with these people?"

"Oh, for heaven's sake, no! You fight them harder than ever, but you pray for them, love them, let your heart be broken for them, and then watch what God does to change you and deliver you from this present darkness. Jack, you and I both know that you're eventually going to get to heaven as a brother in Christ. That will never be lost. But I want to see you filled with the Holy Ghost in the meantime. You'll be crushed if you aren't."

My heart said *Amen*.

I thanked Larry for his advice, which I said I needed and I knew was true. He said he would be checking in on me to see how I was doing. I was now accountable to a flesh-and-blood brother for my behavior and the attitude of my heart. I wished I had learned that earlier, but I knew God was teaching me as I went. At least I was learning. I kept reminding myself of Ephesians 6:13: "Therefore put on the full armor of God, so that when the day of evil comes, you may be able to stand your ground, and after you have done everything, to stand."

In the weeks and months after my initial talk with Larry Poland, the multiple lawsuits against me progressed, like glaciers, through the laborious litigation process. By the fall of 1989, I felt like I was swimming in court documents and countless hearings. As I was treading water in the judicial system, I knew I was barely keeping my nostrils above water. This had gone on for two years now. It felt like much longer.

During all this local litigation, a hearing was scheduled in the Federal Communications Commission oversight subcommittee to the Senate Commerce Committee. They were confirmation hearings for new commissioners to the FCC appointed by President George H. W. Bush.

When I heard these hearings were going to occur, I made a phone call to Gary Bauer, who at that time was head of the Family Research Council in Washington, D.C. The FRC is a profamily Christian organization that was the brainchild of Dr. James Dobson. I had met Gary Bauer in the White House in 1987 when I was asked to join a group concerned about the distribution of pornography in America. Gary Bauer had been a top domestic policy adviser to President Ronald Reagan and had met with us that day. We were supposed to have met with President Reagan, but as Gary Bauer told us at the time, "The president decided to invade Honduras today, so he's a bit busy. You're stuck with me." It turned out that God had a plan and knew it was more important for me to meet Gary Bauer than the Gipper.

I introduced myself to Gary Bauer on the phone and reminded him of our meeting in 1987. I told him that hearings were coming up in the Senate Commerce Committee for the new commissioners and that I understood shock radio would be discussed with the nominees. Gary Bauer said that was his understanding as well.

I told him what was going on in Miami, explaining that I had been battling this for more than two years. "Do you have tapes of the worst shows?" Gary asked.

"Yes, I do," I told him, "plus transcripts of some of the worst segments of the shows, as well as an explosive letter from the Adam Walsh Foundation complaining to the FCC about the content of the shows."

"Get me all of that, Jack, and I'll see if I can alert the subcommittee to our concerns."

True to his word, Gary Bauer submitted to the subcommittee his own sworn, written assessment that shockingly indecent material had been broadcast, and was still being broadcast, on the radio in Miami. He included the Adam Walsh Foundation letter as an exhibit to his sworn testimony.

The day after that hearing, a person who was at the hearing told me that there was a virtual explosion in the hearing room when the subcommittee members heard the written sworn testimony from Gary Bauer. He'd put his name and his reputation on the line regarding what was going on in Miami.

Senator Daniel Inouye, a Democrat from Hawaii, was irate and said he couldn't believe such garbage could find its way onto the public airwaves in the United States. He said he planned to go over to the Federal Communications Commission and demand that something be done. And then he did just that.

On October 9, 1989, the Federal Communications Commission announced that it was levying fines against three Miami radio stations for the airing of indecency: the first station that Rogers had worked for, a second station owned by the same company as the first, and the station to which Rogers had moved. The federal government had agreed that this broadcast material was over the clear line set forth in *Pacifica* (the "George Carlin seven dirty words" case).

That day, the FCC handed down what amounted to the first decency fines ever levied by the commission in the history of this country.

As a result of this decision by the federal government, the radio stations and their operatives dropped all the lawsuits that were pending against me. How could they sustain these suits when the federal government had in effect said that my characterization of these shows as indecent was correct?

The Florida Bar still tagged me with an item of wrongdoing, however. Back in 1987, I had had a phone conversation with the executive vice president of the radio network whose station was orchestrating death threats against me. I had called him and asked him to make this stop. The bar felt that I had violated the rule against "a lawyer communicating with another party who had an attorney." At the time, I thought that was a phone call I had to make to protect Patricia and myself. In fact, bar rules allowed one party to contact another directly, so I still don't believe I did anything wrong, either morally or technically. Beyond that, the outside, private counsel for the radio station had, in fact, authorized me to contact this man, given the life-threatening situation. My mistake was not getting that okay in writing. The bar disciplined me with a reprimand that I should not have talked with him.

The bar also found that during this two-year time period, I had filed a document in a case that I had not fully researched. Are mistakes made by those on the right side of a war? Yes, they are, and I had made them, but I had also learned from them. The great danger is that the person who is "fighting the good fight"—as I believe I was—will allow Satan to convince the soldier that his mistakes disqualify him from being worthy to fight at all.

The Accuser tells us the great lie that we are, in our own heart of hearts, so evil that it is the height of hypocrisy to identify and then fight for standards of conduct and morality because we ourselves are flawed.

I know that I have more in common in my very nature with the shock jocks whom I have fought than with the Holy One who made us both. But that is no reason not to acknowledge Him and the "more excellent way" (1 Corinthians 12:31, NASB). He holds out for all sinners, of whom I am chief.

It is *because* of my sin, not in spite of it, that I have fought against an industry that would, for money and for even darker reasons, devour the innocence of our children.

Jesus said, "If anyone causes one of these little ones who believe in me to sin, it would be better for him to have a large millstone hung around his neck and to be drowned in the depths of the sea" (Matthew 18:6). My hands are not clean, because I am a fallen creature in a fallen world. But just because my hands are dirty does not mean that God would not have me do what I can, grubby hands and all, to tie that millstone around the necks of those who would hurt the little ones.

I felt as if what I was doing was actually an act of love to warn those who were so deeply enmeshed in dangerous sin about the consequences of that sin. It would not be loving of me to simply wave pleasantly to these people as they were about to drive their car off a cliff.

I held on, then, through two years of travail because I could not shake the desperate hope that somehow God would deliver me from my enemies. If God's eye is on the sparrow, then surely His eye was on me. Others had turned my fight for children into a fight against Jack Thompson. I did not want this to be about me, but they had adopted a "shoot the messenger" strategy. Thankfully, it had not worked.

This was not a battle "against flesh and blood, but against the rulers, against the authorities, against the powers of this dark world and against the spiritual forces of evil in the heavenly realms" (Ephesians 6:12), as the apostle Paul identifies spiritual battle. And what I found was that bad things—discouraging events—often follow closely on the heels of encouraging events. I had won this battle about what could and could not be on the public airwaves in south Florida. The next battle would truly be about Jack Thompson.

7

IS THIS LAWYER INSANE?

I received a letter from the Florida Supreme Court, informing me that a judge who had presided over one of the lawsuits filed against me by the radio station had decided to act upon the assertion in this lawsuit that "Jack Thompson is obsessed with pornography as evidenced by his opposition to it, and that he is, by virtue of this obsession, impaired in his professional judgment and thus mentally incapacitated by that obsession and unfit to practice law."

This was not a joke. The letter was real.

The judge who had seized upon the mental illness assertion in this lawsuit was Richard Feder, a respected judge in the circuit court of Dade County. He took the bait put into the lawsuit, swallowed it, and ran to the Florida Bar, which then asked the Florida Supreme Court to act upon the assertion that I was mentally ill by virtue of my "obsession."

As I read the letter, I felt as if all the blood had drained out of my allegedly deranged head. I knew I needed to find out why Judge Feder would do such a thing.

I found the answer in the well-stocked University of Miami Law Library. As I began to research, I discovered that Feder had formerly been chairman of the American Civil Liberties Union of Florida. I thought back to the first presidential debate in 1988 between then vice president George Bush and Governor Michael Dukakis, in which Bush said of Dukakis, "he is a card-carrying member of the ACLU," an organization whose position is that child pornography is protected by the First Amendment to the U.S. Constitution.[1] It was a killer strategy that for all intents and purposes helped take Dukakis out of the race. Bush had been prepped for that debate by a number of people, but it was Bill Donohue who had given him that attack line. Donohue is now president of the Catholic League and author of a great exposé on the ACLU called *Twilight of Liberty*.

I discovered while reading Donohue's book that Richard Feder was the ACLU official who persuaded the national ACLU to change its policy on child pornography and declare it to be First Amendment speech!

Judge Feder, then, was also the man who made it possible for Vice President Bush to utter his child pornography line in the debate. Child pornography is literally the raping of children in front of video cameras.

As is true with many people who labor under a bias, Judge Feder could not recognize his own predilection. He should have recused himself from presiding over this lawsuit the second it hit his desk. Instead, he used it as an opportunity to try to get me disbarred. This experience led me to understand an abiding rule: Never seek the resolution of a dispute over public policy within the judicial branch. The judiciary is filled with First Amendment absolutists and tunnel-visioned ideologues just like Judge Feder. Lawyers tend to be to the left of other citizens, and judges tend to be even further to the left. There are exceptions, of course, but the exceptions prove the rule.

So this sitting judge who took an oath to uphold the laws and the constitutions of the State of Florida and of the United States had tried, through the ACLU, to depathologize and decriminalize pedophilia. He was now trying to pathologize my Christian activism. His weapon of choice was the Florida Supreme Court, which oversees the Florida Bar and the lawyers it regulates.

Maybe Judge Feder was right after all, because I have to admit that as I read the letter from the Florida Supreme Court, I thought, *This can't be happening—I truly must be losing my mind. This can't happen in America.*

But I had not lost my mind. Others had lost their balance. We had a sitting judge who had an ideological ax to grind. He found a willing accomplice in the Florida Bar, which had missed an earlier opportunity to nail me for an allegedly illegal wiretap.

The Florida Supreme Court had added an extra twist of the knife, ensuring maximum pain. The Florida Supremes, as they are called by lawyers, declared that "Mr. Thompson must agree and submit to, in short order, any and all psychiatric testing deemed appropriate by the Florida Bar, or he shall immediately have his license to practice law suspended." In other words, agree to our testing immediately—don't try to fight this—or we'll suspend your license to practice law even without the testing.

John Longino, a young Christian lawyer and a member of Key Biscayne Presbyterian Church, offered to help me in all this. I shall forever be indebted to this brother who, in a time when the stewards of my profession were coming after me on the basis of my sanity, stepped up and said he wanted to help. Proving I had some sanity left, I accepted his offer of legal representation.

John's reasonable advice was to fight this order of the Florida Supreme Court and try to get a federal court to issue an injunction blocking it, even if it meant that my law license would be suspended temporarily.

I thought about it, prayed about it, and told him: "John, these pornographers have been saying for months and months now that there is something wrong with me. They have said publicly that nobody in his right mind would 'obsessively' fight them the way I have. Now not only has a judge bought into that, but the entire Florida Supreme Court has as well. Let's not fight them. Let's win this thing by submitting to any testing they want to do. I can live with the results because of two things: I think they'll find I'm sane, but if they don't, then God is big enough to get me through even that. Besides, Patricia would probably like to find out if I am crazy!" The last comment was said with a smile, but all this hurt a great deal to say. I knew it was right to play the game as those who made the rules required me to play.

The apostle Paul, in his letter to the Romans writes: "Everyone must submit himself to the governing authorities, for there is no authority except that which God has established. The authorities that exist have been established by God. Consequently, he who rebels against the authority is rebelling against what God has instituted, and those who do so will bring judgment on themselves. For rulers hold no terror for those who do right, but for those who do wrong" (13:1-3).

It seemed to me that submission to God meant submission even to those who were trying to prove I was fighting the distribution of pornography to children because I was mentally ill. This was difficult to do, but I was reminded that Jesus went to the cross in submission to God the Father *and* the civil authorities. In Mark 12:17, Jesus says we must render unto Caesar what is Caesar's—even if Caesar is a psychologist or a psychiatrist, I concluded.

So against the advice of my good lawyer who only wanted to help me, I chose to submit. This was one of the hardest things I ever had to do, because I would be examined by a psychiatrist as well as a psychologist chosen solely by the Florida Bar. Doing this either took faith or the blind trust of a madman. We were all going to find out which it was. If these doctors concluded I was mentally ill, my ability to practice law in any meaningful sense would be over.

I met each of the two doctors on different days, a few days apart. This felt pretty weird, visiting professionals to find out if I was mentally ill and unfit to practice law. The radio station's lawyers had thrown into the mix the idea that my behavior suggested not just mental illness but also "brain damage." The bar wanted that determined one way or the other as well. When I told my parents that, they laughed, and then they cried. "Jack," my mother said, "we didn't drop you on your head. How did you do well in school if you have brain damage?" Good question.

The psychologist chosen to examine me asked me to click a little device, like a counter, first with my right index finger and then with my left index finger. I could do it much more quickly with my right hand than with my left. "What's this test about?" I asked him.

"To determine, preliminarily, whether you might have brain damage on one side of the brain or the other," he said.

"How'd I do?" I asked when it was finished.

"You did fine. No brain damage, but you're the most left-hemisphere dominant person I've ever tested, which explains why you can click it so much faster with your right index finger. The amount of differential is huge."

"That doesn't indicate brain damage?"

"No, it merely indicates that the left side of your brain, which controls the right side of your body, is highly developed," he said. "The left side of the brain is where analytical thinking occurs. The right side is the artistic, creative, intuitive side of the brain. I can tell not only from this physical test, but also from your answers to my questions, that you are very analytical in your thinking. In other words, if you see that something is true, you follow through on what you know to be true. People like you tend to be rather persistent." Tell me about it. Tell my wife about it. Tell the pornographers about it. At that moment I wished I had a more dominant right hemisphere.

Of course, all of South Florida got to read about this testing as well. The radio station attorneys shared the story with the *Miami Law Review*, which at the time was read by most lawyers in South Florida. The paper ran a prominent article about my sanity. Just what you want your fellow lawyers to be reading. In addition, *Miami New Times*, a countercultural, left-wing, giveaway newspaper with paper boxes all over the county, had its own deliriously happy account of how the crusading antiporn lawyer was about to be found insane by the Florida Bar and Supreme Court. Forget the notion that bad publicity is good publicity as long as your name is spelled right. This was bad publicity, and there was nothing good about it.

Once the examinations and tests were complete, I waited about ten days for the results. I felt as if I were waiting for a jury who had my fate in their hands to come back in and hand down their verdict.

Finally, the written results came enclosed in a letter from the Florida Supreme Court. The psychiatrist and psychologist concluded, independently of one another, that "Jack Thompson suffers from no delusions. . . . He has no feelings of paranoia. . . . There are no obsessive thoughts and no obsessive behaviors. . . . He is above average in intelligence. . . . He is simply a lawyer and a citizen who is rationally animated by his activist Christian faith."

The Supreme Court pronounced the issue of Jack Thompson's sanity now closed.

Often when I tell this story in a radio interview or in front of an audience, I end with this: "And so, ladies and gentlemen, I now stand before you as the only officially certified sane lawyer in the entire state of Florida."

But I also point out that I sued the Florida Bar for this nonsense, this willing participation by those who are supposed to regulate the legal profession for the protection of the public, not to protect the porn industry. When I sued the Florida Bar, the bar's insurance carrier was appalled at what had been done to me. The carrier ordered the bar to pay me twenty thousand dollars in damages for the experience. That payment was a matter of great satisfaction, because it memorialized the fact that the bar had allowed itself to be hijacked for no good reason.

By then, Clarence Thomas had been confirmed and was serving on the United States Supreme Court. During his confirmation process, he was accused of having sexually harassed Anita Hill, with references to hard-core pornography. He was dragged through the mud, and in his angry soliloquy to the Senate Judiciary Committee that saved his nomination, he said the proceedings had been "a high-tech lynching for uppity blacks." I felt I had just come through an attempted high-tech lynching of an uppity Christian. It was the worst thing I had ever been through.

I remember one night during law school watching a popular late-night television program on NBC called *The Tomorrow Show*, hosted by Tom Snyder. The show came on right after *The Tonight Show* with Johnny Carson. Snyder's guests that night were a number of individuals who had gone through their own horrible experiences that should have resulted in their deaths. One fellow had been adrift at sea with no water for over a week. Another man, an airport worker, had been sucked through a jet engine on a plane parked at the gate and come through the turbine blades out the other side. Incredible, death-defying stuff.

The most astonishing guest was a man making his first skydive. When he jumped out of the plane neither his primary nor his reserve chutes opened. His body achieved "terminal velocity," hitting the ground, totally unprotected except by his clothes, at about 120 miles per hour. He had sustained more than two hundred fractures of his bones, including multiple fractures of his skull. His face looked almost two-dimensional, perfectly flat, as if he had been run over by a steamroller.

Each of these guests, after facing a near-death experience, now had an unshakable, irrational belief that he was invincible, that he was "bulletproof." I can still remember the words of the skydiver: "I know it's not true, and I know it's not normal, but now I feel that I simply cannot be killed, by anybody or anything."

After I got my letter from the Florida Supreme Court informing me that I could hold on to my law license because I was, after all, sane, I thought about those guests on Tom Snyder's show. At times during this travail I felt like the skydiver looked—utterly flattened by the whole experience. But I had survived it.

For better or for worse, I think it was a blessing to have gone through the experience of being publicly labeled insane and then vindicated. The liberal publications that gleefully went after me on the insanity issue never published anything about my exoneration. But that was okay. The people I cared about knew.

In all the fights that have come my way or that I've instigated since, I have always had the unshakable sense that no one could kill me, at least not spiritually or in any way that mattered.

Is this arrogant, foolish pride, or is it something else? How must David have felt in the years after he slew Goliath? I'll bet he felt that no challenge was so daunting that God would not protect him. All he had to do was remember the day that he stood in that open field, a young boy, face-to-face with a deadly giant. He undoubtedly remembered, and he was buttressed by the memory.

That is what the insanity ploy that failed did for me, and I am thankful for it. As the common saying goes: "What doesn't kill you makes you stronger." As God Himself says in His Word: "In all things God works for the good of those who love him, who have been called according to his purpose" (Romans 8:28).

But is a feeling of invincibility a blessing, or is it a dangerous curse? I believe it is a blessing, as long as one remembers where the protection comes from. It says in God's Word that we are not to fear those who can harm only the flesh (see Matthew 10:28). How do you get to that point? By going through an experience in which one's enemies could have and should have, by all reckoning, harmed you but did not.

I do know this. The feeling of ultimate safety has been exhilarating in the subsequent battles. It lets me sleep at night—at least most nights. As I drift off, God reminds me: *Jack, they took their best shot, and they failed. I am with you, always.*

8

THE 2 LIVE CREW

On New Year's Day 1990, Patricia and I were invited to the festive Coral Gables home of Mike and Pat Thompson, our hosts for a small holiday supper.

Pat was a dedicated Miami public school teacher; Mike, a widely known conservative political activist who had been Dade County's Republican state committeeman for years. If there had been a state title in Florida of "Mr. Conservative," Mike Thompson would have worn it. Mike had narrowly lost his own run for Congress in 1966 and 1968 and then again for lieutenant governor of Florida in 1974. Forgoing any future aspirations for political office, Mike turned his remarkable political skills to assisting others, serving as Ronald Reagan's Greater Miami campaign chairman and adviser for his 1976 run for the White House.

Mike managed and was chief debater for Anita Bryant's successful and nationally watched effort in 1977 to repeal the Dade County gay-rights ordinance. Mike also created the powerful TV ads for conservative activist Phyllis Schlafly's victorious multistate campaign to defeat the Equal Rights Amendment to the U.S. Constitution and turn that liberal campaign into a failure.

Mike was and is what every political activist ought to be—an ideo-
logue in every good meaning of that word, full of constructive ideas
and totally committed to winning and winning fairly. Conservatives
had learned to turn to Mike Thompson for ideas on how to win their
battles in the public square. Mike embodies, almost to a fault, a maxim
favored by Ronald Reagan: "There is no end to what can be accomplished if no one seeks the credit."

Mike also has hosted a number of public-affairs radio and TV talk
shows. When my radio fight began, Mike had the biggest audience of
any weekend talk radio host in South Florida. Off the air, Mike gener-
ously gave me invaluable advice on how to win against an adversary I did
not initially understand. Mike's inside knowledge of the radio industry
and its vulnerabilities to public pressure was indispensable to me in gen-
erating public support for my efforts against shock radio. I would have
been flying blindly without him. I knew God had sent me this expert in
the radio industry when my fight with the radio industry began. This was
not luck. This was Providence.

Mike became more than a helpful confidant and adviser. He became a
friend whose many "Jack, one day this nightmare will end" encourage-
ments helped get me through each new twist in the battle. Mike and I
shared a last name, common distant Scottish ancestral origins, and a love
of politics and conservative values (even our wives have the same name).
But it was Mike's encouragement during my fight with the radio industry that turned us into the spiritual blood brothers neither of us ever had
in the flesh.

Mike's help to me in the trenches forged in me the love I believe fellow soldiers must feel for one another after going through war together.
How do you not love someone who helped get you through combat?

The fact is, the people God has sent me in my fights with the entertainment industry have been precious few, but precious nonetheless.
Mike is a Christian who is fond of quoting Edmund Burke: "All that is
necessary for the triumph of evil is that good men do nothing." Mike has
an activist view of Christianity—that we are to be light and salt—that

agrees with my own. The fact that I, a fellow Christian, would "fight the good fight" against the entertainment industry and claim the name of Christ seemed to encourage Mike as well.

When Mike told me that my efforts encouraged him, he articulated something that I began to sense as well—that perhaps my battle was having some spiritual consequence beyond the radio industry. Maybe God was using what I was doing to actually encourage Christians and other people of faith to believe that there might be room in the public square for people acting on a religious impulse. I was not the only one fighting these fights, but I was trying to do my part. Maybe the counseling advice Lottie Hillard had given me to follow my passion was helping others as well with what they were trying to do. I will never really know this side of heaven, but I had a growing sense that I was part of something bigger than my own little fight in my corner of the world.

Mike and I both thought that if there was room in the public square for a culture war, then maybe the public square, rather than just the church, was a place in which the expression of Christian values could actually bring people to the gospel. I was beginning to believe that. I believe it now more than ever. In other words, holding up God's values to the world served to remind the world and the souls in it that there is a God who must not and cannot be mocked. This to me is not some social gospel. It is *the* gospel—that God really is there and that He stands for something here and now.

So it was on that New Year's Day 1990 that Mike Thompson pulled me aside after a midday dinner to show me something he had received the day before in the mail.

"Jack, this is a mailing I just got from the American Family Association [a grassroots Christian public interest organization in Tupelo, Mississippi, with affiliates in a number of states]. I'm on their regular mailing list because their president, Don Wildmon, was on my show once. It's a transcript that Dr. James Dobson's Focus on the Family has done of some of the songs from a rap album called *As Nasty as They Wanna Be* by a

Miami rap group called 2 Live Crew. Just read this. You're not going to believe it."

I had heard of 2 Live Crew, because in my 1988 political race against Janet Reno for Dade County state attorney, a female rap group was on the Luke Skyywalker record label rapping about Reno's efforts against "deadbeat dads." Luke Skyywalker was the stage name of Luther Campbell, the man who had created 2 Live Crew and the Miami record label.

Mike was right. I was stunned to find what was on this album, which the AFA said had already sold 1.1 million copies, primarily to teenagers. The songs celebrated treating women like dirt, and this message was emanating from my hometown of Miami and being distributed around the planet, *primarily to children*. There was nothing on this album but sexual material.

After he gave me time to read this disturbing mailing, Mike said this: "Jack, you've got to do something about this."

He was right, at least in suggesting that *somebody* had to do something. But why me? I had just come through a bruising fight with the radio industry, and I wanted to get on with my life, get on to make a living as a "normal" lawyer again and try to get my practice back.

"But Jack," Mike insisted, "if you don't take on these guys who are selling this obscene album to kids, then who will? You know how to do this. You can do to the music industry nationally what you did to the radio industry locally."

Oh no, I thought, *not another crusade*.

"Mike, I'll have to think about it and pray about it. I need to figure out if I want to do this." In the back of my mind was the fresh memory that when I wrote that first letter to the radio station, God had not revealed to me what was going to come my way. I trusted God, but I was not sure I was up to this, whatever "this" might turn out to be.

That night, I asked God to show me what—if anything—I should do about this new challenge. Then I slept on it.

I woke up thinking there was something I should do. I felt a peace about doing something about this album, and I felt no fear about doing it. I felt anger, but it was not a personal anger. Rather, I had a coolheaded resolve that adults who were selling this album to kids must not get away with it.

My experiences in life have taught me that decisions are not made solely on the basis of what seems rational, practical, or doable. Decisions are also made based on intuition, feelings if you will, that seem to suggest a course of action. Man is neither pure emotion nor pure intellect. He is both, with a spiritual facet thrown in as well. At that time, it simply felt right to me that I should do something. I felt as if I must do something. *If I did not do something*, I thought, *who would?*

The one thing I knew I had to do was prove that this incredibly filthy album, available as a record, tape, and CD, was actually being sold to minors, people under eighteen.

Why was this important? Because I had learned in my radio fight that federal laws dealing with broadcast standards were based on the ancient and still widely accepted notion that in this free society adults should pretty much be allowed to consume whatever "entertainment" they want. But when it comes to what is sold to children, that's another matter altogether.

For centuries, children have been a "protected class" of individuals in the law. Kids can't buy alcohol in the United States before they are twenty-one, nor can they buy firearms. They can't vote or buy tobacco until they're eighteen, and they can't drive cars until they're sixteen. Why? Because all civilizations, and ours is no exception, have recognized that children are not simply "small adults." They're children who are impressionable and should be protected from "entertainment" that might be especially harmful to them. There is certain material, including sexually themed material, that is just inappropriate for kids to see or hear.

I have stood in front of college campuses and asked, "How many of you think there ought to be live, real, fully-visible-in-every-detail sex between consenting adults on broadcast network television at 7 p.m.?" Invariably, a few hands in an audience with hundreds of people go up. But the vast majority of hands belonging to today's *college students* stay down.

So I am able to say this in response: "Then let's not kid ourselves that any society, including our free society, cannot and should not have lines about what sexual material is put into the public domain for children to consume readily. We need to decide where those lines should be, not whether there should be lines."

I was successful in the radio fight by proving that the shock radio material was harmful to kids and thus punishable if aired to children. *Surely,* I thought, *that must be the way to go when it comes to this album*—to show that an adult album was being sold to kids and that its content was not only appallingly inappropriate for children, but illegally being sold to them.

So first I checked the law. The law in Florida, then as now, is similar to the laws in forty-eight other states. It prohibits the sale to minors of *anything*—pictures, movies, books, sculptures, even sound recordings—depicting sexually explicit details.[1]

I learned in doing my legal research that it is far easier to prove that certain entertainment is sexual material harmful to minors than to prove that it is "obscene" and thus prohibited even for sale to adults.

Florida law requires the "three-prong test" for obscenity. In order to be called obscene, material must (1) appeal to the prurient interest of the consumer, (2) be below the local community's standard of what is acceptable entertainment for adults, and (3) be utterly devoid of any serious literary, artistic, political, or scientific content. In other words, obscene material must be so gross as to revolt a community to the point that it says no adult should be able to get his or her hands on it.

This struck me as a great standard and a useful working definition, for rather than embodying some rigid, unchanging rule, it allows each community, as mores change over time, to define obscenity on a case-by-case basis.

When I handled medical malpractice lawsuits, for example, we judged the doctors on the standard of care they owed patients in their particular health-care community. Standards of practice change from one community to the next and can change, through the passage of time, within each community. Jurors in communities identify and enforce such standards in civil suits all the time. The same was, is, and should be applied when defining obscenity.

But I didn't even want to go that far. I just wanted to proceed on the standard that this stuff, when heard by children, would constitute a harmful, warping view of sex as something you do *to* a woman rather than share, in love, *with* a woman. This album, *As Nasty as They Wanna Be*, was a graphic description and celebration of a kind of sex that a man can force upon a woman for his satisfaction. This is not a message that any child should hear, because the effect would be to normalize such behavior.

I didn't want this fight to be about my musical tastes or about my sense of right and wrong. I wanted this to be what it had to be—a fight over what the law said and whether the law was being violated. This was not my standard; this was the standard enacted by the state of Florida and embodied in its laws. I knew I couldn't back away from this fight when I heard 2 Live Crew's Luther Campbell on Mike Thompson's radio show. If it had been a boxing match, Campbell's corner would have thrown a towel into the ring to end the bout early on. One of the most memorable exchanges started with Mike asking Luther, "I see you have a big gold cross on a chain around your neck. How is it that a Christian feels comfortable portraying women in this way and selling that portrayal to children?"

Campbell replied, "I'm not a Christian. I'm a Baptist."

Campbell went on to explain that if the retailers chose to sell the album to kids, "that's their business. I won't let my own kids listen to it." Those words would come back to haunt Campbell.

I knew God was calling me to engage in this battle.

⚠️

As I began to research what a fight against 2 Live Crew would entail, I realized that my arsenal included an extra bonus. It was the "Tipper

Sticker" found on the *As Nasty as They Wanna Be* album. In the mid-1980s Al Gore's wife, Tipper, had joined forces with Susan Baker, wife of James Baker, who had served as chief of staff and then secretary of the treasury for Ronald Reagan and secretary of state in George H. W. Bush's administration. Tipper and Susan had become concerned about the sexually explicit records that were being sold to children. At that time, Mrs. Gore was recognized as a conservative Democrat, just like her husband, a senator from Tennessee. While in Congress, Gore had a strong pro-life record on abortion. He had an 84 percent anti-abortion voting record and voted pro-life twenty-seven times.[2]

Since then, Al and Tipper Gore have become decidedly more liberal and pro-choice, but back then Tipper spoke for millions of parents in identifying and trying to do something about explicit records being marketed and sold to kids.

The Gores spearheaded hearings in Congress about the problem, and after both sides had their say, the record industry agreed to allow the Parents Music Resource Center, founded by Tipper Gore and Susan Baker, to review all record albums and determine whether their content was such that it should bear a PMRC warning label on its cover that read:

PARENTAL ADVISORY: CONTAINS EXPLICIT MATERIAL. MAY NOT BE SUITABLE FOR ANYONE UNDER 18.

I believe this solution was really just a compromise by all accounts. Both sides thought that if parents were being warned that a record was inappropriate for their kids, then that was enough of a solution. But it was no solution. In fact, it might have even made the problem worse. I found that no record stores anywhere were refusing to sell the 2 Live Crew album to children, even though it featured a PMRC sticker. In fact, one of my favorite political cartoons to come out of what came to be called "the 2 Live Crew Controversy" depicts two kids, appearing to be about ten years old, standing in a record store. One of them is holding a record and saying to the other, "This one's no good. It doesn't have a

warning label on it." In other words, since there was *no legal sanction* attached to the sale of an adult album to a child, the sticker actually became
a sales tool alerting kids to what they should not have but would most as-
suredly want. For kids, parental warnings translated into "buy me!" Besides, any kid who would buy such an album on his own would not likely
run to his parents and say, "Look what I just bought!"

I decided to use the fact that there was a Tipper Sticker on this record
against the record to show that the sticker was in effect an admission that
it was totally inappropriate for children. If I could show that, despite the
sticker, it was being sold to children in Florida, I could then impale the
album on its own packaging.

I called Rev. Tommy Watson of the First Baptist Church of Perrine in
South Dade County, the same church in which I had shared my story
about my fight against local shock radio. I asked Rev. Watson if he knew
of a family in the church who might share my concerns about this album
and had a teenager who would be willing to go into a local Miami record
store and buy this album with money I would provide. "Yes," he said, "I
have just the family."

I called the family and spoke with the parents and then their sixteen-
year-old son. The boy said, "This would be cool. I have classmates in
school who listen to that album all the time. I think it's disgusting. It's very
disrespectful to girls and women. I've told them that. They just laugh."

I arranged for the boy to meet me at Spec's, a large music store, which
at the time was part of a chain of such stores in the Miami area. I gave him
the money, and as I stood near the cash registers, he went right to the album, picked it up, marched up to the cash register, and with no questions
asked, no ID requested, he was able to walk out of the store with his copy
of *As Nasty as They Wanna Be*, with its label warning parents that this
might not be appropriate material for their kids. There were no parents in
sight.

I then went to all of the local television stations and the *Miami Herald*
with a news release telling what I had done and why—that I had done
what in law enforcement circles is called a reverse sting to prove that "an

album that contains sexual material and that is labeled as inappropriate for children is being sold to children in mainstream record stores on Main Street America."

Only one media entity in South Florida, WSVN Channel 7, at the time an NBC affiliate, thought this was a story. The reporter who was assigned the story was a young reporter by the name of Michael Williams. He called and asked me to meet him at the store where I had done the sting.

Williams came with a cameraman. He interviewed me right in front of Spec's as I told him what I had done and why. He then did a brilliant thing. He interviewed a boy who was fourteen as he came out of the store with his mother. Williams showed the mother and the boy a copy of the album, with the nearly naked women on the cover and some of the explicit lyrics on the back. "Do you have this album?" he asked the boy.

Remarkably, he said, "Yes, all my friends have this album."

His mother looked at him and said, "You have this album? Kids can buy an album like this?"

"Yes," said Williams to the astonished mother, "any kid can buy this album anywhere." It was clear that the mother was annoyed with her son and annoyed with the store.

This whole story, brought down to the appropriate level of a family issue, aired on that night's evening news. In short order, what one station recognized as a news story was indeed news to others in the media. Even the *Miami Herald* recognized it as a story and did a small piece about the antipornography crusader Jack Thompson, a descriptive phrase they often used for me. At least they spelled my name correctly.

The local news coverage had given me what I needed—corroboration.

Armed with that as backing, I then wrote a letter to each of the sheriffs for each of the sixty-seven counties in Florida and told them that enclosed they would find the lyrics to an album that was being sold to children across the state and across the country, as reported by the local Miami media. I also told them that I had called a number of record stores in their various jurisdictions and found that indeed this same album was being sold to children, no questions asked, in music stores there. I added that in my legal opinion such sales constituted a violation of a specific criminal statute in Florida—Section 847.012—and that such sales of "sexual material harmful to minors" could and should be identified and prosecuted. I concluded by stating that this album was so thoroughly sex and nothing but sex that it might even be obscene and thus contraband for sale to adults. With that, I wanted to underscore how inappropriate it was for children to get their hands on it. But this was a "sound recording," and as far as I could tell, there had never been a determination by any court of law that a sound recording was "harmful to minors" or that a sound recording was "obscene" for sale to adults. *We were going to find out if such a thing was possible*, I thought. The statute provided for such a determination, but the uniqueness of the question and the situation was intriguing, and I also thought it was important.

I was wrong—wrong in thinking nothing would happen.

I got a call from the sheriff's department in Lee County, whose county seat is Fort Myers, on the southwest coast of Florida. A deputy said their department was interested in joining this battle against 2 Live Crew. "I am thankful that you are, but you are the first sheriff's department to call. Can you tell me why you're interested?"

"Sure can. There was an incident over here that made the papers. A schoolteacher at Fort Myers Beach Elementary School was on the playground during recess recently, and she heard a bunch of kids describing sex acts to one another in what sounded like a song. It freaked her out. She asked where the kids had heard all that stuff. Turns out there was a ten-year-old boy who got his hands on 2 Live Crew's *As Nasty as They Wanna Be* and taught the lyrics to his classmates. Some parents asked our department what could be done about this album that is out there, available to kids. We weren't sure. Now you've given us the answer."

This stunned me. I had sent letters to sixty-seven sheriffs, expecting not a single one of them to do anything with it, and yet here was a sheriff's department that had been looking for precisely what I had given them—a transcription of the album and a legal analysis of why selling this album to children violated a Florida criminal statute.

Instantly, I felt God was at work. I realized that all the radio trouble had been worth it, that it had prepared me for another fight. This fight might be even bigger, it might have more consequence, and it would likely require me to be smarter and more astute than I had previously been. I had been a student in the radio fight, it seemed, so that I could be a smarter student in a subsequent classroom. *God*, I prayed, *what is it You are going to do this time?* I was both excited and scared to find out.

The sheriff's deputy had told me that they were going to take my letter, as well as the transcribed lyrics and the album itself, before a local judge. They would ask this judge to answer two questions: (1) Is there probable cause that this album is sexual material harmful to minors? and (2) Is this album "obscene" under *Miller v. California* (and thus illegal to sell even to adults)? The deputy told me he would let me know what the judge decided.

Late on a Friday afternoon I picked up a message on my answering machine from a Fort Myers television reporter. As "luck" would have it, I was not in Miami but actually in Fort Myers when the call came. Patricia's parents were vacationing there, and we had driven up to spend some time with them. I returned the call to the reporter for WINK-TV, a CBS affiliate, who told me, "Mr. Thompson, a Lee County judge has just entered an order finding probable cause that 2 Live Crew's *As Nasty as They Wanna Be* is obscene. The sheriff's department has issued a warning to all record stores in Lee County that any sale of this album—to a child or an adult—will be considered a criminal act. We want to interview you by phone for this, since you're in Miami, and we want this on the evening news."

"Actually," I told him, "I'm in Fort Myers right now."

"Can you be here in one hour?"

"You bet."

This would be my first live television interview, and although I knew the issue was extremely important, I was still scared to death.

Fortunately, I had little to fear. The interview went well; the interviewer was fair, giving me plenty of opportunities to share the details of our case. He was, in fact, quite shocked when I shared some of the content of the album.

The next day, the Fort Myers newspaper ran a front-page story about the judge's probable cause ruling. The story noted that the court ruling that a sound recording was obscene was unprecedented. The Associated Press picked up the story, and it appeared across the country.

The bottom line was this: America had just learned that obscene records were being sold to children in mainstream music stores on Main Street America. If we did not have a "culture war" before this, I was pretty sure we might have the beginnings of one now.

Thank You, God of coincidences and surprises. I was now sure that none of this was happening by chance, and I was glad of it.

When this story popped up all over the country, I got a phone call from an African American woman in Sarasota, Florida, who said, "Mr. Thompson, I tracked you down because I wanted to thank you. Did you know that this last Easter Day parade in Sarasota, some young kids calling themselves 2 Live Crew marched down the street in the parade pretending to engage in anal intercourse?"

I hadn't heard that, I told her. But it was clearly proof that selling adult sexual material to children had an effect, and in a very public way.

Within days, the Lake County sheriff, whose jurisdiction is northwest of Orlando in the central part of the state, contacted me and asked me to meet with some of his deputies. I drove over and talked to his force about the album's content and what they could do, legally, to stop its sale. Shortly thereafter, a judge in Ocala echoed the decision by the judge in Fort Myers and entered an order declaring *As Nasty as They Wanna Be* "probably obscene" and thus illegal for sale to adults as well as children.

What could be passed off as an aberrant or idiosyncratic ruling in one place could not be so easily dismissed as such now that two judges in two different jurisdictions had made the same ruling. There was one more such ruling to come.

In what was still the winter of 1990, Broward County sheriff Nick Navarro put my letter, the transcript of the album, and the album itself before a Broward County circuit court judge. Broward's county seat is Fort Lauderdale. This judge handed down the third order declaring that 2 Live Crew's *As Nasty as They Wanna Be* was "probably obscene." With this ruling, the second most populous county in the state joined the battle. This was significant because this portion of the state—Palm Beach, Broward, and Dade counties—had a reputation of "anything goes." But here, in the land of *Miami Vice*, a judge had listened to the album and had determined it was way over the line, which in South Florida is really saying something.

9

AS OBSCENE AS A COURT WANTS IT TO BE

With three court rulings claiming *As Nasty as They Wanna Be* was probably obscene, Luke Skyywalker Records really began to feel the pressure. Not only had the record been pulled off store shelves in the three counties with court orders, it was removed from stores in the rest of the state as well. Other sheriffs were reading the papers and seeing the television reports on the controversy. I was thankful that law enforcement was acting upon the issue. The supply of records was quickly drying up not just in Florida, but also in other states because of what was becoming national news coverage.

Enter the American Civil Liberties Union. In my experience, this civil rights group focuses so much on freedom of speech that it often ignores the content of that speech. I don't know if Luther Campbell contacted the ACLU or vice versa, but either way, the union between a music pornographer and the ACLU was a marriage made in hell. The ACLU's lawyer in all this was Bruce Rogow, a law professor at Nova Southeastern University who sports bow ties and a mustache-less Abe Lincoln beard.

Professor Rogow brought what is called a declaratory judgment action in the federal court for the Southern District of Florida in Fort Lauderdale. Rogow sought a federal court ruling that *As Nasty as They Wanna Be* was *not* obscene, and thus was protected as speech by the First Amendment. The ACLU figured that the federal judiciary, with judges typically more liberal (with life tenure) than state judges who were elected, would be more likely to rule in its favor. This was a perfectly legitimate strategy, as there was clearly a federal constitutional issue at stake here.

The ACLU also petitioned the court to be *amicus curiae*, which is Latin for "friend of the court," and entitles someone who is not actually a party in a lawsuit to file documents to inform the court about certain issues, facts, and legal authority. In this way, both the ACLU lawyer, who was representing 2 Live Crew as his client, and the ACLU organization as a public-interest entity could participate in the case and use it as a platform from which to posit their views on these First Amendment issues.

If the ACLU was going to be a friend of the court, I thought the lawyer responsible for bringing this controversy to a boil should be counted as a friend of the court as well, so I petitioned the court for that status. The ACLU objected, but the court granted my petition.

The ACLU, Rogow, and 2 Live Crew were delighted with the judge to whom the case was randomly assigned. They all told the media how pleased they were that this judge was assigned to this case, calling him a "friend of the Constitution." In other words, they felt very confident that this federal judge would agree with their view of the First Amendment. He was Jose A. Gonzalez Jr., appointed by President Jimmy Carter, roundly praised as a liberal judge who interpreted the law to guarantee civil rights to expand freedoms rather than constrict them. The defendant in the case was Sheriff Nick Navarro, who had put the album, the lyrics, and my letter before the Broward County judge. Navarro was known, by friends and foes alike, as "Nick at Nite" because of his penchant for drug busts and other high-profile police work timed and publicized in such a way as to maximize the possibility that his work and his face would wind up on the local evening news. Navarro was a self-promoter, and this gave me pause. How committed was Navarro to winning this case? Was he just in it for the publicity, or did he really care about the fact that adult sexual material was being sold to children? We would find out in short order.

Another thing that gave me pause—a very long pause—was that this issue had morphed from a "sexual material harmful to minors" case into an obscenity case, which meant that the album would be judged as to whether it was contraband for adults, not just harmful to children. I knew from my radio fight that there was incalculably more agreement across the political spectrum that sexual material should not be sold to kids. There was far less consensus as to what was obscene for sale to adults.

This put me in a battle along lines that I had not chosen, but it was the battle as now framed. I had to fight it, like it or not. I thought the album was indeed obscene, but I knew that hurdle, both in societal views and in the law, was much higher. Knowing that was the issue, off to court we went.

Judge Gonzalez set the case for trial in May 1990. As soon as the trial began, there was national and worldwide news coverage. Never before had there been a trial with the possibility that a sound recording could be held obscene. The earlier proceedings in Florida were just probable cause hearings. This would be a full-blown trial on the issue of whether the album was obscene. The media thought this was a possibility both absurd and remote.

I liked being in this situation much more than the radio wars I had just come through, as the issue that was front and center was the specific entertainment product being distributed willy-nilly to adults and children alike. The issue was not Jack Thompson, nor my alleged insanity, but rather it was a specific product that had everyone's attention.

This made the stakes more manageable for me personally—at least it felt that way. I also felt, quite honestly, that this was so clearly a right versus wrong issue that I took some delight in noting that all the "important" and "influential" people, especially the self-appointed opinion molders in the national media, were full of scorn for the notion that a sound recording could possibly be obscene.

Saturday Night Live even did a skit on the 2 Live Crew controversy, with guest host Kyle MacLachlan, who had starred on *Twin Peaks*, portraying me as the quintessential religious fanatic. *Wow*, I thought, *if we're being lampooned on SNL, we must have somebody's attention.*

⚠

During the federal trial, Professor Rogow put an English professor from Harvard on the stand. This professor compared *As Nasty as They Wanna Be* to the earthy content of Chaucer's *Canterbury Tales*. He also introduced evidence from "experts" that rap music was simply black culture misunderstood and not appreciated by white America, that the effort against 2 Live Crew's album sprang from racism.

As an *amicus curiae*, I was not allowed to participate in the case in any fashion. I would just be allowed to express what I knew of the law and the facts and the issues raised by both sides in written memoranda submitted to the court. Friends of the court can be ignored by the court and often are. What really mattered most was what was and wasn't going on in that courtroom.

The only witnesses that Navarro's team put on the stand were detectives from Navarro's office who had precious little knowledge of what was on the album.

Navarro's attorney put absolutely no evidence before the judge, who was trying the case without a jury, as to any of the three prongs of the *Miller* obscenity test. Absolutely no evidence at all. In other words, no experts and no fact witnesses were provided to the judge as evidence that this was sexual material appealing to the prurient interest of the consumer and that it was below this local community's standards for such material.

My instinct is always to give law enforcement the benefit of the doubt, but when you have a situation such as this in which the law enforcement community is involved in a case and appears to be botching it, the benefit of the doubt evaporates. This was a battle with significance beyond the

Broward sheriff's office, but it didn't seem like they understood that. The sheriff was doing nothing, as far as I could tell, to win this case.

As I watched the case unfold, it seemed that Sheriff Navarro was totally and intentionally lying down—taking a dive. The trial was nearly over, and only one side had put on a case; I wondered if Sheriff Navarro, this "Nick at Nite," really only wanted the headlines, not the fight. It certainly seemed that way. For when the fight came his way, he did what he could to get it over with as quickly and as quietly as possible.

When I realized what was going on—that a local sheriff had tried to hijack this issue only to fly it into the ground—I called Sheriff Navarro's attorney and offered him experts who could put into evidence proof of the three prongs of the *Miller* test. This attorney, John Jolly, was not the least bit interested in any help, and he told me so.

I filed a motion alerting the court. In that motion, I said to Judge Gonzalez that Sheriff Navarro was, for whatever reason, "taking a dive," which did a disservice to the people he had taken an oath to protect. Secondly, I provided to the court a case that established the precedent that although rare, an *amicus curiae* could actually introduce evidence in the form of live witnesses in the courtroom. In other words, I had found a law that would allow me to jump into that courtroom and try to save the case with experts who could address all three prongs of the *Miller* obscenity case.

I concluded by saying to the judge, "You may find, Your Honor, this album obscene, but such an order will never survive an appeal by the ACLU and 2 Live Crew, because there will be absolutely no evidence on the record to sustain such an order by you."

Judge Gonzalez, despite the precedent found in the case law that would have allowed me to do so, denied my request to put on that evidence. 2 Live Crew and its attorney now had an open field.

The trial was concluded, with no meaningful case put on by Sheriff Navarro, and Judge Gonzales told everyone, including the media, that he would have his verdict in a matter of days or weeks. So we waited. On the morning of June 21, 1990, the call came from the judge's secretary that I should be in his courtroom in an hour. The judge had made his decision. I called Mike Thompson, and we rode up to Fort Lauderdale from Coral Gables just in time to enter the courtroom with 2 Live Crew, the ACLU's lawyers, and all the media and members of the public who could cram themselves into that small room.

Before we went into the courtroom, Bruce Rogow saw Mike and me and began to grin.

As we went into the courtroom, my lawyer's instincts and training told me that Rogow probably had plenty to grin about.

Shortly after Mike and I took our seats, Judge Gonzalez came into the courtroom. We all rose, and then he said this: "Bailiff, lock that door at the back of this courtroom. All of you here are going to read my sixty-two-page opinion, and you're going to get a lesson in the First Amendment. You will be allowed to leave when you're done with the lesson."

My blood ran cold. A federal judge was saying that we were all going to get a crash course in what many federal judges believe—that the First Amendment, not as I believe the Founding Fathers construed it but as modernity now interpreted it, was there to protect pornographers, not children. Court personnel were expeditiously handing out copies of the sixty-two-page opinion to all in the courtroom. Mike and I waited for ours at the far end of a row, as if we were receiving the collection plate during a church service.

When we got our copies, Mike started reading on the first page. I knew better. I knew that the punch line was at the end. I immediately turned to the last page and read these words:

ORDERED AND ADJUDGED THAT 2 LIVE CREW'S ALBUM *AS NASTY AS THEY WANNA BE* IS OBSCENE.

I was stunned. I immediately looked at Luther Campbell, Bruce Rogow, and Robin Blumner, who was the South Florida head of the ACLU. They had gone to the back page as well. They looked as if they had just received some terrible news—and they had. My eyes met Bruce Rogow's. The smile was gone.

Apparently others had read the back page as well, because gasps were heard all over that locked, packed courtroom. This liberal, ACLU-praised judge had just ruled that a record album was obscene. The courtroom started to buzz. The judge banged down his gavel and said, "When you are done reading this order in silence, you will then be allowed to leave. Not before then. There will be order." Silence fell once again, as only pages could be heard turning. We were in the Church of the Constitution.

I went to the front of the opinion, which began with this: "This is a classic disagreement between those who say 'Anything goes' and those who say 'Enough already.'"

Somewhere before the punch line at the end, Judge Gonzalez addressed the issue of what Sheriff Navarro did not do—that he did not introduce a shred of evidence that the album was obscene. Judge Gonzalez dealt with that this way: "This court [meaning this particular judge] has presided over obscenity cases before, and this court's experience is substantial enough to know, based upon its clear understanding of what is obscene and what is not, and after listening to this album in its entirety, this court can, with assurance conclude that this album is clearly obscene, in that it contains sex and nothing but, appeals to the interest of the consumer only in that regard, and is below the community standard of Palm Beach, Broward, and Dade Counties for such material."

In other words, Judge Gonzalez was saying that he knew obscenity when he saw it because he had seen it before, and this album was obscene. Period.

I appreciated, more than anyone could possibly know, that this federal judge had applied his common sense to an uncommonly filthy adult product marketed to children. But my exhilaration with the verdict was tempered, almost immediately, with the fear that the judge's good sense would not ultimately be enough to sustain his ruling. There was nothing in the court record from the defendant, Sheriff Navarro, showing that the album was obscene. I knew this could have terrible consequences on appeal.

In the meantime, however, I knew that the world had just been given, as if on stone tablets brought down from Sinai, the first federal verdict in history that a sound recording was obscene.

When the courtroom's lesson on the First Amendment was over, Judge Gonzalez ordered the doors unlocked, and the media made a mad dash for pay phones (in that pre-cell-phone era) and to cars to get to their employers.

Set up outside the courtroom were all the electronic media, ready to broadcast live whatever the court had just decided. John Zarrella of CNN saw me and beckoned me to come over to where he was standing on the courthouse steps. We did a quick, live interview. "Mr. Thompson, you're the one who got this ball rolling," he said. "What does it mean?"

"It means that if this adult album, which is being sold to children, is not even legal for sale to adults in the region of the country identified with *Miami Vice* where anything goes, then this album is clearly obscene in Topeka, Kansas, and anywhere else in America."

At that point, Luther Campbell saw me being interviewed, put his face in front of mine, and shouted an obscenity at me, directing me to engage in a certain sexual activity. *Pretty brilliant way to convince America that you're a responsible recording artist,* I thought.

⚠

With this historic ruling, my life, which had been changed by a local fight with a radio station, was altered even more by a national fight with the recording industry. Suddenly, I was living a completely different life, at least in the short run.

I got a call the very next morning from CNN in Washington. They wanted me to fly up that day to Washington, D.C., to appear on *Crossfire*. *Crossfire* was then hosted by Michael Kinsley "on the left" and by Pat Buchanan "on the right." The show's producers wondered if I would be willing to be a guest on the show.

"Are you kidding? I watch *Crossfire* almost every night," I told them. "I would walk there if I had to."

When I got to CNN's studios an hour or so before the live broadcast, I was told to go to makeup. Other than the immediate postverdict sound bite, I had never been on national television before. Now I was to be made up by a makeup artist. This was almost too much to process! In the makeup room I met Michael Kinsley, who was surprisingly pleasant, cordial, and funny. *Maybe this isn't going to be so scary after all,* I thought.

I was feeling pretty calm when I was done in makeup and told to hurry down to the studio in which I would sit with Kinsley and Buchanan. On the way there, I passed Bernard Shaw in the hallway. He was reading something with his reading glasses pushed down on his nose. He was not wearing a suit jacket, and his tie was loosened. He looked very much like a journalist, which of course he was. Bernard Shaw had deservedly come to everyone's attention in 1988 when he asked Governor Mike Dukakis, in his second debate with Vice President Bush, if he would drop his opposition to the death penalty if his own wife, Kitty, were raped and killed. The question started the ascendance of Shaw's star, whose zenith was reached when he bravely reported live from a Baghdad hotel—at great physical risk to himself—the first bombardment of that city during the opening moments of the 1991 Persian Gulf War.

When I saw Bernard Shaw, I felt the same way I did as a teenager when I went to see the Cleveland Indians play the New York Yankees and got so close to Mickey Mantle that he could have heard me sneeze. I was starstruck, but what made it more unnerving was that I was not a spectator, really. I was to be a participant, and as much as I cared about the issue that brought me there, the weakening in my knees that came with seeing Bernard Shaw made me want to be on a plane headed back to Miami—right then.

Bernard Shaw looked up from his papers and stopped walking. There must have been something about my green color that convinced him I was to be a guest on *Crossfire.*

"Hello, Mr. Shaw. How are you?"

"I'm fine, and you'll be fine too." As he started to walk again he said, "And by the way, call me Bernie."

"Thank you, Mr. Shaw." I couldn't even get that right.

The butterflies that were flying in my stomach were not flying in formation. It had to look more like bumper cars in there.

I walked maybe thirty more feet and through some doors into the studio for the *Crossfire* broadcast. Some members of the technical crew were there to meet me. They told me that the two hosts would be in within moments. We were five minutes or so from airtime. I looked around. Everything was black except for the brilliantly lit desk at which I would sit between the two hosts "on the left" and "on the right" of me, with the person on my left being the person "on the right" to the audience. It all made me feel off balance.

The contrast between the light and the dark reminded me of what a near-death experience must be like, as described by some who have escaped death's jaws while unconscious: speeding down a pitch-black tunnel toward light. But the light at the end of this tunnel seemed to me like the proverbial locomotive. I wandered over to a darkened corner of the room and began to pray. This was too much for me. I was not ready for this. God had put me into a place I didn't think I could survive. I was about to go on national television, for the first—and I prayed the last—time, with the strong likelihood I would mess up in front of hundreds of thousands of people, and that was if I did not pass out first.

My eyes were closed when I heard someone come into the room and someone else say, "Hey, Pat!" Pat Buchanan had arrived before Kinsley. He made a beeline for me.

"You're Jack Thompson, aren't you?" he asked.

"Yes, sir," I managed meekly.

"You're about to throw up, aren't you?" Pat Buchanan had diagnosed my stage fright perfectly. I had been in plays as a kid, had already appeared on the Fort Myers TV station, and had done dozens of radio and newspaper interviews. None of that had felt like this. I truly thought I *was* about to throw up.

I nodded in reply. Pat Buchanan, who was not treating his question nor my answer flippantly, put his right arm around me and tightened it in a hug. "Look, what you have done with this 2 Live Crew thing is important," he said. "I'm proud of you. Millions of people are proud of you. You're going to do great here tonight, because remember this: If Kinsley gives you a hard time, I'll slug him."

At that, I involuntarily laughed. Pat Buchanan's eyes twinkled as his face crinkled into a grin. And immediately I felt the blood return to my head. *I can do this*, I thought.

On the jacket of Pat Buchanan's recent book, *Where the Right Went Wrong*, written fourteen years after this *Crossfire* appearance, the well-known commentator Fred Barnes, a conservative who disagrees with Pat Buchanan on a number of issues, says "Mr. Buchanan has a secret weapon: charm."[1]

Indeed he does, and that day Pat Buchanan used it to save my suddenly public life. I will never forget the kindness shown me that day first by Michael Kinsley, then by Bernard Shaw, and finally by Pat Buchanan.

There were three guests for the interview. One was Bruce Rogow, live via satellite from South Florida, and the other was Jello Biafra, a performer in a rock group called the Dead Kennedys. We parried back and forth about what the verdict meant, with the other two claiming that the First Amendment protected the album.

I left the interview studio and then CNN headquarters almost skipping. I was so glad that I had survived this experience. I did not do great, but I wasn't a disaster either. I wondered if I would ever do an interview like that again.

I soon found out that the answer was yes. Following that CNN interview was a whirlwind of national television appearances in the span of a couple of weeks, including ABC's *Nightline* the next night to debate the national head of the ACLU, Nadine Strossen. Strossen began by talking about how great the album was. I asked her if she had ever listened to it. She admitted she had not. The interview seemed to go downhill for her after that. Another guest on that *Nightline* was Bruce Rogow, of course. The host, Ted Koppel, said to Rogow, "Now Professor Rogow, I know you believe that this album is true art. . . ." I interrupted, I am sure rudely, and said, "No, he doesn't!" Rogow laughed, I believe because he knew that I had blurted out the truth.

I was then invited to be a guest on ABC's *Good Morning America*. ABC flew me up to New York the night before, and I arose at 5 a.m. to be driven to the studio. I waited in the green room before being hurried to a sofa on the set where I was to be interviewed by Joan Lunden. Just before we went on the air, she leaned over and whispered, "Jack, I have young children. As a mom, I want to thank you personally for doing this."

A day or so later I was on *CBS This Morning*. The interviewer—or more accurately, the referee—was Paula Zahn. She fielded the debate between William Kunstler and me. Kunstler was a high-profile criminal defense lawyer who represented the Chicago Seven after the Chicago riots in 1968 following the Democratic National Convention. He was well-known as a liberal political activist. Although the discussion grew quite heated at times, I felt as if God was giving me the answers.

In my debate with Kunstler that morning, he called me a "book-burning Nazi," to which I responded by calling him a "liar" in suggesting that the First Amendment protects the distribution of pornography to children. Kunstler looked like he had been hit with a burning book. He was stunned that anyone would give it back to him. It must have been good theater, because the CBS people cancelled the upcoming commercial break, cancelled what was supposed to be the next segment of the show, and let us two lawyers try to eviscerate one another on national TV. Paula Zahn was great, just as I would have expected from a lady who grew up in Canton, Ohio, where my folks live.

I then appeared on *The Phil Donahue Show* with Luther Campbell himself. Campbell, of course, called me a racist. I was glad that he had because I wanted the opportunity to prove him wrong. I told a story about the first time my life had ever been threatened. It had been in 1969 when, as student mayor for a day of my all-white Ohio suburb, I had called for open housing for people of all races. I understood racism, and I was determined to prove that this fight had nothing to do with racism.

Campbell then told Phil that *Nasty* was just a party album, that it did not depict violence against women. Phil Donahue called Luther's attention to his own lyrics, pointing to the vulgar words up on the screen as he talked. For once in his life, Luther Campbell had nothing to say.

The national media was shining light on a very dark place in America's popular culture. American parents, it seemed, were beginning to understand that filth was being marketed and sold to children on Main Street America.

And so it went for a dizzying month or so—lead stories on the front page of *USA Today* and other papers, television appearances, and even a mean-spirited, lengthy hatchet job by the *Miami Herald*. After weeks of missed meals and running on adrenaline, I found that I had lost fifteen pounds, a noticeable loss off a frame that was thin to begin with.

My wife, Patricia, was happy for me. We both felt as if this 2 Live Crew fallout was a blessing from God for our faithfulness during the radio wars.

In the fall of 1990, *Billboard* magazine, whose reporter, Bruce Haring, really put the 2 Live Crew controversy on the national news front burner, graciously gave me the opportunity to pen a first-page guest op-ed on the meaning of the controversy and where it would lead. The recording industry, it seemed, was listening to someone they considered an enemy.

The television appearances spawned a college debate and lecture tour on well over a hundred campuses in which my favorite and best opponent was Bob Guccione Jr., the son of the founder of *Penthouse* magazine. Bob was himself the owner and publisher of music-oriented *Spin* magazine and was the real draw on the campuses, not I. But Bob was and is a charming man who obviously gets along with conservatives quite nicely, as he dated right-wing siren Ann Coulter for some time. This was all fun, all exhilarating—and it was important in advancing the cause I felt called to. The college debate tour also provided me with income, as colleges were paying me and my various opponents to come to their campuses to address the topic of music censorship. The income was appreciated and, frankly, had a spiritual significance for me as well. I felt as if God was rewarding me in a tangible way for being faithful. I obviously had not taken on the radio stations and the recording industry for the purpose of making money, but it made me feel better as a husband that I was able to contribute to the income of our two-person family in this fashion.

Surprisingly, standing up in front of hostile crowds was also a little exhilarating for me. It always gave me an adrenaline rush when I walked into a huge hall filled with two thousand students. But at one school, Arizona State University, I walked onto the stage, only to see a banner streaming across the wall that read "F— Jack Thompson!" I knew I had my work cut out for me there, and the banner kind of made my point that our culture might have a problem.

The hostility also made me a better speaker, as I was learning to communicate in the sound-bite culture of today. In a courtroom, I could talk more deliberately. But college campuses and *Crossfire* required urgent talk now. It is a skill that can only be developed through experience, and I was enjoying the experience.

Without a doubt, however, now that the 2 Live Crew verdict was entered, I was identified by the mainstream media and on college campuses as Public Enemy Number One of the Constitution. God and I both knew better, and there was a certain amount of mischievous fun that comes from being misunderstood and then being given the opportunity to prove your critics wrong about who you are and what you stand for. I was having the time of my life. I was glad that I had taken Lottie Hillard's advice to follow my passion.

Even beyond the personal satisfaction, the 2 Live Crew case had given me an opportunity to talk face-to-face with tens of thousands—and on TV, millions—of people about what deeply troubled me and others: the marketing and sale of harmful adult entertainment to children. What began with a letter from a libertarian lawyer to a local radio station had come to this. I was amazed.

The legal side of the 2 Live Crew matter came to a not-so-happy conclusion—as I had predicted and had warned Judge Gonzalez. The U.S. Eleventh Circuit Court of Appeals in Atlanta, in hearing Rogow's appeal for 2 Live Crew, found that because there was no evidence submitted by the sheriff at the trial, there could be no sustainable finding that the album was obscene. The court did not rule that the album was *not obscene*, as wrongly reported by the liberal media, but rather that Sheriff Navarro *did not try to prove* that any of the three prongs of the *Miller* obscenity test were present. I could not disagree with the ruling. You have to prove an album is obscene in order to make that label stick.

Navarro's office then took an appeal to the U.S. Supreme Court. He really had no choice, as he had begun a legal fight and he at least had to go through the motions to finish it. Given the high-profile nature of the case, the Supreme Court agreed to hear arguments on the case. I knew what the ruling would be. The Supreme Court ruled, as had the Eleventh Circuit, that the album had not been proven obscene. The media, of course, with huge headlines, reported that the High Court had ruled that "The Album Is Not Obscene!" But in reality, this was not what the Court was saying. What the Supreme Court had done was analogous to their getting a case in which it was alleged that the world was round rather than flat but not being given any evidence by the party claiming it was round. Although the legal battle was ultimately lost, I believed that a more important battle, one fought in the public square, was won. The 2 Live Crew controversy was, in many ways, the opening battle in what some have—correctly, I believe—called the culture war. America learned through this controversy that pornography was not just available to adults, but also to children. Adults were shocked to find out what was really on this album, as some newspapers actually printed the lyrics. Light was being shown into the darkness, and people were being aroused from slumber.

What had we accomplished through this flap over an album? In my opinion, the "decency movement" and the "entertainment industry" had been like two ships passing in the night. The passengers on the deck of the decency ship had been wringing their hands and pointing their fingers at what was going on on the other ship. Those on the entertainment ship were laughing at and waving to those on the other vessel. I felt that I had grabbed the wheel of the decency ship and rammed that other ship, convinced that the time for talk about how bad pop culture had become was over. It was time for consequences for those who had made it that bad. This strategy of acting upon the facts rather than just identifying the facts annoyed the entertainment industry. It also annoyed many in the decency movement, including people identifying themselves as Christians. Many claimed that to proceed as I had was judgmental, unloving, and not the role of Christians in society.

I disagreed. In my mind, it was lead, follow, or get out of the way. No more talking. Talk is cheap. It was time to stop playing defense and start playing offense. It was time to win this culture war.

Within days of the trial verdict in the 2 Live Crew case, George Will wrote a column on his customary last page of *Newsweek* about all this, calling the 2 Live Crew episode proof of "America's slide into the sewer."[2] The article was so well done and captured the essence of the problem—that America was not exactly a shining city on a hill in these regards—that it was read by Bob Dornan, a California congressman, into the Congressional Record on the floor of the House of Representatives.

To say I was looking to make all this happen is, to paraphrase C. S. Lewis in *Surprised by Joy*, to suggest that I was a mouse looking for a cat. I had no idea, when any of this started, that it would be such a big deal. How could I? What I knew then, and what I know now more than ever, is that while this battle was a very big deal, Jack Thompson was not a very big deal. God used me, despite my middling abilities and my shortcomings as both a person and as a lawyer. I realized that if God could use me, then He could use anyone. This had not been an ego trip. This was a trip God had graciously taken me on. The battle had been His. What a thrill it was to see it up close.

10
COLONEL CAN-DO

In May 1992 my phone rang, and when I picked it up, the voice on the other end said, "Jack, this is Ollie North."

I was momentarily stunned. Either this guy was a great mimic or it really was Lt. Col. Oliver North. I decided to assume that he was the real McCoy until he proved otherwise.

"Colonel North, it's an honor to speak with you. What can I do for you?" As he began to tell me the reason for his call, I knew this was indeed the man who had stood Congress and the country on their ear during the Iran-Contra hearings. His voice even cracked repeatedly like it did during the hearings.

"Jack, I followed what you did in the 2 Live Crew case, and like a lot of other Americans, I appreciated it. Besides being involved in making security devices, bulletproof vests, and the like for law enforcement officers, I am now the head of an organization in the Washington, D.C., area called Freedom Alliance. Freedom Alliance gets involved in the questions of the day and puts forth what we think are the conservative answers to those questions."

He went on to explain that there was a song out there by the rapper

Ice-T called "Cop Killer." "Police across the country are upset that this song advocates killing cops. They are getting organized, trying to put together a boycott against Time Warner, which is distributing the song on Ice-T's album *Body Count*."

Officers had talked to Oliver North about the issue since he was dealing with law enforcement agencies every day. It seemed natural for him to get involved, not just because of his dealings with the police but also because of his public concerns about the current state of American pop culture. "I think we do have a problem in this country with popular culture that is increasingly violent, filled with sexual content, and marketed to kids," he said.

"I have two questions, Jack. First, is there anything you can do to help us, given your familiarity with the rap music industry? And second, how much would you charge us to help?"

As I paused to respond, I was struck by how incredibly direct and to the point he was. He told me the facts, told me the problem, and asked me what to do. His was a mind trained to formulate an objective and go for it. I understood why he had been a part of a can-do White House.

"Colonel," I began, "let me address the fee issue first. God did not send me into relatively safe battles against the pornography industry and the music industry to turn around and charge real soldiers—who are real heroes. I will not charge you for my time and effort. After what you did for me and my country in Vietnam and elsewhere, that's the least I can do."

"We'll argue about that later," Col. North said, "but thank you. Now, tell me what we can do." Col. Can-Do was back on duty.

"I've heard a bit about this flap, but I'm not as on top of it as you are," I told him. "Remember I haven't done any legal research or fact-checking, but I'll give you my initial thoughts. First off, Time Warner is the company that distributed 2 Live Crew's pornography. Kids copycatted that album. I even received a call from a girl who told me that a friend of hers was raped in school by a gang of boys while they played *As Nasty as They Wanna Be* on their boom box."

I told him about the woman who called from Sarasota about the kids at the Easter Day parade. "Time Warner can't say then that music products they have distributed have not influenced kids to do things. So it is useful that the target here again is Time Warner.

"Secondly, the possibility that someone might copycat this song— killing police officers—causes two problems for Time Warner. One, civil liability on the part of Time Warner to any surviving family member of a police officer killed by someone responding to the call to murder police, and two, criminal liability on the part of Time Warner for soliciting people to kill police officers."

If we could show that there was a "clear and present danger" posed by the song to police officers, then a criminal court might entertain a prosecution of Ice-T and Time Warner for solicitation of murder. A civil court might also be able to enter an injunction prohibiting the sale of the album on which "Cop Killer" was found because it constituted a plausible, imminent threat to human beings.

I knew we would need to come up with a *legal* argument that would fairly portray what Ice-T and Time Warner were doing as *illegal* and thus stoppable through the operation of the law, either in a civil or a criminal court.

"We don't need any more hand-wringing on issues like this, complaining that these songs are *morally* wrong and should stop," I told Col. North. "We have to hit them upside the head with hard, cold laws. That's been my plan, my method, in every one of the fights I've been in. And it works."

I said I would need to listen to the song and do a bit of legal research, but that I would get back to him within a couple of days.

"That will be great," he said. "I look forward to working with you and meeting you. In case you hadn't guessed it, I think this is important."

"Thank you, Colonel. I think it is important too."

"God bless you, brother," Col. North said.

As soon as I hung up, I had goose bumps all over my arms. A number of things hit me all at once. Someone I considered to be a real American hero had just called me and asked for my help. Second, here was more confirmation from God that the journey that had begun as a fight with a local radio station and taken me into battle against the record industry was now leading me to a fight with Time Warner, the largest communications company in the world. David's giants seemed to be getting bigger. I was, in a word, thrilled. I knew that God was in all of this. The call from Col. North felt like an endorsement of what my life had become.

Off I went to the music store and then straight to the University of Miami Law Library yet again.

At the library I found a number of state laws that made it clear that it *was* a crime to advocate killing law-enforcement officers. Also, many states, I found, treated law-enforcement personnel as a special class of individuals, and if you harmed or killed one of them there were harsher penalties than if you had killed a civilian.

This made sense, not because a police officer's life is more precious than that of a civilian citizen, but because there is a reasonable state interest in protecting, with great vigilance and deterrence, "the thin blue line" that keeps mayhem from the rest of us, so that we can *all* be safer. In the states that recognized this rationale, then, there were enhanced penalties for harm done to police—sort of like "hate crimes legislation" for cops.

Armed with this knowledge, I reasoned that we could argue that since many jurisdictions embody in their laws a special protection for police, any entertainment or speech that advocated killing them could be stopped by an injunction and prosecuted criminally. I liked what I was finding.

Finally, I found in researching the federal law—statutes passed by Congress—that the Smith Act, passed in 1940 shortly before the United States entered World Word II, might be of use to us in this instance. This federal statute, which makes it a crime to advocate the violent overthrow of the government, was clearly aimed at those who were part of an ideological movement—such as Communism—and who call on others to help achieve that objective by killing "peace officers" or other agents of the government.

But it seemed to me that we could use the Smith Act in our case against Ice-T and Time Warner in order to show that talk of violence like this is not idle, consequence-free chitchat, but is actually designed to bring about what is a real possibility—murder of law officers—and thus poses a threat to law and order. The law was clear. You can't target law-enforcement personnel in that way.

Some would consider applying a Cold War criminal statute to a recording company a reach, but I did not think so, for there had arisen within the music industry a category known as gangsta rap. Ice-T was smack in the middle of that genre. These rappers were very clearly advocating destroying the government of the United States by violent means. During my college-debate tour, I had appeared more than ten times with a rapper known as Professor Griff. Before he went off on his own, Professor Griff was a member of the gangsta rap group Public Enemy. Professor Griff advocated tearing down the whole system by force. A rhyming, rapping Marxist.

After I finished this legal research, I returned to my office to listen to Ice-T's *Body Count* album and in particular the cut "Cop Killer."

What I heard was shocking:

I got my ski mask on. . . .
I got my twelve gauge sawed off.
I got my headlights turned off. . . .
I'm 'bout to dust some cops off.
Die, die, die pig, die![1]

This was not some twisted discussion of how bad cops make life worse for those living in the inner city. The album was a clarion call for the killing of police officers, regardless of color, regardless of whether they were "good cops" or "bad cops." The album was a crystal clear call for killing cops as a class of citizens in order to tear down the system. I had even found a *Newsweek* article in which Ice-T admitted the idea was, in fact, to encourage people to kill cops. This was worse than I thought it would be. I called Col. North the next day to let him know what I had found out.

"Well done. When can you get up here? I want to spend a day with you before you go to Beverly Hills."

"What's in Beverly Hills?" I asked.

"The annual Time Warner shareholders meeting in July. We'd like you to go there, if all goes well, to speak on behalf of Freedom Alliance and law officers everywhere. Reed Irvine has stock proxies, which will get both of you into the meeting. The proxies will let you speak on behalf of the shareholders who have given you their proxies. Here's Reed's phone number. . . . Call him and then work with my assistant to come up with a day that we can meet up here." This was getting even more interesting.

I called Reed Irvine right away. Reed had founded Accuracy in Media in 1969 to have it serve as a watchdog, of sorts, on the liberal bias in the media. Reed told me the date of the shareholders meeting in Beverly Hills, that it would be in the Beverly Hilton, and that he had enough stock proxies for himself, for me, and for one other person.

"The plan is to have all three of us speak to try to persuade Time Warner to pull 'Cop Killer' from store shelves," he said.

"Great. That sounds interesting. Who's the third person?"

"Charlton Heston."

"Really?" I asked incredulously, my brain working quickly to find a connection between Heston and this case.

"Yep. Chuck is a friend of mine, and he thinks this must be stopped. But first, as I understand it, you're to meet with Ollie in D.C., and then you and I can meet when you come up here. We'll go over final plans then."

Off to Washington, D.C., I went to spend a day with Oliver North. He wanted to get to know me better so that he might feel certain it was a good idea to hitch his considerable wagon and reputation to a lawyer from Miami whom he did not know. That was okay with me. I would have done the same thing.

I went to Col. North's Guardian Technologies International offices in Sterling, Virginia, which was where he oversaw the manufacture and distribution of Kevlar vests and other law-enforcement protection equipment. For the most part, I just tagged along with him, talking about the Ice-T matter in extended moments sandwiched between the pressing needs of his day.

He recorded some radio commentaries for Freedom Alliance that would run on stations around the country. He was driven to appointments and we talked in the backseat of the car about many things. He had bodyguards at all times. I could remember that at one moment during the Iran-Contra hearings there was a loud bang in the hearing room. Col. North instantly, reflexively ducked. Abu Nidal, a terrorist who would die years later in Iraq, had put a price on North's head. As I rode around Washington with Oliver North and his bodyguards, I thought, *This is pretty cool! I'm riding with Ollie North!* Then it dawned on me that if somebody tried to take him out, there was a good possibility I'd be taken out in the process. And the bodyguards were paid by Col. North, not by me, so I would not be their first priority. I wanly smiled to myself. Oh well, it was fun in the meantime.

During the course of that day I met with Cliff Kincaid, who worked with Col. North and also with Reed Irvine at Accuracy in Media. Cliff, a talented writer, commentator, and all-around good guy, spent time prepping me for my trip to Beverly Hills. Everything was a go, and Cliff seemed pleased to hear my legal analysis and what my presentation before the Time Warner shareholders would be.

That evening, Col. North sat in for Deborah Norville on her nighttime syndicated radio show on the ABC Radio Network. Fairly recently, she had left NBC's *Today* show. As her fill-in, Oliver North chatted exuberantly late into the evening with his callers, many of whom began by saying "semper fi," which is short for the Marines' slogan of *semper fidelis*, Latin for "always faithful." "Semper fi to you, ma'am," he'd respond. The audience, by and large, loved "Ollie," and Oliver North made it clear he loved them. *Where does this guy get his energy?* I wondered. He was older than me and seemed to have twice the energy that I did.

When the radio show was over, we went upstairs at the ABC building because Col. North wanted to say hello to some of the crew at *Nightline*. I took note. Oliver North didn't want to miss this opportunity to be friendly with folks in the mainstream media. When he popped into the television offices there, everybody's face lit up. They knew "Ollie," and they obviously liked him, despite any differences of opinion. Col. North had the common touch, which is not so common in famous people.

And I liked him as well. But I sensed I was not seeing the whole Oliver North. There was clearly a shield up of some kind. He was understandably wary of anyone he really didn't know. Still he was fun to be with, courteous almost to a fault, and incredibly smart. On the way to my motel, from which I would leave early the next morning, the rigors of the busy but typical day for Oliver North began to show. He began, with a creeping weariness, to talk less like a laser-focused, wisecracking former soldier and more like a man eager to get home to his "best friend" and wife, Betsy, and the sleep he obviously needed.

We began to talk about "fighting the good fight" in the public square, something he had obviously already done, and which I was now trying to learn how to do as well.

"Jack, God Himself knows the mistakes I made, the mistakes I continue to make trying to be a good soldier for Him. My heart is never pure because I'm a fallen man," Col. North said. "That is why I serve Christ. I know I am imperfect. I have served my country imperfectly. I served President Reagan imperfectly. I regret any mistakes I have made. But I have tried to do the right things, as God has given me the light to see, through my imperfect eyes, what the right thing is. It is fun to be with a brother in this Time Warner matter. Two imperfect brothers trying to do what God seems to want us to do. Before you go home tomorrow, let's pray right now that we do the right thing."

And so we prayed, with Oliver North doing the praying. I felt the presence of the Holy Spirit. We were two souls looking for guidance and encouragement. Oliver North, brave soldier, praying a humble servant's prayer. No wonder soldiers followed this guy into battle.

⚠

On July 16, 1992, I arrived in Los Angeles, checked into a hotel in Beverly Hills, and went to bed to recover from the transcontinental flight and prepare myself for what was sure to be an interesting next day.

Before I went to bed, however, I called Patricia, to make sure she was all right. She was pregnant with our first child. When I had agreed to go to California, I had done so with some fear that she might go into labor while I was gone, even though the baby was not due for two weeks. My medical malpractice work at the local hospital had taught me that those due dates were mere guesses. The baby could theoretically come anytime, and I wanted to be in the delivery room. I had gone through all the birthing classes with Patricia, and I didn't want to miss a thing.

We had talked together about whether or not I should go to California. "You must go," Patricia had said to me. "Colonel North is depending on you." Oh boy, my wife was pulling rank on me. So I went. I was relieved to hear that all was well and she was not feeling anything out of the ordinary.

The next morning I met with Reed Irvine and some other folks for breakfast before we walked across the street to the Beverly Hilton where the annual shareholders meeting of Time Warner would be held.

Because the mainstream media had already begun to cover the "Cop Killer" controversy, Time Warner had made a calculated decision to address the issue at its shareholders meeting, hoping that once their critics had been heard their voices would be forgotten.

On the eve of this shareholders meeting showdown, the *Wall Street Journal* had published a lengthy opinion piece written by Time Warner chairman Gerald Levin. The piece claimed that Time Warner knew better than its critics what real art was and that Time Warner would "never abandon its artists at the expense of the First Amendment."[2]

Later I also wrote an op-ed piece, this one for the *Washington Times*. Here are portions of that opinion piece, which ran in the summer of 2002, just days after Heston announced he was suffering from Alzheimer's disease:

MY DAY WITH CHARLTON HESTON

The news that Charlton Heston may have Alzheimer's disease saddens, but his announcement, when I saw it, brought a smile, which caught my tears. I had seen this man at his brilliant best once before.

It was July of 1992. Reed Irvine, chairman of Accuracy in Media, enabled Mr. Heston, me, and others to address the annual Time Warner shareholders meeting in Beverly Hills.

This was in the midst of a law-enforcement boycott of the communications giant for its sale of rapper Ice-T's "Cop Killer" album, which advocated the murder of police.

Minutes before the shareholders showdown, I was ushered into a breakfast hosted by Mr. Irvine, who said, "Jack, this is Charlton Heston." "It is an honor to meet you, Mr. Heston," I said, shaking a hand stronger than my own. . . .

We marched down the street to the Beverly Hilton, site of the shareholders meeting. A block away we saw the police officers, holding boycott signs. When the officers spotted Charlton Heston, a cheer went up. I looked up at him, next to me. His face hardened in an instant, his pace quickened. He waved regally, as we entered the hotel, his set jaw crowned by a tight grin. Chuck was no longer Chuck. Moses was in the building.

Out of our pockets we pulled our shareholder papers to show the guards posted at the doors, but they proved unnecessary. One man's fame parted security like water.

When Mr. Heston entered the meeting hall, filled with what must have been three thousand shareholders, a din spread. His stature extended to more than his height. On the stage was the new Time Warner Chairman Gerald Levin, who, after a few preliminaries, announced the first agenda item—Ice-T's "Cop Killer." Mr. Heston stood. Derisive cries of "Sit down, Moses" rang out, followed by much laughter. This was a tough crowd, in a tough town. Mr. Levin said into the microphone: "The chair acknowledges Mr. Heston."

He began: "I'm here as a shareholder, but I speak as a private citizen and the public artist I've been most of my life. I think I understand the rights and responsibilities of both identities. I'm here to condemn this company's response to the growing clamor across the country. I condemn the responsible officials of this company. . . . In the end, of course, the buck stops at the top. At Gerald Levin . . ." Mr. Heston was making this personal, man against man, reprising his role of Moses, but this time confronting a first-time pharaoh. The catcalls stopped. Drama had sucked the air out of everyone's lungs but Mr. Heston's.

He quoted, verbatim, Ice-T's graphic descriptions of killing police officers, regardless of their race. Mr. Heston in his brilliance knew that the lyrics were the most effective indictment of the album, and that few in this room had ever heard them. He then read at length the words of a song on the same album that described the rape of Al and Tipper Gore's niece.

Mr. Heston understood that targeting cops may be one thing in Hollywood; targeting a liberal Democrat's female family member for rape, a politically incorrect crime, is quite another. Rhetorical genius.

An audible gasp filled the room. The shareholders realized, in the twinkling of an eye, that they had been ready to defend an album they had never heard. Now they were on Mr. Heston's side.

Knowing the crowd had turned, Mr. Heston then concluded by skewering Mr. Levin with an echo from Senator Joe McCarthy's Army hearings. "Have you no decency, sir?" Mr. Heston had an ear for history as well. Finished, he started to walk backwards, exiting the hall, facing Gerald Levin, staring him down. This bit of athletic adroitness was the capstone on the most stunning oratorical performance I had ever witnessed.

The crowd agreed, as they went crazy, breaking into wild applause, many of them standing. Charlton Heston had convinced them he had come not to take their money but to safeguard both it and their honor.

Charlton Heston, in that summer of 1992, lit the fuse on the "culture war" with an overdue response to the entertainment establishment's assault upon, among other things, law enforcement. With the [9-11] heroics of New York's "finest" and "bravest" then years later, Mr. Heston's defense that day of our defenders seems a prophecy worthy of Moses.[3]

After Mr. Heston spoke, I was supposed to speak. That was the arrangement worked out ahead of time with the Time Warner brass. But instead Mr. Levin, either by inadvertence or design, gave the floor to someone else to talk about the Ice-T matter. I was put at the end of the speakers list. I knew enough about public meetings that when time was short, the folks at the end of the list got axed. I had not come all the way out to Beverly Hills from Miami, a distance of 3,200 miles, to be a victim of some parliamentary rules shenanigans.

As soon as the unknown person speaking after Mr. Heston was done with his mild comments defending Time Warner, Chairman Levin again acknowledged someone other than me to speak.

"Point of order, Mr. Levin!" Here I was, in a room of hundreds of people I didn't know, and I was about to tell the most powerful man in the most powerful communications giant in the world that he had screwed up. My stomach was in knots.

"Mr. Levin, my name is Jack Thompson. I'm an attorney here on behalf of Oliver North's Freedom Alliance, and I am supposed to speak next!"

All of the crowd's bile that had been stored up for Mr. Heston but could not be vented upon "Moses" was now projected upon this lawyer from Miami.

"Shut up!" I heard. "Go chase an ambulance somewhere else, you jerk!" And so on. Tough town indeed.

Mr. Levin, knowing he was once again before a friendly crowd, intoned into the microphone, "Whoever you are, you're out of order. I give the floor to this man up front, right here." Checkmated. No, not quite. Years of attending Cleveland Browns and Cleveland Indian games in cavernous Municipal Stadium had given me enough volume to kick up my voice a notch. I cranked it up to the level I could achieve if Jim Brown had just run for a winning touchdown.

"Mr. Levin, I've come here from Miami, Florida, where my wife is nearly nine months pregnant with our first son. I have a plane to catch to be with her today. She could be in labor right now. If you make me miss the birth of my first son, then that will be on you!" The volume of my voice frightened even me.

Some voices from the crowd said, "Let him talk." Levin paused and finally relented. "Go ahead, Mr. Thompson, you have three minutes. We surely don't want you to miss your plane," he said sarcastically.

Aware that nobody could follow Charlton Heston with anything approximating his rhetorical brilliance, I made my legal point quickly. I said, with as much of a lawyer's demeanor as I could muster, that what Time Warner was doing violated various state and federal criminal statutes prohibiting the solicitation of the murder of police officers.

Furthermore, I said, if some prosecutor somewhere did not heed our warnings, some person might heed Ice-T's call to kill. If that happened, Time Warner could be sued, and every law-enforcement officer in America and I would help the bereaved widow of the slain officer.

"Ice-T is simply a criminal sociopath who can rhyme. Time Warner is knowingly training people, especially young people, to kill," I said. "One day this company will pay a wicked price for that."

I was done. There were more shouts of "Go back to Miami and take care of your kid; we can take care of our company," and so forth. I walked over to Reed Irvine, thanked him for this opportunity, and rushed off to the airport. I had done what Oliver North wanted me to do. I had made the legal argument, but Charlton Heston had stolen the show.

I called Col. North before I got on the plane and told him all had gone reasonably well, but I noted that I was doubtful that Time Warner was going to budge. For all the splash that Mr. Heston had made, I felt Time Warner was going to dig in and wait for the storm to pass. After all, Levin had written in the *Wall Street Journal* that he would do just that.

⚠

Upon returning to Miami, I found myself immersed in the final preparations for the arrival of our son, putting finishing touches to the nursery, getting baby clothes, and buying diapers. This was a "surprise baby" God had given us relatively late in life at the age of forty-two. Patricia had not gone into labor. She was in fact overdue, and had developed gestational diabetes, which we both knew was not a good thing.

While we were waiting for our baby to be born, I received some great news. Time Warner had done an about-face. The Time Warner board decided to pull *Body Count* from store shelves worldwide, reconfigure it, and rerelease it without the song "Cop Killer."

It turns out, according to news reports, that the great opera star Beverly Sills was on the Time Warner board at the time and was sitting there in that hall listening to and watching the proceedings.

After the big shareholders meeting, the board had met, and Sills, a true artist, had made the point to the board that advocating killing police is not "art." She said that Time Warner could be sued and that if somebody died as a result of this record, then Time Warner *should* be sued.[4]

We had given people on that board the facts to move that giant in a certain direction, and they had done just that. We had won!

Not long after receiving such good news, we were blessed with more: On August 2, 1992, Patricia delivered a healthy baby boy by cesarean section. As I held my newborn son, John Daniel Peace Thompson, I was thankful that the birth had not come sooner. I had a feeling it would not be the last thing my son did for me.

Later that year, because of our role in the Ice-T case, the American Civil Liberties Union declared Oliver North and Jack Thompson two of the ACLU Censors of the Year. I am more proud of that formal honor than any I have ever received. As Joseph Conrad said, "You shall judge a man by his foes as well as his friends."

Ice-T, whose real name is Tracy Marrow, was dropped months later from Time Warner's record labels. Since then, he has portrayed a policeman on the popular television series *Law & Order: SVU*. And some say God doesn't have a sense of humor!

11

HURRICANE

Dear John:

When you were three weeks old, on August 24, 1992, your mother and I wrapped you in a blanket and huddled with her parents in our Miami home's dark hallway as Hurricane Andrew approached us and millions of others. I was afraid, John, for I did not know what would come with the dawn.

I had been more afraid than this once, five years earlier, when people threatened to kill me, to end my career as a lawyer, and to ruin what had been a happy life. That human hurricane went on for five years, not just one night. There were nights I could not sleep because of the winds of worry howling in my head.

Eventually the men who meant me harm were stopped. I did not stop them. The One who fashioned the ocean out of which came Andrew stopped them. Deliverance once suggests deliverance again, so I was not as afraid for my family in that hallway as I might otherwise have been. There were butterflies in my stomach as I looked at you sleeping in that blanket, but at least they were flying in formation.

When I was twelve, which you are now, I began to think seriously of what I should like to be when I grew up. I wanted to be in politics. Three years earlier on Election Day 1960, I had stood on my playground in Bay Village, Ohio, with a

"Nixon for President" sign before I went into my first class. I was a little Republican. I wanted, eventually, to be a big Republican on a big stage.

As I grew older and went off to college, I remember always wanting people to like me. It is a natural thing to want to be liked, to be popular, even to be respected. But I found, John, that in the midst of wanting to be liked by everyone I had to do something that would wind up making many folks hate me and some of them threaten to kill me. This is a hard thing to do, to turn your back on what you want to be. It's so hard, in fact, that the One who led me to that choice was clever enough and wise enough not to show me what writing one letter would do to change my life. If I had known, I never would have acted. Fear is real.

In the middle of the consequences of that choice, a person in the news business asked your dad this: "Would you be surprised to know that the media in this community hate you more than any other person who lives here?"

"No," I told him, "I have known that for quite some time. What shocks me is that you would be so honest as to tell me. Thank you."

John, your dad is still hated by the "important people" in this corner of the world. He has to go to news organizations outside this community in order to be heard and to be believed. It says in the Bible that "a prophet is honored everywhere except in his own hometown" (Matthew 13:57, NLT). I'm no prophet, but I have some truth that others near me do not want to hear. I also have a "name recognition" problem. Too many people around here know who I am.

So I owe you an apology, John. As you grow older, people will dislike you because of who your father is. Even though they don't know you, they will treat you unkindly because you are the son of someone they think they know.

Even if people do not know whose son you are (my advice is not to tell them), there is an awfully good chance that you will make enemies on your own. You are a fearless truth teller. It is this strength, this virtue, that will make others uncomfortable, not your flaws.

You must always do your level best to speak the truth in love. You will not always be successful, but you must try. If you speak the truth in anger, do not be disabled by the guilt you will feel. The truth is still the truth, and it must be spoken. You will be forgiven the anger, so you can speak the truth again with a clear conscience down the road.

You must never think of yourself as better or more righteous than anyone. The people who have hated me and who have targeted me for harm because I have spoken the truth have claimed, for years now, that I think I am better than they are, that I must think I am holy. I know better and you know better, for as my son you have seen my flaws. No, the only difference between your father and those he has fought is that I am a sinner and know it and have resolved to do something about it. I am just one beggar telling other beggars where to find bread.

John, my life has turned into something I did not intend. To say that I planned this life is like saying I planned Hurricane Andrew. My life has swept me to places I did not want to go, but now that I am here, I cannot imagine wanting to be anyplace else. I have traded being comfortable for being used. Just as He does not tell us how bad it will get, God also does not tell us how deep the joy will be, for if we knew we could not stand the waiting for it. It would be worse than the almost unbearable desire to get up early for Christmas morning.

The greatest miracle in my life before you were born was that your mother ever got to the point of loving me. Whenever I have fought with men who have treated women badly and made money doing so, I have fought them because of what she has meant to me. Any man who hurts women hurts someone such as your mother. That is not to be abided. Enemies must be made when your mother and other mothers are at stake. It is a small price to pay.

Whenever I have fought with men who have put in front of children "entertainment" that hurts them, I have thought of the harm done to my own child and to other children just as precious. I have done what I have done not only to protect children like you, John, but also to protect those who are doing the harm. To stop them is to love them, whether they realize it or not.

This life of mine has been shattered and then put back together again in part, I think, so that I could be a better father for you. What I know for certain is that my life is richer because you are in it and because God is the one who put you there. Your mother and I could not have planned you any better. God planned you perfectly.

Fondly,
Dad

⚠

From August 1992 until John went off to school, my job was to be his stay-at-home father. When my wife and I had found out that we were expecting, we, like all couples, had to figure out how we were going to cope, in practical ways, with this surprise. In other words, we had to decide who would be the primary caregiver—my wife, me, or a nanny/day-care provider.

We decided I would be the one to stay at home. It made sense. Patricia had a great job, and my professional life, jumbled by a radio war and other efforts stemming from that endeavor, was less structured, to say the least. We didn't go the day-care or nanny route because we didn't have to. Besides, I had persuaded myself that I could practice law out of our home on a part-time basis while raising our son. I had absolutely no basis for concluding that I could do that, and boy was I wrong!

Our son was colicky for a full year after he was born, so our sleep patterns were piecemeal. I was so worn-out that when he went down for a nap, I would take one too.

What I thought would be the relatively easy job of taking care of one boy proved to be the hardest job I have ever undertaken. There is no close second. I gained a deep appreciation for my mother, who raised two kids, three years apart, and for my mother-in-law, who raised four children, of whom Patricia is the eldest. I also came to believe that women are much, much better at this primary care provider role. The nurturing instinct is pretty deeply buried in most men, and I was no exception.

I learned some other things as well. I realized that my son, like other children, was both a sponge and a parrot. He absorbed and then mimicked everything he saw and heard. This close-up observation of the monkey-see, monkey-do reflex deepened in a profound way the concern that I had been acting upon before John came along—that "adult" entertainment is harmful to kids because they will consider appropriate pretty much whatever they see and hear. Then they will replicate it. This explained why women—mothers—were generally far more supportive of my efforts against the entertainment industry. They had seen the problem in the acting out of their own children.

I also learned, as a stay-at-home "Mr. Mom," that I had a lot to do with the development of my son's personality, at least the part explained by nurture and not nature. This was frightening, because it was a daunting responsibility. My impatience with my son's colic and other "imperfections" was a constant rebuke to my impatient nature.

The mistakes that I was daily making in raising him, mistakes of all types, made me appreciate and love my parents more, because I realized that any "mistakes" they may have made in raising me were only the result of their just trying to do their best.

As I watched John quickly grow from baby to toddler to little boy, the thing that frightened me most was realizing how much it would devastate me if any harm came to him—from any source. I came to realize then, as I do now, that I would be willing, almost as a reflex, to give up my life to save him or protect him. Being a father seems to give you no other choice, really. When you see your child for the first time, it's as if a switch gets thrown on inside you and you then have a new task: protect this life at all costs. I understood that I would never have a more important job than this one.

It is natural and appropriate, I think, when you become a parent to reflect upon what you would have done differently if, let's say, you had been a parent ten years earlier. I can tell you what I would have done differently in my fights with the entertainment industry, and it is this: I would have had a greater sense of urgency because I would have had a deeper sense of the danger. Pop culture seeks to unteach the many good things that loving parents are trying to teach their children every day. This is dangerous.

Maybe that is one reason why I do not sleep quite as well now as I did before I was a father. I now have a sense that society and its culture affect not just the public square. They affect precious little lives who increasingly swim not in fresh waters but in pop pollution.

I'm now a dad. How can I not be concerned about other little ones as if they were my own?

12

PADUCAH

In March of 1998, the country was stunned to learn that two young boys had lured classmates outside of their middle school in Jonesboro, Arkansas, and then proceeded to mow them down with gunfire. Four students and a teacher were killed in the attack.

Sadly, this was not the first school shooting incident we had witnessed. Four months earlier, three students had been killed by fourteen-year-old Michael Carneal in Paducah, Kentucky.

Like most Americans, I noted that these school shootings were happening, but I assumed they were just reflective of the increasing lawlessness in society generally and among teens in particular. I didn't think "entertainment" had anything to do with these shootings.

But on June 17, 1998, I came across a news story in *USA Today* pertaining to the Jonesboro shootings. The story recounted the testimony before Congress of Debbie Pelley, a teacher at the Jonesboro school.

According to Debbie Pelley's testimony, one of the shooters, thirteen-year-old Mitchell Johnson, had always been a respectful student, never exhibiting any kind of violent behavior before this incident.

As I read the story, my eyes were drawn to this statement: "In a discussion with seventh grade classes the first day [we] were back at school after this tragedy . . . [we] explored possible reasons Mitchell could have committed this act. The students said that Mitchell had been listening to gangster rap music, and in particular, to Tupac Shakur."

She went on to say that students had seen Mitchell making the gang sign on the cover of Shakur's album *All Eyez on Me*. She also shared some of the lyrics that the boys had been exposed to, including, "I got nothin' to lose so I choose to be a killer. . . ."[1]

"I believe the message coming out of the tragedy in our school in Jonesboro, Arkansas, is that even the good schools and responsible families can no longer protect their children from our society," Debbie Pelley said. "Violent music is only one aspect of our culture, but a very significant one that seems to have gotten very little attention in the recent school tragedies."[2]

I decided to try to find Debbie Pelley's number so I could tell her how much I appreciated what she had done, not only for Jonesboro, but also for the nation, in expressing her concern about the possible role of violent rap lyrics in altering teenagers' behavior. Ms. Pelley's congressional testimony recalled for me my concern about Ice-T and his "Cop Killer" song, but her words were much more important, because she was able to link a specific tragedy that had already happened to a specific album. In other words, she had proven correct those who had been warning that something like this might happen. I wanted Ms. Pelley to know I had been fighting in that trench for a while and that she was, in my opinion, on the right track and brave to be on it.

When I finally connected with Debbie Pelley, even though I did not know her, I could tell that she was weary, depressed, and discouraged.

"People think that I'm crazy to suggest that a rap song could lead to killings," she said. "They're saying in my hometown, which I love, that I'm somehow trying to excuse what these boys did by trying to explain it, by pointing to a piece of the puzzle. I'm not trying to excuse what they did. I'm trying to prevent it from happening again, anywhere."

"It sounds like people want to blame the messenger," I told her. Then

I shared the story of the girl who had been raped by a gang of boys while listening to the 2 Live Crew album. "Surely if music can lead to rape, it can lead to shootings."

"I agree," she said. "But now I'm the enemy in this town."

"Hang in there," I told her. "It's not easy carrying a hard message." Somehow she didn't seem encouraged. She did suggest I talk to a man who lived in Jonesboro by the name of Lt. Col. Dave Grossman. "He knows more about this than I do. He's helped me understand and explain what I already know." I told her that I would contact him.

After playing phone tag a bit, I caught up with Dave Grossman.

"Col. Grossman." As soon as I said his name, I realized that the last time I addressed someone with that title I was addressing Oliver North. I got a chill up my spine, as I suddenly felt as if maybe God had something in store for me with *this* colonel as well. I was soon to find out. He interrupted my opening sentence. "Please, call me Dave," he said. "I'm not in the army anymore. I'm a civilian, just like you. How can I help you, sir?" It was obvious that this former military man had not lost his military speech habits.

"Please, Dave, call me Jack."

"Okay, Jack, what's up?"

"Dave, Debbie Pelley, a teacher at your middle school there, suggested I give you a call. As a lawyer, I've been involved in efforts against the entertainment industry for eleven years now. I was encouraged by what Ms. Pelley told the Senate Commerce Committee. I want to know if I can help on this in any way."

I began to tell Col. Grossman some of the things I had been involved in, when suddenly I heard this loud sound on the other end of the line.

"Hooooooooooah!" Grossman exclaimed. "I've been waiting for a long time to talk with a lawyer like you about this. I didn't think there was such an animal!" Excitedly, he continued. "Let me tell you all that I know about this, if you have the time."

"Are you kidding? I have all the time in the world." But before he began, I had an urge to tell Lt. Col. Dave Grossman something. I can't really explain why I felt compelled to tell him this bit of information right then. It didn't make sense to say this, but urges rarely do "make sense." That's why we call them urges.

"Dave, I think I should tell you that although I'm a lawyer, I am also a Christian, what some would call a 'born-again Christian.' I prefer just 'Christian,' because as a follower of Christ, I'm a brother with anybody who claims His name, regardless of any other label."

Dave responded with an even louder "Hooooooooooah! Here's what you can call me: brother! I'm a Christian too. This is one reason I am so passionate about this issue. There is a darkness spreading through American culture, into the hearts of our children. I think God has brought you and me together to do something about that."

I had goose bumps all over, talking with this brother in Christ on the phone. I remembered something my former pastor, Steve Brown, had said. "If you feel the urge to share Jesus, do it, even if it seems to make no sense. You don't want to regret not having shared Him."

Dave and I were off and running, soon to be running in tandem. Dave said he was going to give me a crash course in violent entertainment and its effect on kids as well as its role in school killings. He began: "I was an Army Ranger. I was trained to kill other human beings, and the men I served with were trained to kill other human beings. I never, as far as I know, killed anyone, but I served with and was around those who had. It takes a toll, killing other human beings. There is a cost, a price that is paid by a human being when he is trained to kill, when he does kill."

Dave explained that when he left the Rangers, he became a professor on "the psychology of war" at West Point. His teaching there led him to write a book called *On Killing*. Nominated for a Pulitzer prize, the book recounts how a man is trained to kill and what the consequences are of training him to kill. Dave had coined the word *killology* to describe the body of knowledge about killing, what it takes to make a killer, and what it costs to be a killer.

"I was in the triage units that were slapped together in Jonesboro," he said. "We can talk about Jonesboro, but the case I really want to talk with you about is Paducah. I was an expert in that case." Dave Grossman had not testified at Michael Carneal's criminal trial, but the expert who had been called to the stand, Diane Schetky, had provided chilling testimony. A world-renowned forensic pediatric psychiatrist, Schetky had interviewed Carneal and determined that he had been immersed in violent entertainment. She found that Carneal was enthralled with the movie *The Basketball Diaries*, which had a classroom shooting scene. In fact, when the first officer responding to the scene put handcuffs on Carneal, he asked him, "Michael, why would you do this? Where did you get the idea for this?" Carneal said simply, *"The Basketball Diaries."*

Schetky also found that Carneal was an avid player of violent video games, including the game *Doom*. Michael Carneal obviously had some other things going on in his life—a thwarted romance and some bullying—but no drugs and no history of violence, Dave Grossman told me. But the movie and the violent video games, according to Schetky, gave Carneal a powerful message that to kill people in your school with whom you have certain "issues" would be fun, cool, heroic, and consequence free. Schetky found that the violent entertainment Carneal consumed wound up consuming him. Carneal's mental state fed into his passion for violent movies and games, and they in turn grew him into someone more interested in violence than he otherwise would have been. The "heroes" in the violent entertainment became, in effect, powerful role models for him.

"But the appetite to kill is only half the puzzle," Dave said. "The other half is this: How is it that Michael Carneal was able to kill so efficiently?"

"Are you going to tell me that Carneal learned *how* to kill by playing a video game?" I asked. "If you are, Dave, I'm skeptical of that. I don't think a video game can teach you how to kill."

"You should be skeptical, but you don't know what I know. Just listen, and you can draw your own conclusions." Grossman pushed on, undeterred by yet another skeptic: "Any firearms expert will tell you that a gun novice—and that is what Carneal was—will unload his gun into a target until he gets a visual confirmation that the target is disposed of, literally on the ground. Then he will move to the next target. If Carneal had done that, had done the natural, intuitive thing, he would have unloaded his weapon into just one student, killing—at best—one. But he did not do that. He fired once at one student, then moved instantly to the next. And then moved instantly to the next."

Michael Carneal had played *Doom*, which teaches you to fire at one target and to instantly move to the next target, never pausing. According to Dave Grossman, this form is totally unnatural, a learned way to shoot. "Carneal learned how to kill efficiently playing *Doom*," he said. "You can explain the shooting accuracy by chance, by mathematic probabilities. You can't explain the method by math."

All I could say was "Wow." Grossman then said something else. "Michael had one more bullet in his clip. It was an eight-clip gun, but he forced nine rounds into the clip, which you can do. He fired eight times, but after the eighth shot, a classmate ran up to him and said, 'Michael, stop!' Michael stopped, and dropped the gun to his side."

"Why would he do that?" I asked, not knowing what in the world the answer would be.

"Because Michael was acting out the game, and a voice intruded into the 'game' that is not part of the game. Reality invaded the killing, invaded the video game Michael was in. Eyewitnesses say it was as if he was in a trance. He had a totally flat affect on his face, as if he were playing a video game, calmly picking off targets, one by one. But when the voice entered that 'game,' then reality crashed in and the game was over. Michael obeyed instantly, which is not exactly what you would expect a highly motivated killer to do."

"Why didn't you testify at the trial?" I asked.

"The defense decided not to use me. The families of the victims, though, know what my testimony would have been, and they're not too thrilled with me. They think I am trying to excuse what Carneal did."

"That echoes what Debbie Pelley said to me about Jonesboro. She says she is trying to warn people so others won't die."

"Hooah," Dave Grossman said, more softly this time. "The parents of the three precious girls who died are upset with me because what I had to offer was an explanation for the deaths of their daughters that was outside of Carneal himself. I think Carneal is to blame, but he is not the only one to blame. I was retained by Michael Carneal's parents to help prove that Carneal was influenced by certain violent entertainment products. He was literally *trained* to kill those girls. I'm encouraged to hear that there is a lawyer somewhere who knows there is a problem with popular entertainment. You really ought to call the attorney in Paducah who represents these parents. I think they're fixin' to sue the entertainment industry, at least I've heard noise about that. I think you could help them with what you know. They don't want to hear from me.

"They need to hear from you, because lives *are* at stake. The boy who took their daughters from them was not the only one responsible. That is a hard thing to swallow, the notion that the boy who destroyed a huge part of their life is not pure evil, but we've got to let people know that evil from an outside source helped turn him into someone—into something—he had not been before it entered his life. Michael Carneal was a killer trained by an industry to kill."

I thanked Lt. Col. Dave Grossman for his time and his service to our country, thinking both of his service in the military and in this new battle.

"My brother, let's pray before you go." Dave prayed fervently for the two of us. I was deeply moved by the words of this intense man. He prayed, among other things, that we would be able to "fight the good fight" together. When I heard those words, I knew I was right where God wanted me to be.

As we said good-bye, Dave said, "Jack, my favorite Bible verse on all this is Galatians 6:9: 'Let us not become weary in doing good, for at the proper time we will reap a harvest if we do not give up.' Stay staunch, my brother. Hoooooah!"

I bid Dave Grossman good-bye, warning him that I would be calling him again. I had a sense something would come of this, and the fact that I didn't know what it was worried me and energized me at the same time. Once again, into an unknown place I went.

⚠

I started by calling Mike Breen, the attorney for the parents of the three slain girls in Paducah.

Mike Breen was a successful personal injury lawyer in Bowling Green, Kentucky. I told him I had some information that might help him win his case, and then I told him about standing before the board at Time Warner's annual shareholders meeting. I explained our argument at the time that if someone were to act upon Ice-T's call to kill cops, then Time Warner could theoretically be sued for having recruited and encouraged the killer. Time Warner also happened to be the distributors of *The Basketball Diaries*. I told Mike that testimony in this case would be all the more relevant because Time Warner had already recognized the risk involved in producing "entertainment" that promotes violence. Mike Breen took it all in. "I think your testimony would be very helpful. We didn't know about you. Let me talk with my clients, and I'll get back to you."

Several days later, Mike called me back. "The parents of these three girls want to meet you. We're all thinking about making you co-counsel with me in the case. You have expertise on this issue that we just don't have. When can you come to Paducah?" I was floored. I had not expected this. But when God was doing the leading, I had learned to expect the unexpected.

I arranged with Mike the date for my trip and then settled down to do a little research about the Paducah shootings.

I found that there were far more school shootings in America recently than I had realized. Paducah was just one in a string of many school shootings that had begun to pop up around the country. Each incident was known to the public by the name of the town in which it had occurred, just like many of the battles in our Civil War: "Bull Run," "Antietam," and "Gettysburg." There was "Pearl," Mississippi; "Jonesboro," Arkansas; and "Bethel," Alaska. Some of these events I had not heard of, but I knew the people in those towns had suffered and been changed by them. Killings had come to their towns—and even worse to their schools, which they thought were safe.

As I researched the Paducah shootings and others around the country, I found that the killers were almost without exception boys between thirteen and seventeen years old. In nearly every instance the violence seemed to come out of the blue. Often, the shooter's classmates said things like "He was the last person I would have thought would do something like this. Nobody had a clue." And "he was kind of quiet, kept to himself, not very popular. He was bullied sometimes. He was into some pretty bizarre music. He was into computers and video games," and so on. It sounded like pretty normal stuff, frankly, for kids of this generation. But I couldn't help but remember what Dave Grossman had told me: Those video games were not just fueling a possible appetite to kill but were perhaps even training children *how* to kill.

I had to get myself to Paducah, so I quickly made arrangements for our son's care while I was gone. I was thankful that he would not be playing video games in my absence, since that product had not yet invaded the life of our six-year-old boy.

⚠

I went to Paducah and met Mike Breen and the six parents of the three slain girls. I thought I knew a bit about the school shootings. I found in meeting these parents that I knew nothing about their loss.

What I met were six human beings whose lives had been utterly turned inside out. These were simple but very bright people. They were in terrible pain, but somehow they were holding up. As soon as we sat down to talk, they made sure I understood that they were all believers in Christ. I told them that I was as well.

They told me a bit about themselves and their daughters—Jessica James, Nicole Hadley, and Kayce Steger—and what it was like not to have them. When it was time for me to talk, Mike Breen asked me to tell what I knew about Time Warner and the recklessness of the entertainment industry. I looked at these parents with their sad, weary eyes. My heart ached for them.

"I have a son," I said. "I cannot imagine life without him. If this had happened to me, I think I would have found a way to kill Michael Carneal."

Before I could stop myself, I began to sob, in part because of my anger at the needless loss these parents were suffering, and in part at the tremendous sorrow I saw in their eyes. Joe James spoke: "Jack, we appreciate that. We get through this a day at a time. We pray for Michael Carneal as best we can. We want to do something with our loss. Mike tells us you might be able to do that."

So I told them about my own history with Time Warner, the FCC, 2 Live Crew, and Ice-T. I also told them about the recent information I had gathered about video games, although I did not mention Dave Grossman since he was the one who was hired by the parents of Michael Carneal. I did not want understandable emotion to get in the way of these six parents hearing me. I said that I thought there was merit to Mike Breen's idea that a lawsuit could and should be fashioned to prove that the entertainment industry took a twisted boy and twisted him more, and in fact trained him to kill.

"Sounds like you've been talking to Colonel Grossman," one of the parents said, smiling.

"Well, I have," I admitted. "Jonesboro led me to him, and he led me to you."

Sabrina Steger, the feisty, smart, take-charge mother of Kayce, jumped in.

"Look, Michael Carneal killed our daughters. Nothing is going to change what he did to them and to us. What we think is that there is plenty of blame to go around here for the loss of our daughters, and we think not only Michael Carneal should be held responsible. We think his parents are responsible. We think the movie people are responsible. We think the Internet porn he consumed played a role. And we know the video games trained him how to kill our daughters. This is not about the money. No money will bring our three daughters back. We don't want this to happen to anyone else. We want to do something with our loss. We want to teach the entertainment industry a lesson. We think enough kids have died in our schools."

Amen, I thought.

⚠

I went back to Miami to prepare a complaint that we would file in the federal court in Paducah in an effort to prove that the entertainment industry trained a boy to kill. I had never seen such a complaint, let alone drafted one. But these parents wanted a lawyer "crazy" enough to draft that complaint. I knew I would have to try.

I did just that, identifying the three categories of entertainment products that Michael Carneal consumed, which then consumed him. When Diane Schetky had interviewed Carneal in his jail cell, she determined that he had come under the powerful influence of three categories of violent entertainment. One was Internet-provided images of violence, primarily against women, which Carneal had downloaded onto his computer. All but one of Carneal's targets were females.

Another piece of Carneal's entertainment and motivational puzzle was the movie *The Basketball Diaries*, starring a young Leonardo DiCaprio. This is a movie based on the autobiography by the poet and punk musician Jim Carroll. The movie includes a classroom shooting scene nowhere to be found in the book. It's the most cinematically compelling scene in the movie, filmed in slow motion in order to make it more mesmerizing. When asked—before the Paducah killings—why this scene was placed in the movie, the director said "We wanted to jazz up the movie more for teens." This was quite an admission, since the movie was rated R by the Motion Picture Association of America and thus was inappropriate for anyone under seventeen. Schetky found, in speaking with Carneal, that he had identified powerfully with the character played by DiCaprio.

Finally, Michael Carneal was a devotee of violent video games, including the M-rated[3] *Doom*. Carneal's appetite to kill, according to Schetky, was fueled by the games, and we knew we could prove, in speaking with firearms experts, that Carneal's counterintuitive, unnatural shooting technique of one shot per target—one shot per student—was acquired from the video games.

I prepared the complaint based upon these facts. It was a product liability case, and we hoped to establish that adult-rated violent entertainment had helped warp Carneal into becoming a motivated killer.

At the core of this theory were the video games, which were different from the other two categories of violent entertainment in that they imparted not just an appetite to kill, but also a skill to kill. They were dangerous products, especially in the hands of a child. Dangerous to whom? Dangerous to anyone who might get in the way of someone like Michael Carneal.

The lawsuit prepared and ready to file, I flew back to Paducah, Kentucky, to do just that. The day we filed it, April 12, 1999, Mike Breen and I held a news conference with all the parents and Christina, sister of the slain Nicole Hadley.

Before we walked into that news conference, Mike and I met with the families and prayed. I felt, in that circle of prayer, the calming power of the Holy Spirit. I thought of the fight with the radio stations. I thought about the efforts against 2 Live Crew and Time Warner's Ice-T. All of these seemed like individual battles important in their own right, but as we prayed, I could see that they were all part of a plan that led all of us to this day in Paducah.

We then walked to the large room in which the news conference was about to begin, and I was unnerved a bit by what I saw. There were easily twenty different news organizations representing the print media and the electronic media, local and national. At the podium, the microphones formed what looked like the many snakeheads of Medusa's hair.

Taking all of this in, I could feel the butterflies in my stomach start acting up again. The calm that had come with prayer was gone. I was not frightened, but I was apprehensive. The adrenaline was there, for good or ill. But then I remembered Pat Buchanan, who had put his arm around me nine years earlier and told me that this work was important. I reminded myself that I had done this before. I knew that God was there and would give us all that we needed to do this work. We were not alone. *We* were ready to do this.

And we did. Mike Breen began by explaining why the lawsuit was appropriate from a legal and constitutional sense. Mike did an excellent job sounding like a lawyer, and a good one at that. It was then up to me to convey the passion we all felt against an entertainment industry that we hoped to prove had contributed to the deaths of these three girls. I wanted the members of the media assembled there that day to hear, in my voice, the anger that we felt.

"We intend to hurt Hollywood," I said. "We intend to hurt the video-game industry. We intend to hurt the sex porn sites."

Indeed we did intend to do just that. Only time would tell if we would succeed.

Within hours of the news conference, an NBC *Today* show producer called. They wanted to interview us the next day about the lawsuit in Paducah. We scheduled the interview, and I hurriedly returned that evening to Miami.

The next day, I found myself in front of a camera in the NBC Miami affiliate's studio. Three of the Paducah parents—Gwen Hadley, Sabrina Steger, and Joe James—were uplinked by satellite from Paducah. Although we were separated by distance, we were together in our purpose and our goal.

Today's Matt Lauer seemed to be in our corner as he asked us to explain our lawsuit. We explained how dangerous we felt these movies and video games were and the role they had played in Michael Carneal's killing binge. We expressed our fear—a prediction—that other boys in other American high schools would do the same thing or worse.

Little did we know how accurate this prediction would be.

13

60 MINUTES AND MORE

One week after our *Today* show appearance, I was sitting at my office desk when the phone rang. It was April 20, 1999.

"Turn on your TV," Mike Breen said.

"Why? What's going on?"

"Just turn on the TV."

"Which channel?"

"Any channel."

I reached for the remote and turned on the television. The set, tuned to CNN, popped to life.

Live images, shot from a helicopter, of children running out of a building filled my screen. I had no idea what the building was or why they were running.

"Mike, what's going on?" I asked again.

"Somebody is shooting students in a high school in Littleton, Colorado. They don't know who it is, but they know people have been killed."

"Oh no!" As we watched together in silence, a cold chill went through me. "Mike, we predicted this a week ago."

"Why do you think I called? Stay by your phone. They'll be calling."

But I had a call to make first. I got the phone number for the Jefferson

County Sheriff's Department in Colorado. I called and was quickly connected to the officer on duty who was manning the phones.

"Sir, my name is Jack Thompson. You don't know me. No reason you should. But eight days ago I was on NBC's *Today* show with three of the parents in Paducah, Kentucky, whose daughters were shot and killed in the school shootings there on December 1, 1997, and—"

"I'm sorry, Mr. Thomas, but we're a little busy here right now. We have a school shooting, and we're trying to investigate who did this and why. Let me get your name and number, and maybe somebody can call you back once we do our preliminary investigation."

I didn't bother to correct his mispronunciation of my name, given the fact that he had more important things on his mind at the time.

"But that's why I'm calling. I think I know what you'll find if you know what to look for. If this is a student, then he's probably a video gamer and into other violent entertainment, just like Michael Carneal was in Paducah—"

"Mr. Thomas, this isn't Paducah, and you're not a law enforcement officer, are you?"

"No, sir, it's not Paducah, and I'm not in law enforcement. I'm a lawyer, and I apologize for that."

He laughed. "So what do you want? We're kind of busy here right now."

"Please, sir. Just get this suggestion to the investigators: Get a search warrant and specify on it that you want to search for any and all entertainment materials that might be in the homes of whoever is doing this, especially if it is a student. That includes home computers, video games, anything that might have influenced him or them to do this."

"Why?"

"Because from my research on the Paducah case, I have reason to believe that school shooting—and now possibly this one—was the result of a teen filled up with violent entertainment and trained on violent entertainment—video games—to kill."

"I'll pass it on."

"Do you want my phone number?"

"No, we have what we need. Good-bye."

⚠

At roughly the same moment that I was speaking to the officer in Colorado, shock radio host Howard Stern was broadcasting live across the nation from New York. His show was being heard on dozens of radio stations while he looked at the same images I was watching on television.

Howard Stern laughingly told his audience, "I don't know who's doing this, but I'll tell you one thing. If I were this guy, or these guys, whatever, I'd be sure to bang these chicks before I killed them. Look at some of these broads. They're hot!"

⚠

My phone rang. It was Michael Radutzky, a producer for CBS's *60 Minutes*. "Jack, are you aware of what is going on?"

"Yes, my co-counsel Mike Breen just called me and told me to turn on my TV. I'll bet you right now the killer is a student who has been trained on the same violent stuff that Michael Carneal was into in Paducah."

I had just talked to Mike Radutzky the week before. He had said that *60 Minutes* was very interested in the connection we had drawn on *Today* between violent entertainment and school shootings. They were planning to put together a segment in September and had asked us not to talk to any national electronic media before the show aired. They wanted the exclusive.

Of course we had agreed to that a week ago. We were thrilled at the opportunity to get this message out to our nation's parents on *60 Minutes*. But now it was going to be hard to keep that promise to *60 Minutes* because of what was happening in Colorado. The fact that we had predicted such an unfortunate event just eight days ago would not go unnoticed, of that I was sure. In fact, this call from *60 Minutes* confirmed that.

"Mike, I know we had an agreement, but I don't see how we can be quiet for five or six months about all this. This is a very big deal. We can't be silent in the midst of more and more of these school shootings happening when we have an explanation as to why."

As I was talking, the call-waiting function on my phone indicated a new call was coming in. I looked down at the caller ID and it told me I was right to expect other media to call.

"Mike, I've got another call. It's from New York. You know somebody else in the media has figured this out. I'm going to have to talk with them. I have no choice. The parents in Paducah want to get this message out now more than they want to be on *60 Minutes*."

"Jack, that's why I called. We want to do a crash." I had no idea what he was talking about.

"What is a crash?" I asked, ignoring the other call from New York.

"A crash is when you do a show that would normally take you three months to put together, and you do it in three days. We want to fly you all to New York. We want to do the piece this week and have it on *60 Minutes* this Sunday."

"You've got to be kidding. How can you do that?"

"We can do it," he said. "We're *60 Minutes*. We've done harder things than this. Do you agree?"

"Of course, but I have to contact the clients and Mike and figure out their schedules—"

"*This* is their schedule now."

"I know. They'll be there."

We had not hoped for tragedy, but we had known in our bones it would happen. The Old Testament prophets had predicted calamity. Did that mean they hoped for it in order to prove that their predictions from on high were correct? No, I don't believe so. They dreaded what they knew to be true.

We had connected the puzzle pieces in Paducah. And I believed the same pieces would be revealed in Littleton, Colorado, as well. My heart ached as I thought about what the parents in this Denver suburb would now be facing.

But even in the midst of this horrible event, I could see the hand of God. For out of this tragedy, we were going to get the opportunity to tell the nation what we had discovered in Paducah. And maybe, armed with this knowledge, I'd never again have to look into the eyes of parents like Joe James and Sabrina Steger.

⚠

As we were readying for our trip to Manhattan to tape *60 Minutes*, our worst fears were confirmed. Investigators quickly revealed that the perpetrators at Columbine High School in Littleton, Eric Harris and Dylan Klebold, had trained on *Doom*, the very same game on which Michael Carneal had trained, to prepare for the worst school shooting in American history. In their videotaped suicide note, Klebold and Harris brandished their shotgun and said they had named it after one of the characters in their favorite game. Harris said "it's gonna be like [expletive deleted] *Doom*, man."[1]

Further, Klebold and Harris were so enamored with *The Basketball Diaries* that they had videotaped their own version of the classroom shooting scene. Not only were Carneal and Klebold and Harris into the same kind of violent entertainment, they were also consumers of the same *specific* violent entertainment.

With all of that as part of the breaking news coming out of Littleton, Colorado, we headed to Manhattan to sit down with *60 Minutes'* Ed Bradley, the correspondent assigned to do this story in just a few days.

We did the interviews, and Mr. Bradley could not have been more cordial, more professional, and more insightful. The producer and his assistant told me that Lt. Col. Dave Grossman had sat down with Mr. Bradley the day before and had taken him around to video arcades. What Grossman told and showed Bradley had unnerved the veteran newsman.

Ed Bradley, like so many adults in America, had no idea what kids were playing. He had no idea how dangerous that play was. The glazed eyes of the kids in the arcades as they blew away pixelated humans provided an image more disturbing than anything we could say.

The producer and his assistant thanked me for putting them on to Grossman, because Grossman had "hit it out of the park," to use their phrase. It began to appear that *60 Minutes*, based upon the enthusiasm we were hearing from the producers, was going to air a story that suggested that violent entertainment may indeed spawn violence, including school shootings.

Now it was the turn of the Paducah parents and their two lawyers to explain to Ed Bradley what our lawsuit in Paducah was about. Ed Bradley interviewed me and Mike Breen side by side. I can honestly say it was the worst interview I have ever done. I hate being taped for anything because it gives editors the opportunity to make you look like a fool. My words came with difficulty. I could not quite get beyond the fact that I was going to be on *60 Minutes*, and when the rubber hit the road sitting there in front of Ed Bradley, I felt as if I were in a car without a steering wheel.

Having completed the interview, I said to the producers off camera how poorly I had done and apologized. One of them said, "Don't worry. We can make people look great. And by the way, you did fine." I did not do fine, but I appreciated the pep talk. It also reminded me that this was not about me. It was about three dead girls in Paducah.

When the parents were interviewed by Mr. Bradley, the key moment came when he asked all of them, "Isn't it a parent's responsibility to keep his or her kids away from this violent entertainment?"

Joe James, the father of Jessica and husband of Judy, was the homespun philosopher among the six parents. He looked at Ed Bradley in his friendly way and said: "Ed, I'm trying to figure out what I did wrong as a parent. I had my daughter in school, and she was in that hallway at a pre-school prayer meeting. If I hadn't raised Jessica right, she'd be alive today."

There it was in a father's reasonable response: Parents can raise their children, but they can't raise other parents' children. The entertainment industry, far too often, is raising them, and our children, the children who have responsible parents, might be in their crosshairs. Don't blame us for that.

As Sabrina Steger, the most fiery of all six of the Paducah parents, added in response to another question from Ed Bradley, "There's plenty of blame to go around."

Our *60 Minutes* "crash" ended, and we all anticipated its airing that Sunday. It was the lead segment, and it was powerful stuff. We thought that most people viewing it would conclude that violent entertainment helped spawn Paducah and Columbine.

The Paducah families were hopeful that all of the news coverage of Columbine and our prediction of it based upon what had happened in Paducah would serve to convince our federal judge that our wrongful death lawsuit had merit.

However, it was not to be. The judge never even let us get to first base, as he granted the various defendants' motions to dismiss without even allowing any evidence from our side.

Yet the judge, rather remarkably we thought, based his ruling on a very narrow reading of Kentucky tort law, claiming that it was not foreseeable that any child would ever act out any violent entertainment—ever.

We found this a bizarre ruling, in light of our prediction of Columbine before it even happened. If we could predict it, surely the makers of the products that trained and inspired Carneal, Klebold, Harris, and the school shooters before them should have known the danger of their adult products in the hands of kids.

We appealed the federal judge's ruling to the Sixth Circuit Court of Appeals, where we lost again. The appellate court did not rule, thankfully, that adult-rated violent entertainment marketed and sold to children is First Amendment speech, but it did affirm the trial court's interpretation of Kentucky's tort law on this issue.

There was only one thing left to do to keep the case alive. We appealed all the way to the United States Supreme Court. The High Court refused to hear our case. We received that disappointing ruling nearly four years after we filed our case in April 1999.

The Stegers, Jameses, and Hadleys were obviously disappointed. The entertainment industry had contributed to the deaths of their three daughters, but the entertainment industry had slipped off the hook. For the parents in Paducah, this fight was over.

As I write this, more than six years after that *60 Minutes* appearance, the invasion of violent, M-rated video games into the youth culture is deeper than ever. Schools are far less safe after Columbine, not more safe. In fact, in May 2005, Rockstar Games announced its intent to release a new game called *Bully* that will follow the story of a troublesome schoolboy in reform school as he tries to stand up to bullies, gets picked on by teachers, plays pranks, and even tries to get the girl.

Now more than ever, the time has clearly come for us to strike back at the video-game empire.

14

IS IT RIGHT VERSUS LEFT
OR RIGHT VERSUS WRONG?

On January 26, 2000, all of the Republicans vying for their party's presidential nomination stood on a stage in New Hampshire—with that state's primary scheduled to be held six days later. The moderator of the debate was NBC news anchor Tom Brokaw.

Earlier that same evening, I had appeared on *NBC Nightly News*. Correspondent Pete Williams interviewed me in a taped segment on the apparent connection between violent video-game play and a spate of recent school shootings. NBC apparently chose me to give voice to the video game/school shooting link because of the Paducah case.

Once it had become known that Dylan Klebold and Eric Harris had been immersed in violent entertainment, and because there had been an unprecedented number of school shootings leading up to Columbine, President Clinton ordered the Federal Trade Commission to determine the extent to which adult-rated entertainment products—explicit music, violent and sexually charged movies, and violent video games—were marketed to children.[1]

Therefore, by the time of this Republican candidates' debate in New Hampshire, Columbine had become a campaign issue. By then, *Colum-*

bine was a name that meant certain things to certain people, and candidates knew they had to convey to potential voters what it meant to them.

The public had expressed increasing unease with the direction popular culture seemed to be heading. A major national poll in the summer of 2000 indicated that the number one domestic issue on the minds of most American voters was the moral drift of our society and the role popular culture was playing in that drift. Four years later, exit polls in 2004 indicated that the number one issue on voters' minds was "values." Americans seemed to have an abiding concern that America was becoming disconnected from morality.

President Reagan's great speechwriter Peggy Noonan had given voice to this concern on the pages of the *Wall Street Journal*, just three days after Columbine: "With Columbine, a line has been crossed for American parents. They now realize that the popular culture in which their children are swimming is raw sewage that is hazardous to their health, even to their safety."[2]

All of this set the New Hampshire debate stage for Tom Brokaw to ask his first question:

"Today *Time* magazine, the newspapers and television and radio were filled with the blood-chilling accounts of Eric Harris and Dylan Klebold and the videotapes that they left behind before they engaged in that cold-blooded massacre at Columbine High School. In those videotapes, they invoke guns and video games and movies. Now if past patterns are any guide, all three of those industries will disclaim responsibility for what happened. . . . Do you think that the gun industry, the video game industry, and Hollywood have any role in what happened?"

The front runner for the Republican presidential nomination, then Governor George W. Bush responded: " . . . There is a problem with the heart of America. One of the great frustrations in being governor is I wish I knew of a law that'd make people love one another, because I'd sign it."[3] Bush followed that bromide with some additional comments about how his administration would be profamily, but as to the connection between school violence and violent entertainment, Governor Bush had nothing to say and offered no solution, at least not one that his government, if he was elected, was going to offer.

Bush's answer illustrates a schism found in both major political parties, a divide between those who think "making people love one another" is the first and only solution to the corrosion of popular culture and those who view the entertainment industry's actions as predatory and harmful. In other words, the latter group sees this problem as an assault to be stopped by any appropriate means, even with government help, if necessary.

Upon hearing Bush's response, I had no doubt that he was in the first group. As someone in the second group, I was dismayed. There are two kinds of conservatives. There are those who think government has a role to play in opposing all of America's foes, both foreign and domestic. And then there are those who say they believe in original sin, but not when it rears its head in a corporate boardroom. The corporations-can-do-no-wrong group believes, in effect, that the commercial marketplace doesn't really need law enforcement, and certainly not when it comes to pushing adult-rated entertainment at kids behind their parents' backs.

There is a respectable philosophical and ideological basis for the notion that better parenting is the sole answer to the entertainment industry's assault on our children and that government must have no role in stopping that assault. It is called, in a word, libertarianism. The libertarian wing of the Republican Party ardently and reflexively opposes all efforts of government to interfere with business and the marketplace in which it operates. There are variants of libertarianism and differences among their respective adherents, the most extreme of whom would repeal all drug laws and all prostitution laws, but the basic overarching principle of libertarianism is that government must not interfere in individual choices.

The probusiness facet of this philosophy was enunciated by Calvin Coolidge: "The chief business of the American people is business." In fact, morality, according to libertarians, should have nothing to do with business calculations. And no one should tell anyone else what to do in making business or "lifestyle" decisions.

The day that Paducah parent Sabrina Steger testified before the Senate Commerce Committee about the role that *Doom* played in training Michael Carneal to kill her daughter, a popular talk radio host went after her by name, mocking her as part of the crowd of people who "blame anybody but the perpetrator, who are gutting this nation's bedrock principle that people ought to take responsibility for their actions."

Sabrina Steger wasn't blaming Michael Carneal for the killing of her daughter? Rush needed to talk with Mrs. Steger about that one. Sabrina Steger's point, which she made to the Senate, to national television audiences, and to anyone else who would listen, is that kids who kill kids should be held accountable for what they do, and the adults who make, market, and sell murder simulation devices to those kids ought to be held accountable for their recklessness as well. In other words, Mrs. Steger was for accountability *across the board.* That strikes me as a rather enlightened conservative position. After all, the fellow who sold Klebold and Harris the guns was held criminally accountable for selling weapons to minors. This gun dealer did not pull the trigger, but he equipped those who did.

The schism, then, between the libertarians and the social conservatives, turns on how one answers this question: Should a society use its government to protect children from those who would harm them?

American society has determined that children must not be sold alcohol, cigarettes, or firearms. Why? Because those products are harmful to them and to those around them. How, then, can a libertarian conservative say with a straight face that the sale and marketing of a product that desensitizes a child to killing and that actually trains him how to kill more efficiently should not be regulated, especially when that product sports an age-rating label that says it is harmful to children? The video-game industry puts an M (for "mature") rating on a game and then markets it to kids under seventeen. That is fraud. It's also recklessness that should have consequences.

Who are these social conservatives who are often the most outspoken about the problem caused by the marketing of adult entertainment products to children? They tend to be part of the religious right, which for some is a derisive term.

I refer back to Edmund Burke's famous dictum: "The only thing necessary for the triumph of evil is for good men to do nothing." Arguably the father of social conservatism, Burke's writings informed the thinking of this nation's founders, who wrote much about liberty but also about virtue as indispensable to the preservation of liberty. For them, virtue would never allow corporations to declare open season on children. Government should protect children, not just corporations, and surely not corporations that prey on children. That would not be liberty. That would be license.

The libertarians, for quite some time, have been rising in the ranks of the Republican Party. That explains why, in the run-up to the 2004 presidential election, social conservatives within President Bush's party grew restive with his refusal to acknowledge that a culture war was raging. This refusal is somewhat surprising at a time when radical Islamists claim American culture is depraved. We might do well to take a look at whether our popular culture gives those Islamists a propaganda weapon.

But given President Bush's response to that question in New Hampshire in January 2000, no social conservative Republican should be surprised by this largely libertarian president's failure to see the culture war in the context of the war on terror. It only stands to reason that if a presidential candidate was not troubled enough by the entertainment industry's role in Columbine to want to do something about it, he would also not be troubled by the overall coarsening of our current culture.

Yet there is another major political party in America. The Democrats, and more generally liberals within that party, have their own schism over the culture war. That divide tends to be expressed in discussions about the Constitution, specifically the First Amendment and what it means.

Some in the Democratic Party seize upon the following language in the First Amendment to the United States Constitution: "Congress shall make no law . . . abridging the freedom of speech, or of the press. . . ." These people see those words as an absolute, total prohibition against government at any level—local, state, or federal—restricting the marketing and sale of any "communication," even violent, adult-rated and labeled entertainment, to children.

In my opinion, there are a number of problems with that view, the full exposition of which would require an entire book. But let me briefly share the two most obvious flaws. I believe the First Amendment was framed by the founders to operate as a guarantee of *political speech*, that is, communication that deals with public issues—with *ideas*—which have or could have a political, governmental, or societal consequence. In other words, the First Amendment is a guarantee that the government will not, in any fashion, outlaw or impair the flow of *ideas*.

The First Amendment was never intended to be a guarantee against government restrictions on *nonpolitical* speech. Proof of that can be found in the fact that laws prohibiting obscenity, libel, and other categories of harmful speech—including even political speech that poses a clear and present danger of violence—predated the Constitution and were widely understood to be left unprotected by the First Amendment.

Indeed, this latter-day notion that the First Amendment protects all forms of communication, even obscenity and child pornography, comes in part from a failure to read or acknowledge the entire text of the First Amendment. Here is the rest: "Congress shall make no law . . . abridging . . . the right of the people peaceably to assemble, *and to petition the Government for a redress of grievances*" (italics added).

That last phrase—"the right of the people . . . to petition the Government for a redress of grievances"—guarantees that local, state, and national governments, through the efforts of private citizens, may, among other activities, pass laws to address what are perceived to be grievances or problems within society.

Such a grievance, for example, is the creation and distribution of obscene material. The United States Supreme Court has repeatedly ruled that it is constitutional—within the meaning and sweep of the First Amendment—for citizens to petition their local, state, and federal governments to pass laws to criminalize the sale of obscene material, even making the mere possession of child pornography, not just the sale of it, a criminal act. The ACLU, on the other hand, officially maintains that the possession of child pornography is a basic constitutional right guaranteed by the First Amendment.

It would be a strange First Amendment, indeed, if a constitutional provision that guarantees the right of the people to pass laws doesn't really mean that people can pass laws, even laws that pre-Constitution America considered necessary and proper. Indeed, our Supreme Court has declared restrictions on commercial "speech" to be constitutional and justified. In *Miller v. California*, for example, the Supreme Court defined obscenity and ruled it to be contraband. Apparently, Congress *can* make a law that abridges speech and press. If that speech is not expressive of an idea, then it is unprotected. What is the "idea" conveyed to a child in a video game that trains him to kill? It is more akin to an appliance—a murder simulator—than to speech.

Yet all entertainment is "speech," according to First Amendment absolutists. In this claim, they find themselves in league, arms locked on this issue, with libertarian conservative Republicans. Republicans arrive here largely because of a probusiness, don't-tell-anyone-what-to-do mentality, and Democrats lock arms with them largely because of a strained historical view of the Constitution. One should note that these liberal ideologues do not embrace an absolutist view of the Second Amendment to the Constitution. Guns can be regulated and even banned outright. The fact is that all of the Constitution, including all of its first ten amendments known as the Bill of Rights, must and can be harmonized, as anticipated by those who drafted the Constitution and the Bill of Rights.

Libertarians and liberals alike don't want to see what most Americans understand both instinctively and by common sense: that no "right" is absolute. The Constitution, they understand with their heads and their hearts, does not protect a corporation engaged in predatory practices that target children with adult products.

Yet the libertarian mentality wants to knock down anyone who suggests otherwise. The most abiding and hurtful criticism that has been aimed at my efforts to hold "big entertainment" accountable has come from my fellow conservatives and Republicans who claim that no true conservative would do such a thing.

I understand and can even abide better the criticism of the ideologically absolutist liberal, who at least has an idea-driven framework with which he or she comes to this absolutism. Any conservative, however, who claims that the Republican Party's "big tent" cannot abide those of us who want to stop big entertainment's assault on our children is a conservative who is rather loosely educated. He doesn't know his Grand Old Party's history.

The father of the Republican Party, President Abraham Lincoln, led this nation into a Civil War over whether a commercial enterprise known as slavery could or should be abolished by force if necessary. That's not laissez-faire economics. It is the application of morality, in a very real sense, to the marketplace.

Theodore Roosevelt, a Republican, went after business monopolies, rightly noting that corporations could become so large and powerful that they stifled certain American values, including a free market. He was a trustbuster. In other words, business could not be trusted, in certain situations, to regulate itself. Law enforcement was needed on street corners and sometimes in corporate boardrooms. Recent boardroom scandals involving WorldCom, Global Crossing, and others seem to have made that point anew.

Common sense tells us that any human enterprise that is answerable to no one poses a danger to liberty and to virtue. It makes no difference whether that "large and in charge" mentality is resident in government or in business.

We see it now in the media, and this consolidation of the media has even affected my ability to get this message out to the American people. When I try to tell people about the dangers of violent or sexually explicit adult entertainment marketed to children, I often find myself trapped because major entertainment companies now run major news organizations. Disney owns ABC. News Corporation, which owns Fox Broadcasting Co., is also the parent of the Fox News Channel. Time Warner owns CNN, and Viacom owns CBS. If you read between the lines, it's easy to

see that the anything-goes mentality of the parent companies is now finding its way into news coverage—so it's not surprising that we hear fewer
media reports connecting the dots that link pop culture to crimes. Obviously, entertainment companies tend to shy away from news stories that
point fingers at their corporate parents.

Michael Copps, an FCC commissioner, believes that this consolidation of ownership in the electronic media is a dangerous problem that
threatens to choke the distribution of information and news to citizens
in the marketplace.

There are people in both major political parties who know that parents are
under siege in America. What for some is a business or an ideological calcula-
tion is a public-safety crisis for the rest of us. We say: "You will not train my
child to kill, and you will not train some other child to kill my child."

When the next Columbine happens, which may eclipse in its horror
and impact what happened in April 1999, will American parents then tell
the probusiness apologists and the extremist ideologues in their respective
political parties to get out of the way? Will we then say, "We're taking
back our culture, legally and constitutionally. We're going to 'petition our
government for a redress of grievances' "?

In the meantime, because certain vested business and ideological interests thwart even minimal efforts to stop the marketing of dangerous
entertainment products to our children, I believe these interests are fool-
ishly laying the groundwork for what may be a greater contraction of
freedom than they could possibly imagine.

Just as the 2004 Super Bowl halftime show put the entire broadcast industry in the regulatory crosshairs, could the next Columbine lead to
calls to outlaw such entertainment altogether?

If so, the entertainment industry and their apologists in both parties will wonder why they are being targeted. Those of us who know
better, who tried to apply common sense to keep adult entertainment
out of the hands of kids, will be able to say, "We warned you, but you
would not listen."

15

STERN STUFF

September 11, 2001, changed most Americans—but not all of them. One who seemed unaltered by the terrorist attack upon our homeland was Howard Stern, the self-professed "King of All Media." Stern's shock radio show, which he had hosted since 1982, was syndicated nationally by Infinity Radio in the 1990s.

A few days after the World Trade Center Twin Towers collapsed and as rescue workers sifted through the smoldering rubble, Howard Stern encouraged prostitutes to go down to Ground Zero and provide oral sex to the rescue workers while on their breaks.

Call me old-fashioned, but some things are not funny. That was one of them. The morning I heard Stern make this suggestion, I was reminded of a cartoon that appeared in the *Miami Herald* in the early 1990s after my first radio war with a shock jock. The cartoon had been done by the *Herald*'s Jim Morin, who won the Pulitzer Prize for editorial cartoons in 1996. It showed an Old Spanish home in Coral Gables, much like our house. On the front of the house was the inscription "Jack Thompson's House." The caption below read: "Howard Stern announces his radio show will be on the air soon in

South Florida." Coming out of one of the windows of the house was an anguished scream, obviously from me.

When I heard Stern make the Ground Zero joke, I wanted to scream that scream. Instead, I put it in the back of my mind, remembering that Howard Stern was still broadcasting in my community, still trying to shock in order to increase ratings and make money. And once again, I knew that someone needed to do something about it.

⚠

A year and a half later, on April 13, 2003, it was one of those Miami mornings when the calendar says spring but the early morning temperatures say summer. Spring sometimes lasts about two weeks in Miami. Mild winter goes to hot, humid summer—fast. They don't call South Florida's NBA team the Miami Heat for nothing.

That morning, as I always do, I took John, then ten years old, to his school about ten miles south of our home. I always enjoyed this time to talk with him and to look at and comment on the "cool" cars on the road. The radio was not on because it always gets in the way. I dropped him off with a hug.

"I love you, Daddy."

"I love you, Johnny. Be kind to everyone today. I'm proud of you." Johnny saw his buddy Vincent across the playground and raced over to him. I smiled. It warmed my heart to watch Johnny with his friends, talking about the things that ten-year-old boys talk about before school begins.

As I left the school and merged into the heavy northbound traffic that always clogs Miami roadways in the morning, I turned on the radio, although I knew that none of its chatter would be even half as entertaining as that of my son.

I had not heard *The Howard Stern Radio Show* for months. No good reason to listen to it. The last time I had listened to it, or more precisely monitored it, was in mid-September 2001, after the attacks on the Twin Towers.

So on this day, a year and a half later, I happened to be moving down the dial on my radio when I landed on Clear Channel's WBGG-FM 105.9, known as "Big 106" in South Florida. It plays rock music all hours except during the morning rush, when Howard Stern's show airs.

On this particular day, Stern's guests included a man and a woman who were marketing a product called Sphincterine. The discussion went on and on, with graphic references to oral and anal sex, as well as tips for making oral sex more appealing.

Howard Stern provided the man's Web site for anyone who wanted the product. As I listened to this, my reactions went from shock to disgust to anger to resolve. I had heard a lot of indecent, sexually graphic material on the public airwaves in the past fifteen years, but this seemed to be particularly over the line drawn by the U.S. Supreme Court in the *Pacifica* case.

I reached over into the glove box and pulled out a small notebook. While I drove, I scribbled down key words and phrases. I kept thinking about all the teenagers who were probably driving to school right now across the country, listening to this pornographic material. When I reached my office, the interview was just about over. I continued to listen to it, making notes, until it ended with Stern going to commercial. I stayed in the car, determined to find out which advertisers were supporting Howard Stern. There were tons of commercials. It seemed that advertisers were lining up to pay for this "entertainment."

As I sat in my car, I felt a pull that was both encouraging and at the same time frightening. I had felt it before. It was the same mix of contradictory emotions I had felt thirteen years earlier when I heard a similar shock radio show emanating from Miami.

I knew what I was hearing on my radio was wrong. I knew it was illegal. When I turned off the radio, part of me also wanted to turn off my response, but I felt I couldn't do that. I slipped out of my car, determined to do something about what I had just heard.

As soon as I got into my office I contacted a Coral Gables company called Broadcast Quality, which provides audiotapes of certain television and radio programs. I ordered a tape of what I had just heard. I knew, given my past experience, that the FCC prefers both audiotapes and verbatim transcripts of shows alleged to be indecent.

In a couple of weeks I had the tape. I transcribed it, and I shipped the tape, the transcript, and my formal complaint of indecency to the Federal Communications Commission. Years earlier, I had done this very same thing after hearing a local shock jock. That had not been a pleasant time. Doing it again now made me feel a bit sick to my stomach.

I had learned by now to be, as I heard someone once say, "subjectively optimistic and objectively pessimistic" that the FCC would ever do anything about my complaint.

The FCC never sent any acknowledgment that it had received my formal complaint. That was not surprising, as I knew that the FCC had to have accumulated enough complaints from citizens like me about Howard Stern and other illegal, indecent programming on the public airwaves to fill a football stadium to the rim.

⚠

On February 1, 2004, about nine months after the "Sphincterine" broadcast, our family was sitting at home, enjoying the Super Bowl match between the New England Patriots and the Carolina Panthers.

I had left the downstairs living room to go to an upstairs computer to check my e-mail and the news. While I was doing that, my son, who had been watching the halftime show, ran upstairs and breathlessly said, "Daddy, Janet Jackson just took her top off during her dance with Justin Timberlake!" I assured him that he had to be mistaken.

"Johnny, it must have been some sort of trick with the camera or something. They wouldn't do that."

"No, Daddy! It happened. They're all talking about it." I felt the blood drain out of my face as I thought, *Is this how bad it has gotten?* Sure enough, I turned on the TV upstairs, and I heard what had happened.

I returned to my computer, composed a formal complaint to the FCC, and faxed and e-mailed it to the commissioners immediately. I had a feeling I would not be alone in doing this, and I was not. News reports since state that more than five hundred thousand citizens complained to Congress and to the FCC about what they had seen.[1]

FCC chairman Michael Powell was also sitting in his living room with kids from his neighborhood to watch the game. He described the halftime show as being "tainted by a classless, crass, and deplorable stunt."[2] A line had been crossed, not that it had not been crossed countless times before. But this time it had been crossed on the most watched telecast on the planet.

The next morning Howard Stern, who had seen the halftime show, knew what it meant. He told the media, "I'm under attack. Janet Jackson whipped out her [breast] and it's all over."[3]

President George W. Bush, when asked that same morning for his reaction to the halftime show, said, "Saw the first half, did not see the halftime—I was preparing for the day and fell asleep."[4]

But Stern's show was not, as he predicted, quite over—not just yet. Even after the "new normal" for broadcast indecency was ushered in by the Super Bowl, Stern kept doing what he was doing. Maybe he thought his fears had been unfounded, that the coast was clear. Maybe he thought he would survive Janet Jackson after all.

I certainly figured he would. After all, he had survived his Columbine comments. He had survived using the tragedy at Ground Zero to shock his listeners. Stern, if not quite the self-described King of All Media, was undoubtedly the King of All Scofflaws. I believe that part of the reason for that was that many political "conservatives" championed Howard Stern as an asset to the political right because Stern's political instincts, they believed, were largely conservative and reflective of a healthy distrust of government. Conservatives like those at Bill Buckley's *National Review* could put up with Stern's pornography as long as he continued to poke fun at people in power. In the 1990s, *National Review* even ran an article explaining why conservatives should love Howard Stern.[5]

Stern liked New Jersey's Republican governor Christine Todd Whitman, often having her on his show in between visits by female porn stars.

Stern had even bought highway billboard advertising to support Governor Whitman's reelection. How could a true Republican not like this guy, right?

But I was one Republican who did not love this guy. On February 24, 2004, three weeks after America's Super Bowl epiphany, I dropped Johnny off at school and turned Howard Stern's program on. I figured I would hear a cleaned-up Howard Stern, in light of the "new normal," and I was eager to hear it.

Boy, was I wrong. That morning, in the half hour before eight o'clock, Howard Stern's guest included the man who had sexual intercourse with Paris Hilton in front of a video camera and microphone. In order to share these intimate moments with his listeners, Howard Stern streamed the audio and video of the encounter on the Internet. Just what was Howard Stern looking for in such an interview? Sex, obviously, and he got it. After a clearly indecent but typical discussion of all things sexual, which included banter about some of the odors attendant to certain kinds of sexual intercourse, Stern decided to take phone calls from his listeners.

"Have you ever banged any famous n——- chicks?" the caller asked. "What do they smell like? Watermelons?"

I was stunned. But as soon as I heard that, I knew that lightning had just been caught in a bottle. Pornography broadcast to children doesn't seem to trouble some people, but pornography wedded to racism, particularly that which objectifies and demeans African American women—in our country with its history of slavery and discrimination and mistreatment of women of color—is positively incendiary. Airing that incredibly hurtful comment was possibly the worst thing Howard Stern could have done in his career at that moment. I was certainly out to prove how reckless—and wrong—it was.

I bolted to my desk from the car and typed a letter to the FCC recounting precisely what I had just heard. I called the FCC and asked to speak with Jordan Goldstein. Mr. Goldstein was, and at this writing still is, senior legal advisor to Michael Copps, one of the five commissioners on the FCC who for years had been like the proverbial voice in the wilderness calling upon the FCC to get serious about the explosion of indecency on public airwaves. When I told Jordan Goldstein what Stern had aired just minutes earlier, he was shocked. "You have got to be kidding!" I told him, no, I was not kidding.

Mr. Goldstein asked me to fax him my written complaint immediately. "I will take it down to the enforcement division of the FCC and tell them, 'This comes to you with the request from Commissioner Copps that it be taken seriously and acted upon,'" he said.

"It will be in your hands in about two minutes," I told him. I quickly faxed the letter and then sent a copy to the executive offices at Clear Channel Communications in Austin, Texas, on whose station I had heard the broadcast. I also e-mailed the same letter to every Clear Channel executive's e-mail address helpfully provided at their company's Web site.

I had finished my correspondence by late morning on February 24, 2004. The next day, Clear Channel Radio CEO John Hogan released a statement to the national media. The news was startling: Clear Channel had placed Howard Stern on probation, effective immediately, until such time as Infinity Broadcasting, which syndicates the Stern show, gave adequate assurances that decency standards would not be violated in the future.[6]

In the news release, Hogan and his people were meticulous in reciting, verbatim, what Stern had aired, describing it as racist and misogynistic.

I had not listened to Stern in nearly a year, yet I just happened to tune in the very day that he aired the "watermelon" comment. Did I feel God's providence in my tuning in? Call me crazy, but yes, I did.

Did I feel God was in control rather than Howard Stern and Clear Channel when one simple letter sent to a handful of people resulted in the removal of "The King of All Media" from the largest radio broadcaster in America? Call me doubly crazy, but yes, I did. I was not in control. The One who created these radio frequencies seemed to be taking charge of them.

After Clear Channel put Stern on probation, I put out a news release explaining exactly what it was that Stern had aired and why I had acted upon what I heard. Later that week, I found myself on CNN and MSNBC to talk about the events and what it all meant.

Wow, I thought. *This was a lot easier than fifteen years ago against the Miami shock jock. It doesn't get any better than this.*

But I was wrong. It did get better.

On April 8, 2004, less than a month and a half after Stern was put on probation by Clear Channel, the Federal Communications Commission announced that it was proposing a fine in the amount of $495,000 against Clear Channel Communications for the airing of indecency one year earlier, to the day, on WBGG-FM serving the Palm Beach south to Miami market, in furtherance of a complaint filed.[7]

I was certain the fine was the result of my complaint against Stern's "Sphincterine" broadcast. And later, when the Fort Lauderdale newspaper, the *Sun-Sentinel*, contacted the FCC to inquire who the citizen was, they confirmed that it was Jack Thompson. The transcript of the offending broadcast posted on the FCC's Web site was identical to the one that I had filed, right down to the punctuation I used.

In the days that followed, I appeared on several other cable news talk shows. I was no longer nervous, as I had been years before. I knew these programs were a means to an end. Doing these programs was necessary if I wanted to spread the message that there is such a thing as indecency, that it is illegal and harmful, and that there is something a citizen can do about it. I wasn't trying to promote myself. I was trying to encourage others to do what I had done. If every town in America had just one person who would take on the distribution of adult entertainment to kids, the distribution across the country might stop.

I also wanted certain Stern fans to know that I had not been intimidated. These were people who had called me and threatened to kill me after the February 24, 2004, "watermelon" broadcast and the resultant national news coverage. One guy who was a regular on Stern's show had called me over and over, saying he and others could kill me. If it is a sin to want people like that to know they cannot intimidate and threaten people into silence, all the while proclaiming *their* "First Amendment rights," then I need forgiveness for that sin. You cannot be a culture warrior or any other kind of warrior and not enjoy a victory. I was enjoying this, all the while trying to remember Whose victory it really was.

I was grateful that of all the complaints filed with the FCC over the last several years, the one that the FCC had decided to process was mine. It seemed that the FCC trusted me.

Clear Channel, when hit with the $495,000 FCC fine, decided to pay it and announced that Howard Stern was permanently off all their stations nationwide, including the one in South Florida. I was thrilled. *The Howard Stern Radio Show* would no longer be heard in my community.

I figured that was the last time I would have to deal with Howard Stern. Boy, was I wrong.

16

STERN'S BACK

Howard Stern's banishment from the airwaves in South Florida upset his loyal listeners here. After all, children whine when things they like get taken from them, even—or especially—the harmful things.

Because of the "new normal" that seemed to have been ushered in by the 2004 Super Bowl, *The Howard Stern Radio Show* was deemed too hot to handle by Fort Lauderdale and Miami radio stations—all except for one station, WQAM-AM.

This station had put shock jock Scott Ferrall on the air in June 2003 to compete with Stern. It was the same station that put my first radio nemesis on in spite of the fines I got against his shows in 1989 and then kept him on the air despite the fact that the FCC fined WQAM-AM for his show's indecency in 2000, a complaint that was brought by someone other than me.

In other words, it seemed that Beasley Broadcast Group, which owns forty-one radio stations around the country, had a corporate strategy of putting shock radio on the air to increase ratings and thereby increase revenue. Since 1997, Beasley had featured Howard Stern's show on its Fort Myers, Florida radio station, WRXK-FM.

Beasley's corporate policy would surprise some in light of the fact that it also owns and operates a number of Christian radio stations around the country. It didn't surprise me, given the fact that the radio business is as much concerned with what makes money as any other entertainment industry sector. If pornography makes money for a broadcaster in one market and religion makes money for that same broadcaster in another, that company does whatever it takes to reach a profitable bottom line. That surely seems to be Beasley's strategy.

Beasley is a substantial financial contributor to the Republican National Committee. Broadcasters consider this greasing of palms in Washington, correctly or incorrectly, as "protection money" to help ensure against regulatory consequences. The thinking is that a broadcaster with "friends" in Washington is less likely to be troubled by an activist regulatory agency. But sometimes events like Super Bowl halftime shows render that influence ineffectual—at least for a while.

Beasley, however, decided to bring Stern back to South Florida, to a station where the guy who got him off the air there in the first place—me—would surely hear him. On August 16, 2004, with much fanfare and advertising, *The Howard Stern Radio Show* was back on the air from 6 a.m. to 10 a.m., in clear violation of the law that makes it a criminal act to air indecent material on the public airwaves between those hours.

I listened to the show that week and immediately knew that nothing had changed on Stern's show. The show was clearly over the line of what could be considered legally decent. One of Stern's broadcasts featured a female amputee beauty contest, along with tips and advice for helping female amputees achieve orgasm. Real family entertainment stuff from Beasley, a broadcaster of Christian programming.

Beasley had announced that it had in place its own "dump button," separate and apart from the ten-second delay that Infinity supposedly used to excise Stern's indecent material coming out of the New York studio. The reality was that neither Infinity nor Beasley was using its respective dump buttons to keep all the indecency off the air.

The other remarkable thing I heard from Stern was his repeated admission that "there is one lunatic lawyer in Miami who got me off the air down here."[1] I felt that it was Stern's backhanded tip of the cap that he had to make a South Florida comeback because of me. He even noted that he was reading all the e-mails I was sending to his agent, Don Buchwald, in New York.

Those e-mails, starting with one August 16, 2004, conveyed to Stern, to Infinity, and to Beasley each formal complaint that I filed with the FCC. Each complaint detailed the illegal airing of indecency on radio broadcasts of *The Howard Stern Radio Show*.

Beasley quickly struck back. On August 24, Beasley's outside counsel wrote me a letter making it clear that unless I backed off, a bar complaint alleging I was misrepresenting the content of the show and the actions of Beasley would be filed against me and a lawsuit would also be filed.

I had been through this drill before, so I pushed ahead. The bar complaint was filed, which didn't deter me. The plan was to get Stern off the air, despite the threats. If I backed down in the face of these threats, I would never be able to take a stance against this type of illegal conduct again. The other side would know I could be intimidated.

What seemed to particularly upset Beasley was my assertion that the airing of indecent material is a criminal act punishable by up to two years in prison for those involved. I stated to the FCC that Beasley and its counsel were facilitating that criminal activity, all the more so when they made threats against me in order to protect the criminal activity.

The back-and-forth and the distraction of the bar complaint continued well into the fall. It did not comfort me to know that the same bar that had tried to whack me fifteen years earlier and then had to pay me damages was now in a position to deliver payback. Beasley's outside counsel was even publicly asserting again that I clearly had mental problems. *Here we go again,* I thought.

But then something helpful happened, in a way that seemed to be out of the blue. I had learned to expect these surprises from God. In no small way, these surprises kept me going. On November 23, 2004, the Federal

Communications Commission went public with two official actions. The FCC entered into a $3.5 million consent decree with Viacom/Infinity, which syndicates Stern's show. By the consent decree, the FCC agreed to dispose of all complaints of indecency aired by Viacom/Infinity, including the airing of Stern, with the payment of the $3.5 million, in exchange for Viacom/Infinity's (a) admission that it had in fact aired indecent material in violation of the law, and (b) promise to put in place new measures, effective December 31, 2004, to keep indecency off its stations.

In other words, Viacom/Infinity had finally gotten the message that Clear Channel had gotten back in February 2004, when it came to *The Howard Stern Radio Show*.

What the consent decree did not do, however, was wipe out the complaints I had already filed against WQAM for the airing of *Stern*. Beasley was not a part of the consent decree, and thus was not protected by it.

As if to drive that point home to Beasley, on the same day the FCC also entered a $55,000 forfeiture order against Beasley for the airing of indecent material on *The Scott Ferrall Show* in September 2003. I had been one of the complainants.

Michael Copps, one of the five FCC commissioners, wrote of the remarkably "brutal" targeting of citizens by Ferrall's broadcasts, which included a threat to have a man beaten up, his wife raped, and their home burned down with them and their children in it. I had also been threatened and targeted by this same show. In fact, Ferrall had said on the air that I would be beaten up if I went to a Florida Marlins game, which WQAM broadcast on the radio.

The dual FCC actions on November 23 served notice on Beasley that *The Howard Stern Radio Show* was indeed indecent and that the FCC considered me credible yet again when it came to formal complaints about indecency on the public airwaves.

Any responsible or rational broadcaster would have heeded the message sent by the FCC. Not Beasley. One week later, they filed a twenty-million-dollar lawsuit against me.

I informed the FCC that the bar complaint, the lawsuit, and the on-air threats of physical violence were all part of an extortionate plan by Beasley to deter me from exercising my constitutional right to "petition the government for a redress of grievances." Here was a broadcaster claiming that the First Amendment protects indecent broadcast to children but does not protect a citizen complaining about that criminal activity.

I pointed out to the FCC that all of these threats against me, in their various forms, constituted criminal violations of certain federal statutes: Title 18, U.S.C., Section 241, which makes it a felony to threaten a citizen in such a way as to restrict his constitutional rights; and also Title 18, U.S.C., 1505, which makes it a felony to issue any kind of threat that would affect in any fashion a matter under investigation by any federal agency, including the FCC.

The FCC, knowing that its entire regulatory scheme fails if broadcasters are allowed to intimidate citizens, understood, it seemed, what was at stake here. On December 15, 2004, two weeks after Beasley sued me, the FCC filed formal notice that it was opening an investigation of Beasley's alleged "threats, intimidation, and harassment of Jack Thompson."

Encouraged, I asked to inspect Beasley's WQAM-AM "public file." The FCC requires that each FCC-licensed facility maintain such a file to be readily viewed by the public to see what is going on at the station.

When I went through the file, I found a letter from Beasley's outside counsel to its in-house counsel delineating how I was to be harassed. These careless people had not bothered to go through this very *public* file to remove that smoking gun. I found this letter after Beasley's outside counsel had assured me and my lawyer that there was no orchestration of any harassment of me. Abraham Lincoln once wrote that "no man has a good enough memory to be a consistently good liar." Beasley was proof that Honest Abe was right.

I, of course, informed the FCC about what I had found. I also explained how Beasley was threatening me with yet another bar complaint for daring to disclose to the FCC the existence of this smoking gun.

Why would they do this, in the face of all their wrongdoing and in the face of all of my vindication? Because for Beasley, this had become a zero-sum game. Beasley was now looking at the loss of radio station licenses, at least the WQAM-AM license, worth tens of millions of dollars.

Instead of backing off, Beasley then set out to shoot the messenger. They hauled out the big guns and filed a new bar complaint against me alleging, in effect, that I had acted "unprofessionally" in saying things about Beasley and its outside counsel and that I should be punished by the Florida Bar for being such a nasty fellow.

Beasley's law firm, Tew Cardenas, gets the second half of its name from Alberto R. "Tico" Cardenas, former chairman of the Florida Republican Party. He is a close friend of Florida governor Jeb Bush and President George W. Bush, having helped get Jeb reelected in 2002 and George elected in 2000.

I had written Governor Jeb Bush, whom I know, to tell him that his friend Al Cardenas and his law firm, Tew Cardenas, were actively engaged in protecting the broadcast of indecent material to children and threatening me as part of that protective process.

If I were making any of this up, then Tew Cardenas should have sued me for libel, but of course that was not done because (a) what I said was true and (b) a public civil litigation of these issues would reveal what Beasley and its lawyers were actively doing—distributing porn to kids and threatening a citizen who opposed it.

What Beasley and its GOP-wired law firm decided to do, cleverly, was go the regulatory route via the Florida Bar, which had proven in the past its willingness to mess with Jack Thompson.

In the midst of all this, Beasley took *The Howard Stern Radio Show* off WQAM-AM, a move that seemed to acknowledge that I had been right way back on August 16, 2004, when I had filed the first decency complaint against Beasley for airing Stern's show. But Beasley decided to have it both ways. Get clear of Stern and any subsequent fallout from the continued airing of it, but also try to discredit and destroy me in order to get out from under the pending decency complaints I had already filed.

Beasley's strategy was to make Jack Thompson the issue since Howard Stern is indefensible.

Want further proof? On May 10, 2005, Beasley had its on-air morning drive host, Hank Goldberg, who is a frequent ESPN on-air personality as well, tell the audience that he could make sure Jack Thompson had "no kneecaps" in retaliation for my letters to the federal government. It's rumored in South Florida that Hank Goldberg, by virtue of his personal gambling habits rubs elbows with organized crime figures. How appropriate and dangerous, then, that Goldberg, with the full approval of Beasley, would use a mob term for a physical act of extortion— removing my kneecaps.

This was extortion in the light of day. This was how desperate Beasley was, and is, to hold on to its licenses. Desperate people do desperate things.

On August 15, 2005, one day short of a full year after Infinity's *The Howard Stern Show* was placed on Beasley's WQAM-AM, the Federal Communications Commission wrote Infinity and Beasley to inform them that it was pursuing *new* formal investigations of both radio broadcasters for the airing of allegedly indecent material. One incident was on the *Hank Goldberg Show* on WQAM, and the other incidents were on *Stern* broadcasts on Beasley and Infinity stations. I was the citizen complainant in them all. Vindication!

Stern responded with a tirade on his show, and the new FCC actions made headlines across the country. Even Matt Drudge linked to a story at his Drudge Report that "Coral Gables, Florida, decency crusader and Stern nemesis, Jack Thompson" had once again persuaded the FCC to proceed against Infinity, Beasley, and Stern. Another national article correctly reported that a November 23, 2004, Consent Decree between Infinity and the FCC might require that Stern be taken off the air if the FCC took the complaints one step further and issued a "Notice of Apparent Liability."

In a year of fighting with Stern, I felt what seemed like persecution. But Jesus said, "If the world hates you, keep in mind that it hated me first" (John 15:18). Any persecution I have had to endure while trying, imperfectly, to serve Him has been nothing compared to what the world did to Him. His yoke is indeed light, and I consider any pain that has come my way a privilege, because in the midst of it all, I have felt His pleasure.

17

SWEET HOME ALABAMA

On a brisk January day, I received an e-mail forwarded to me by Dave Grossman from one of the thousands of police officers he has trained in the United States and around the world.

This officer's e-mail contained a news story out of Fayette, Alabama, a fairly small town about seventy miles west of Birmingham. According to the e-mail, on June 7, 2003, eighteen-year-old Devin Moore had stolen an unoccupied car. A Fayette police officer by the name of Arnold Strickland came across Moore in the car that night, and things didn't look right.

Officer Strickland ran a check on the plate and arrested Moore without incident, taking him into the tiny Fayette police station for booking. Officer James Crump was there to help Strickland. Devin Moore had no criminal record, and the officers had no reason to believe that anything unusual would happen.

But in the middle of the booking, something terrible did happen. Moore grabbed the revolver out of Strickland's holster and shot him. He then turned on Officer Crump and shot him repeatedly. Both men were killed from a shot to the head.

Moore then came across dispatcher Ace Mealer sitting at his desk in the next room. Moore shot him in the head repeatedly, some bullets going through his hands which were held up to his face in a natural but futile attempt to block them. Mealer was also killed. Bullet holes were later found high in the walls in the rooms in which the three homicides had occurred. Moore clearly was aiming for his three victims' heads.

Devin Moore then grabbed keys to a police squad car, ran out to the parking lot, and fled. Not a good getaway plan. He was arrested shortly thereafter, just as he crossed the Alabama border into Mississippi.

According to a report in the *Tuscaloosa News* written by reporter Johnny Kampis, when Devin Moore was arrested, his response was simple: "Life is like a video game. You've got to die sometime."[1]

Of all the things Moore could have said, why did he say that? I thought I knew.

The news reports gave the name of the local pastor who presided over a memorial service for the three slain men, so I called him and told him that Moore's comment that "life is like a video game" might indicate that the boy was immersed in the video-game culture and might help explain, at least in part, why this senseless act happened. The pastor, hearing my explanation, thought it was important that I speak with Fayette police chief Euel Hall.

Chief Hall called me within a matter of days. He said he was especially interested in my theory because he had just watched his son play the video game *Grand Theft Auto: Vice City*, and when he saw it he said to his son, "That's exactly what Moore did to my three men." Chief Hall asked me if I would take a call from the families of the three slain men, and I said, "Of course."

Things moved quickly from there. I spoke with the attorneys for Devin Moore, who told me that in fact Moore was a devoted violent video-game player and that his favorite game was *Grand Theft Auto: Vice City*.

We then arranged for me to meet with the surviving members of the Strickland, Mealer, and Crump families. I say "we" because I would not be alone in what already felt like an important legal fight. I went to Alabama with Ray Reiser, one of the best trial lawyers I know. Ray and I had practiced together at Blackwell, Walker, Gray, Powers, Flick & Hoehl, where I had gotten my start under the wing of Sam Powers.

Ray had taken me to my first deposition in 1981, and although we are roughly the same age, he knows far more about how to win a case than I do or ever will. Ray does a great deal of medical malpractice defense work, so he knows as much about medicine as a lot of practicing doctors.

Ray had read most of the thousands of e-mails detailing my war with the entertainment industry, and although we hadn't been law partners since we left that large firm, Ray's response, upon hearing about the events in Alabama, was: "Jack, I don't always believe in what you do, but I believe in you. Let's go to Alabama and win this case."

So we went to Alabama to meet with these three families along with their local counsel. I explained, in a half hour or so on a Sunday evening, how I believed that a video game trained Devin Moore to kill their loved ones. As we left the meeting, Steve Strickland, the Methodist minister who was also the older brother of Arnold, said, "I have gone to the jail and met with this young man who killed my brother. I have written Devin's name in my Bible to remind me to pray for him. If we prove that this violent video game contributed to the death of my brother and if Devin Moore is not executed because of that, then so be it. If he has to live so that others won't die, then God will make that clear to us."

In saying that, Steve Strickland was communicating what we all knew: Devin Moore had only two options left to him in his life. He was either going to be executed for three homicides, or he was going to be sentenced to life in prison with no chance of parole. The families understood that "a video-game defense" might help Moore avoid the death penalty. If a jury realized that this was not a premeditated act but rather an impulsive act made more likely by the video game's influence, it would be more likely to spare his life. We knew we needed to file a lawsuit.

We returned to Miami, and I spent the better part of a week drafting the lawsuit. The lawsuit named Sony (who marketed the game with the creator and on whose Playstation 2 the game is played), Take-Two/Rockstar (the designer and maker of *GTA* games), Gamestop and WalMart, retailers where the games were purchased, and Devin Moore, the killer. Ray Reiser and I worked on it and refined it with Alabama counsel Patrick Gray of Nelson, Dorroh, Gray & Newsome, an excellent Tuscaloosa firm.

We returned to Alabama in February and filed the lawsuit in state court. That morning we held a news conference in Tuscaloosa, announcing to the local and regional media that "we intended to put the video-game industry on trial in Alabama."

"This is a lawsuit intended to make every police officer in Alabama safer," Fayette police chief Euel Hall said.

I explained at the news conference, which felt and looked like a replay of the one in Paducah, that we weren't saying that Devin Moore was not responsible for what he had done. What we were saying was that two juries should decide two things: The first jury, in criminal court in the upcoming murder trial, should decide whether Devin Moore was guilty and what his punishment should be—life in prison with no chance of parole or execution. The other jury, in civil court, should decide whether an industry that knows its games are training young people how to kill has any responsibility whatsoever for that training.

After news of our filing hit the front pages of the Alabama papers and television news programs, I sent copies of that Alabama news coverage to Michael Radutzky at *60 Minutes*—the man with whom I had worked six years earlier on the Paducah story.

Radutzky immediately seized the significance of what we were out to do in Alabama; he understood why we might now be able to do in an Alabama courtroom what we were denied the chance to do in a Paducah courtroom. "With Columbine, they can't claim anymore that they couldn't see something like this coming, can they, Jack?" Radutzky asked.

"Michael, you hit the nail on the head. The video-game industry was warned. They have seen incidents like this happening. Sony, Take-Two [the makers of the *Grand Theft Auto* games], and Wal-Mart all have letters from me dated before the triple homicide in Fayette begging them to stop selling the *GTA* games to kids."

"Jack, this is a great story," Radutzky said. "We need to do this story on *60 Minutes*. I want to talk to Ed Bradley. He'll love it. Will you give us an exclusive on this?"

"Are you kidding? Of course. Let me know."

A day later, Michael called me from his cell phone. "Jack, I have someone here who wants to talk to you." Ed Bradley got on the line. "Jack, we need to do this story. We are going to do this story. I'll see you in Alabama."

Indeed he did, along with his *60 Minutes* crew, the very next week. They were going to do another "crash," just as in Paducah, because CBS had decided this was a very big story and one we could not give them an exclusive on forever. Indeed, other national media were already calling trying to get us to come on their shows.

The morning we taped the story in Alabama, Radutzky's assistant Kara McMahon called me early on my cell phone. "Jack, you know Hunter Thompson just killed himself."

Hunter Thompson was the "gonzo journalist" on whose life the *Doonesbury* character of Uncle Duke is based. "I just want you to know, Jack, that Ed Bradley and Hunter were very, very close and Ed is dealing with his grief today. But please don't mention this. It will probably distress Ed further."

When I sat down in the interviewee's chair across from Ed Bradley that morning, I said, "Ed, how have you been in the last six years?"

"Jack, since I last saw you I've had a quintuple bypass," was his only response. He did look thinner and older, but he still had the keen glint in his eye that should make any person about to be interviewed by him wary.

We did the interview, and at the conclusion Ed Bradley said what he had not said after the Paducah interview: "Jack, that was good."

The story aired the next Sunday.

I was hopeful that those who saw it would understand our intent and maybe even decide to join the crusade against such obviously dangerous weapons being thrust into the hands of our children.

"The video-game industry gave [Devin Moore] a cranial menu that popped up in the blink of an eye in that police station," I said to Ed Bradley during the interview. "And that menu offered him the split-second decision to kill the officers, shoot them in the head, [and] flee in a police car, just as the game itself trained [him] to do."

The *60 Minutes* piece also included an interview with David Walsh, a child psychologist who has coauthored a study connecting violent video games to physical aggression. According to Walsh, the link can be explained in part by pioneering brain research recently done at the National Institutes of Health—which shows that the teenage brain is not fully developed. He explained how repeated exposure to violent video games has more of an impact on a teenager than it does on an adult.

"That's largely because the teenage brain is different from the adult brain," Walsh said during the interview. "The impulse control center of the brain, the part of the brain that enables us to think ahead, consider consequences, manage urges—that's the part of the brain right behind our forehead called the prefrontal cortex. That's under construction during the teenage years. In fact, the wiring of that is not completed until the early twenties."

According to Walsh, this diminished impulse control becomes heightened in a teen who has additional risk factors for criminal behavior. Moore had a profoundly troubled upbringing, bouncing back and forth between a broken home and a handful of foster families.

"So when a young man with a developing brain, already angry, spends hours and hours and hours rehearsing violent acts, and then . . . he's put in this situation of emotional stress, there's a likelihood that he will literally go to that familiar pattern that's been wired repeatedly, perhaps thousands and thousands of times," said Walsh.

The week before *60 Minutes* had gone to Alabama, NBC's hit dramatic show *Law & Order: SVU* aired an episode about two kids who were copycatting the *Grand Theft Auto* games, which were given a different name on the show of course.[2]

Law & Order: SVU gave the best analysis I have ever seen, and in a dramatic show, no less, of the copycatting that these games spawn. Ironically, in this episode, Tracy Marrow, better known as the rapper Ice-T, played the part of a police officer, on the special victims unit trying to solve copycat killings inspired by a cop-killing game.

I imagine I was more aware than anyone on the planet of the depth of this irony. More importantly, it reminded me deep down into my bones that God was still there, ready to turn the tables as the God of surprises.

18

BACK TO SCHOOL

At the time of the *60 Minutes* piece about our Alabama lawsuit, our son, John, was in the middle of sixth grade at Palmer Trinity School. The school is a laptop school, which means that every kid has his own laptop on which he does a lot of his homework and that is fully wired to the school community.

Palmer Trinity decided to post on its home page a story about the "Palmer Trinity dad" who was about to appear on *60 Minutes* on an issue that affects teens and their video-game culture.

My son was not thrilled with the attention.

"Dad," he said, "I think it's great that you're on this national show, but the kids are giving me grief about it. Kids I don't even know are coming up to me and bothering me, saying things like 'Tell your dad that I'm not going to go Columbine.'"

To make matters worse for my son, the school had asked me to deliver a speech about all this at the monthly schoolwide convocation.

"Dad," John said, "can't you just skip doing the convocation? Kids are going to really give me a hard time about that." I understood. My son was at the age when he was easily embarrassed by his parents. And now I had been asked to come into the world where he spent most of his waking hours and give a speech that many kids would feel was a preachy sermon telling them they were "bad kids" to be playing violent video games.

My son was getting his first taste of the fallout our family had felt over the last eighteen years, ever since I had taken a stance against the entertainment industry.

I went to the administrators and counselors at my son's school and I said, "Look, I really appreciate this offer to address the whole student body about something that I feel very strongly about. But I have had to pay a wicked price over the years for this stance, and I really don't want my son to have to pay the same price just because his dad has this 'crusade.' I don't want to give the speech and make my son a pariah in his school, but on the other hand, I don't want to refuse and teach my son that the bullies can win. I need some time to figure this out before accepting your offer to speak."

Rita Feild, the lead school counselor at Palmer Trinity, gave me wise counsel. "Jack, talk this through with your son and decide what you should do—together. The school can live with either decision."

So I did that. I told John that I would do my best to give a speech that was not preachy but simply informative. He thought about it for a week or so, then said to me, "Okay, but I hope you know what you are doing. I don't want the kids at my school to hate me." I did not want them to hate him either. I had had my fill of that myself, and I did not want it for my son.

So I wrote the speech, and I went to my son's school to deliver it. I was far more nervous for this than I had been sitting across from Ed Bradley for an interview. I did not want to harm my son in any way by my comments.

I stepped up to the podium and began:

Two years ago I stood at this podium and participated in another Palmer Trinity convocation—a debate over the death penalty. I argued, along with my student partner, that the death penalty was both constitutional and right. I have since changed my mind. I would ask each of you, even if you think you know what I am going to say here today, to have an open mind, because open minds can change when confronted with the truth. Changed minds can change lives, and changed lives can change the world.

America, both as an idea and as a nation, was founded upon a number of truths that used to be self-evident. Much can be forgotten with the passage of time. Let us remember three truths that most Americans used to know:

We used to know that man was created in God's image, and therefore we crave relationship with Him and with other human beings because He craves relationship with us. Life is richer because of relationships—with family, friends, mentors, and partners. Put another way, to know God and to be like Him is to dislike isolation. God wants community with us, and we, created in His image, then want community with Him and with one another. Heaven is a place of gathering, not a place of isolation.

Every person who fled tyranny to come to America learned a second truth. Human beings, when they combine for a purpose other than real community, are dangerous. Our nation's Constitution warns of this truth—that power tends to corrupt and absolute power corrupts absolutely, as Lord Acton warned. Big human organizations pose peril. Big government, big military, big business—all things big and powerful tend to run over human beings in a rush to get even bigger. Today, on the other hand, many Americans tend to trust all things big. Government gets larger, media consolidates, and corporate giants devour, sometimes their own customers.

The third truth we have forgotten is that the love of money is the root of all kinds of evil. Money is not the answer to the problems of life. It is quite often the problem, especially when love of it and what it can buy crowds out virtue. "It is easier for a camel to go through the eye of a needle than for a rich man to enter the kingdom of God" (Matthew 19:24). All of the great religions in the world identify the risks of wealth. In America, wealth is identified as if it were a virtue rather than as a potential threat to virtue.

There is an industry that proves, unwittingly by its rapacious acts, the validity of all three of these forgotten truths. You students are targeted by this industry for harm, and many of you do not know it although many of you are uneasy about it. This industry sees you as a mere means to an end. You are its target.

That industry is the video-game industry. Consider what they do in the face of these three truths. This industry sells you a product that "entertains" you by *isolating* you from others. The *Grand Theft Auto* games, for example, immerse you in a lonely world of violence, cheap sex, and pixelated nihilism. Most experts say it takes more than 100 hours to complete all of *GTA: San Andreas* just once.[1] That is almost more hours than you spend in classes in a month at Palmer Trinity.

Bill Gates, the chairman of Microsoft, has exclaimed, "The cool thing about video games is that they transport you to a world you think is real." It is a lonely world.

How "big" is this industry? It is the fastest-growing sector of entertainment on the planet. It is a big technology, and it is a new technology. We should be wary of things this new and this big, but instead we embrace it, not knowing what the long-term effects of it will be on our community and upon our delicate brains. More on brains in a moment.

As to the third truth, how much do those who run the

video-game industry love money? The video-game industry now grosses fifteen billion dollars a year in sales, more than even the movie industry. You are the primary target of its sales machine. This industry loves money more than you, and it loves money more than life itself. How can I say that? Here's the proof.

A recent episode on NBC's *Law & Order: SVU* dealt dramatically with the causal link between the *Grand Theft Auto* games and teen violence. The police expert in video games said this: "Ever since Columbine, we've known the link between violent games and violent behaviors." The industry knows the link, too, and it couldn't care less.

You need to know that the U.S. military has the video-game industry design its virtual-reality killing simulators for the primary purpose of suppressing the inhibition of new recruits to kill. The gaming industry then turns around and sells some of these same games to you. It knows, then, the potential effect these games can have on teen civilians.

In April 1999 I was on NBC's *Today* show with the parents of the three girls shot and killed by fourteen-year-old Michael Carneal in the school shootings in Paducah, Kentucky. I was asked by Matt Lauer, "What do you fear?" I said, "Matt, we fear that other boys in other American high schools, trained on the same game, *Doom*, will do the same thing or worse." Eight days later, Columbine happened, and it was worse. Klebold and Harris were infatuated with *Doom*. If I could predict this massacre, the video-game industry could as well, but it didn't care.

Carneal in Paducah was taught by the video games to shoot in an unnatural way. He was a gun novice, and all firearms experts will tell you that a gun novice will unload his gun into one target until he gets visual confirmation that the target is down on the ground, and then [he will] move to the next target. If Carneal had done that, he would have killed only one student. Instead he shot at and hit eight different students with eight potential kill shots, all in the head and the upper torso. Even if you leave aside the appetite for violence argument, *Doom* made Carneal a more *efficient* killer.

Many of you have played the *Grand Theft Auto* games. You have a legal right to do so. But the right to do something means you have a choice. I am not here to take your freedom away. I am asking you to see that although you have the controller in your hands, there is an industry that seeks to control you and your choices with clever advertising and fraudulent sales practices. They don't care whether your choices are good ones.

Am I saying here today that video games will turn one of you into a killer? No, that is unlikely, but what I am telling you is that the violent games will harm you in certain other ways without you ever going "Columbine." There is a continuum of harm ranging from bad attitudes, to coarse language, and possibly to bad behaviors that the games can induce. God's Word warns us about putting things into our heads, our hearts, and our souls that may come back to haunt us. This, on our shoulders, is the greatest computer ever devised. Its hard drive forgets nothing. Its hard drive can never be erased. We need to be careful what we put on that cranial hard drive. Consider the science in this regard:

Brain-scan studies—MRIs—at Harvard, Indiana University, and Kansas State prove that your brain does not stop growing, does not stop maturing, until you are twenty-five years of age. (My brain stopped growing obviously when I went to law school. Law school does that.) Further, these brain scans find that teen brains process these games in the midbrain, whereas

adults process the games in the frontal lobes where differentiation between reality and fantasy occurs. The frontal lobes, as
one matures, are the sectors where impulsive behaviors are in-
tercepted. The midbrain is the green light of the brain, the seat
of emotions of the brain. The frontal lobes are the red light
which serves to stop us from destructive, harmful behaviors.[2]

Harvard has found that violent video games are processed in
the midbrain of a teen, not in the frontal lobes where adults
process them. Further, Harvard has found that this processing
structurally joins the violent images to the emotions one feels
while playing the games. Trigger those same emotions in *real*
reality, and the images and the behaviors suggested by them
pop up as strong impulses on how to act in real reality. Harvard
has concluded that that is why teens are far more likely to copycat entertainment than are adults.[3]

The Gallup Poll people did a poll last year. They found that 71
percent of all American teenaged males had played *Grand
Theft Auto: Vice City*. They found that those who had played it
were twice as likely to have engaged in an act of violence than
those who had not.[4] Not necessarily murder. Not going Columbine. But violence of some kind. That poll strongly suggests
that certain video games can have an effect upon behavior.

Om 2004 a school in Michigan initiated a curriculum that included forgoing TV and video games for ten days. Guess how
much the incidents of hitting and other aggressive behaviors
declined? Eighty percent.[5] In 2005 more schools participated
and the majority saw positive results.[5]

The heads of six major health-care organizations testified
before Congress shortly after Columbine that there are hundreds of scientific studies that link violent entertainment to
teen violence.[6] The FBI and the Secret Service found after

Columbine that of all the school shootings they studied, all were at the hands of teens who consumed violent entertainment, especially video games. Bullying was sometimes a factor, prescription drugs were sometimes a factor, but the indispensable, recurrent, one common denominator was the violent entertainment. It provided an appetite to kill, a plan for how to kill, and a headlong flight from community to chaos in the life of the isolated killer. The recent Red Lake, Minnesota, school massacre was at the hands of Jeff Weise who was into *GTA* and *Manhunt*. He uploaded to the Internet two crude versions of these two games as a sort of prediction of what he was going to do. Am I saying Weise didn't have other risk factors? No, but the games fed into his despair and warped it in a certain direction.

Here is another thing that was discovered after Columbine. President Clinton ordered the Federal Trade Commission to study the extent to which explicit music, R-rated movies, and M-rated video games, despite their age-appropriate labeling, are marketed directly and aggressively to teens. The FTC found that roughly 70 percent of all such products are marketed aggressively to you teens, despite the age ratings. Repeated stings by the federal government and by others find that although major retailers say they have policies not to sell M-rated games to anyone under seventeen since Columbine, they make those sales 50 percent or more of the time.

This industry thus is driven by lies. It is fraud to say one thing and do another. The question is not: Why should I, your speaker, trust them? The more important question is this: Why should you, the teens to whom this industry markets its products, trust them when they say their games cannot possibly harm you? Yet this industry hooks kids up to polygraphs to see which killing scenes in games most elevate their vital signs—to see which killing scenes are most physiologically stimulating and thus addictive. They lie about not doing this.

If they will lie about one thing, they will lie about other things. They have the same brain scans Harvard has. This industry knows the harm it is doing. It couldn't care less about you. You are the means to their end—money and growth.

Let me say a word about sex, and now that I have your attention, note this: The video-game industry knows that the sex-control and the violence-control sectors of the brain are physically connected. That is why more and more sexual content is finding its way into violent games. Sex and violence feed one another neurobiologically and make the games more addictive.

Young ladies here today, you need to be concerned about an industry whose best-selling video-game franchise, *GTA,* with fifty million units sold, teaches teenaged males that it is fun to have sex with a woman and then kill her. The *Grand Theft Auto* games turn the world on its head. Bad guys are good guys. Cops are the enemy. Women are to be used and discarded.

You may not play the most violent games, but the industry's plan is to lead you eventually to them. And the games are getting more violent. What used to be M-rated games are now T-rated games, and today's M-rated games are far more violent than what used to be the most violent games. Appetite begets a larger appetite.

Finally, if you are convinced that violent video games cannot possibly affect you, then how sure are you that they will not affect a classmate? Let's assume there is someone at risk in this school in ways that you are not. How sure are you that he will not, for reasons that neurobiology now explains, bring virtual violence to the reality of Palmer Trinity? You may be sure about the inability of the games to twist *you*. But you have absolutely no reason to be sure about *him*. Most of the school killers were "good boys" who had no history whatsoever of violence. Consider Michael Hernandez at nearby Southwood Middle School, a gifted student in a magnet program. One year ago he almost completely decapitated his best friend with a knife.

The day it happened, Channel 4 here in Miami asked me to come into the studio and explain why it happened. I said I did not know, but I suspected the police would find some clues on his computer, and indeed they were there. His murder of Jaime Gough seemed to come out of the blue, but Michael Hernandez consumed violent entertainment, and it may have consumed him. His parents did not believe they had a right to invade his space, to see what he might be into. Ladies and gentlemen, when your parents invade your space to see what you are into, it is because they love you, and they want you to be safe.

The truth is that teens took guns to school for three hundred years in this country to go hunting for their families' dinners after school, without turning them on one another. Something has changed. Something is different about America. Truths are ignored. Entire industries target an entire generation. We live in a country that says tobacco ads cannot be aimed at kids because they might encourage kids to smoke, and yet *interactive* games in which you don't just watch virtual killing but actually *engage* in it cannot possibly lead to aggressive behaviors of any kind. This is fantasy. This is a lie.

Some of you may resent what I have said here today. You have that right. But give me this. I am not here to blame you. I am here to warn you that you need to think for yourselves and not allow a big, isolating, money-driven industry to tell you what life and death are really about. Violence is not cool. Murder is not cool. Raping a woman and killing her is not entertainment. These are all lies. If you are to be angry at anyone, be angry at an industry that treats you as a means to an end and as if you were stupid. You are not stupid. You can handle information and then base your choices on it.

I picked up John at school later that day. He was ecstatic. "Dad," he said, "I had two of my classmates come up to me after your speech and they said, 'We thought your dad was going to be a jerk, but he's convinced us. We're not playing those games anymore.' One kid came up to me while I was with friends, and we were all talking about your speech. This kid started to hassle me about how wrong you were, and all the other kids turned and said, 'Johnny's dad was right. Leave Johnny alone.' Dad, I was proud of you. Thank you so much for not messing my life up at my school."

In the days that followed, I received a number of e-mails from the faculty and administrators and also from some of my son's classmates. Here are two:

Hey Mr. Thompson,
That was a really cool convo.
It was very interesting.
I liked how you answered all the questions kids asked when they thought they stumped you.
The whole convo caught my attention and I paid attention all the time.
Tell Johnny I say hi,
Matthew

Thanks for giving your time to speak in our convocation today. Even though I do not own a video game system personally, I thoroughly enjoyed and agreed with you on everything you talked about. I also thought it was great how you incorporated Scripture into your speech. I believe that what you said may have an effect on the way that my seventh grade peers think and play their video games. Once again thank you. I hope that you can come back to Palmer Trinity School soon and speak to us more.
Sincerely,
Tyler

I wept when I read these e-mails from these two young men. If I could go into a school filled with teens and preteens who are playing video games, many of which are violent, and get two e-mails like this, then maybe we could persuade the powers that be that something must be done to stop an industry from targeting kids with adult-rated products.

Stay tuned.

19

SCAN

Malcolm Gladwell's best seller *Blink* explains how and why humans make split-second decisions every day—sometimes beneficially, sometimes disastrously.

Gladwell calls the brain's ability to take in a lot of information and sort it out very quickly "thin slicing." It explains why a policeman can, in the blink of an eye, make a life-and-death decision to shoot or not to shoot. Gladwell proves, with numerous examples, how we are all programmed by life's experiences to act quickly in situations with what feels like reflective thought, but which is really something quite different. It is the brain "thinking" at hyperspeed.[1]

On March 1, 2005, the United States Supreme Court ruled in *Roper v. Simmons* that it is unconstitutional to execute any criminal who committed his crime while under the age of eighteen. Think what you will of the decision, Justice Anthony Kennedy, in writing for the majority, noted in his decision an important fact:

> Three general differences between juveniles under eighteen and adults demonstrate that juvenile offenders cannot . . . be classified among the worst offenders. First, as any parent

knows and as the scientific and sociological studies . . . tend to confirm, "[a] lack of maturity and an underdeveloped sense of responsibility are found in youth more often than in adults and are more understandable among the young. These qualities often result in impetuous and ill-considered actions and decisions."[2]

Note that Justice Kennedy refers to "scientific and sociological studies" that confirm differences between juveniles and adults as a reason why it would be cruel and unusual to execute a juvenile. Justice Kennedy was referring to neurological studies filed by numerous organizations, including the American Medical Association, the American Psychiatric Association, the American Society for Adolescent Psychiatry, the American Academy of Child & Adolescent Psychiatry, the American Academy of Psychiatry and the Law, and the National Mental Health Association.

The court based its decision on research that proves that brains of adolescents function in fundamentally different ways than the brains of adults. Research using functional magnetic resonance imaging, a kind of MRI scan, has demonstrated that adolescents actually use their brains differently than adults when reasoning or solving problems. For example, adolescents tend to rely more on the instinctual structures, such as the amygdala, and less on more advanced areas, such as the frontal lobes, that are associated with goal-oriented and rational thinking.

In addition, evidence suggests that the regions of the brain that adults use to control and influence behavior are still underdeveloped in adolescents. For example, the prefrontal cortex, which is one of the last areas to develop and mature in adolescents, is involved in the control of aggression and other impulses, the process of planning for long-range goals, organization of sequential behavior, consideration of alternatives and consequences, the process of abstraction and mental flexibility, and aspects of memory including "working memory."

In other words, the United States Supreme Court has now placed in a landmark decision what we knew and wanted to prove in Paducah, what was then suggested by Harvard brain-scan studies done in 1998, and what is now established scientific fact: A person's brain does not stop growing until he is twenty-five years of age. A teenager processes violent entertainment, including video games, in the midbrain and the hindbrain, notably in the amygdala, as shown by an MRI, which is the "seat of emotions" of the brain.

Harvard found that when an adolescent consumes violent entertainment, the images never get processed in the frontal lobes, where differentiation between reality and fantasy occur; instead they remain structurally resident within the amygdala. What is the danger? Teens often feel anger or fear while playing a violent video game. When that same emotion is experienced in real life, the brain calls up the images and behaviors associated with the video game, and the teen may act out, replicate, or copycat those image-driven behaviors. The frontal lobes are not engaged because they simply aren't fully developed in the teen.

That is why, Harvard concluded in its 1999 study, teens are far more likely to mimic the entertainment they see. They are neurobiologically predisposed to do so.[3]

There is now a scientific basis for what I have been warning against since 1987: Adult entertainment, by virtue of its violent content, is far more harmful to kids than it is to adults. Adults know it is virtual violence. The teen brain is not so sure, and the virtual violence can spill out into reality.

The most popular and the most violent video games in history—the *Grand Theft Auto* games—all allow the player to have sex with a prostitute and then kill her by various means to get his money back and win the game faster. How enchanting. Teenaged boys are now provided entertainment that neurobiologically weds sex with violence and trains a boy to act out the two together.

Research has been conducted on neural pathways in the brain called *dendrites*. Dendrites are actual structures akin to wires that are grown in the brain by the repetition of a physical act. If you practice enough at a physical skill, you will literally hardwire the brain to perform that skill without a conscious thought. One study compares these cranial wires to the nubs on a player piano wheel. Hit the play button in the brain, and the brain will direct the human piano player's fingers to produce the music. This is why a world-class concert pianist can walk onto the stage at Carnegie Hall under extreme pressure and play flawlessly. Practice has made perfect.

This is part of the reason that Tiger Woods, having practiced hitting and putting a golf ball since he was two years old, can do so with such extraordinary acumen in the most pressure-filled situations. Woods has a fortuitous combination of both nature and nurture, but without the latter he would not have been able to maximize the former. The early growth of his golfing dendrites made him more adroit than if he had started growing them when he was sixteen.

Dr. John Murray is a professor of developmental psychology at Kansas State University presently on loan to Harvard because Harvard has been given a $500,000 grant to do even more brain-scan studies to determine how juvenile brains process violent entertainment. I have spoken at length with Dr. Murray. He is an expert in the part of the brain called the posterior cingulate which is in the rear part of the right hemisphere of the brain. This is where post-traumatic stress disorder originates. Dr. Murray tells me that the posterior cingulate lights up like a Christmas tree in the MRIs when a kid consumes violent entertainment. Dr. Murray has found that the virtual violence found in modern entertainment is so realistic that the brain cannot differentiate it from real violence and thus is traumatized by consumption of it, particularly so if it is a young brain.

What results from entertainment-induced post-traumatic stress disorder (PTSD)? Copycatting of the violence.

During our *60 Minutes* interview in Alabama, Ed Bradley asked me why I thought a video game helped train Devin Moore to kill three good men. I was able to use science as a basis for my answer: The game gave the killer a *cranial menu* which popped up, giving him the strong urge to kill. It is the catastrophic "blink" response about which Malcolm Gladwell writes in his book.

For me, this newly proven science has vindicated all that I have done since 1987 in my efforts to keep adult-rated and adult-themed violent and sexual entertainment out of the hands of kids. I—and every thinking parent—know that certain entertainment is just not appropriate for children. The intuition that underlies the real meaning of "not appropriate" is that it is in fact *harmful* to children, and now we have the neurobiological evidence to prove it.

If you disagree, consider again Jeffrey Weise, the Native American boy from Red Lake, Minnesota. Was he a boy at risk? Yes. He was a boy with no parents, and he was prone to depression. Not only was Weise fascinated with violent video games, he was also enchanted with the movie *Elephant*, which glamorizes the killing at Columbine. He reportedly used that movie to try to recruit other kids to his killing spree that left ten dead. The media neglected to report the fact that Weise was sixteen years old, yet he had his hands on the R-rated *Elephant*, which was inappropriate (harmful) for anyone under seventeen. Likewise, *Vice City* is M-rated and thus inappropriate (harmful), by definition, to anyone under seventeen.

The director of *Elephant*, when it was released and given the Cannes Film Festival's top prize, encouraged teenagers—young teenagers—to see it. The makers of *The Basketball Diaries* also offered ringing endorsements for *Elephant*.

So many parents seem to have learned nothing from all the evidence that came to us from Paducah, Columbine, and other school shootings. Yet the entertainment industry, especially the video-game industry, has learned plenty. They have learned that more than six years after Columbine, the "coast is clear."

The video-game industry trains children how to kill in a virtual-reality school. Will there be a consequence to such recklessness? We are currently trying to bring about such a consequence in a courtroom in Fayette, Alabama.

In 2004 I appeared on John Gibson's *The Big Story* on the Fox News Channel to explain the copycatting of violent entertainment that is increasingly occurring across the country at the hands of teens.

Toward the end of the interview, Mr. Gibson said, "Mr. Thompson, we've done a little research here at Fox. We have found that entertainment companies are now buying an insurance product called 'copycat liability insurance,' which insures these entertainment companies against losses they fear might come in courtrooms because of lawsuits brought by you and others. My question, Mr. Thompson, is this: Do these companies consider you dangerous?"

I had never been asked that question in quite that way before, but I answered it truthfully and even with a smile. "John, I am dangerous. These companies know what is coming, and I intend to bring it their way."

20

DOES GOD OWE SODOM AN APOLOGY?

Evangelist Billy Graham was once heard to say, "If God doesn't judge America for its immorality, then He owes Sodom and Gomorrah an apology."

Quite a statement. Some might discount it or consider it foolish hyperbole, but we would do well to see if what he has said makes any sense.

Sodom and Gomorrah are identified in Genesis, the first book in the Bible, as two ancient cities filled with sin, including sexual immorality. A word that describes what many consider unnatural sexual acts comes from Sodom: *sodomy*. In 2004, the United States Supreme Court struck down Texas's antisodomy law. Some might say that the Supreme Court's ruling indicates Rev. Graham might have been on to something.

Abraham, the man whom God chose to father the nation of Israel, pleads with God in Genesis 18 for Sodom, asking Him not to destroy it in spite of the rampant immorality of the city. It is a remarkable exchange. There is nothing else like it in Scripture. Abraham begins a bargaining session with God in verses 23-24: "Will you sweep away the righteous with the wicked? What if there are fifty righteous people in the city?"

The Lord responds, "If I find fifty righteous people in the city of Sodom, I will spare the whole place for their sake" (v. 26).

Abraham, obviously emboldened by his ability to get a concession from God, pushes harder, steadily reducing in successive exchanges how many righteous people He must find in Sodom: "May the Lord not be angry, but let me speak just once more. What if only ten can be found there?"

God answers, "For the sake of ten, I will not destroy it" (v. 32).

Following this agreement between Abraham and God, Genesis 19 relates the arrival in Sodom of two angels at the house of Lot. Lot persuades them to stay the night in his family's home. The citizens of Sodom become aware of them, and a gang of men and boys show up at Lot's house demanding, "Where are the men who came to you tonight? Bring them out to us so that we can have sex with them" (v. 5).

Lot refuses and offers his virgin daughters to the crowd instead. The crowd wants the angels, whom they think are men. This is how far the people of Sodom and neighboring Gomorrah had gone. The two angels respond by striking everyone blind, then warning Lot to get his family out of Sodom "because we are going to destroy this place" (v. 13).

The next day, as the sun rises, God does just that, as He "rained down burning sulfur on Sodom and Gomorrah—from the LORD out of the heavens" (v. 24).

As Abraham looked upon the devastation from a distance, I wonder what he thought. *Apparently there were not even ten righteous people in Sodom.*

Fast-forward thousands of years, past the hundreds of greater and lesser civilizations, to the United States of America—the greatest by many measures, and certainly the most powerful of them all by any measure.

This is a nation founded by voyagers seeking religious freedom, proclaiming the God of the Bible, the God of Abraham, the very God who destroyed Sodom and Gomorrah. This is a nation that President Reagan repeatedly referred to as "a shining city on a hill," another clear biblical reference (see Matthew 5:14).

The founding document of an independent America proclaims the existence of God Himself, and the inalienable right of His created ones to "life, liberty, and the pursuit of happiness." The Declaration of Independence stands for a great number of things, and one of them is that there is a God.

Is America further down the road of immorality, the "road to perdition" than was Sodom? Good question. The virtual violence of video games manufactured, marketed, and sold for the entertainment of children at least equals the violence provided to the masses in the Roman Colosseum.

More and more, homosexuality is not even considered a sin but rather an "orientation" determined in the womb. God, then, cannot possibly judge someone who has been dealt such a hand by heredity, can He? AIDS is for many Americans more of a medical issue than one of morality. We just need more dollars spent on research, many argue. We don't need our consciences enlightened. We need not deal with "sin." Sin is treated as if it were a four-letter word.

Sexual activity of all kinds, in all settings, by all Americans, even those too young to have any idea of its consequences, is spawning not only disease but also unwanted life. Tens of millions of those lives have been terminated in the womb before they have even drawn a breath of fresh air. More have died at the purposeful hand of Americans than died in Sodom and Gomorrah at the hand of God. Talk about a holocaust. America's Supreme Court has authorized one.

What of America's "popular culture"? America's "King of All Media," Howard Stern, is just one example of entertainment in America. Stern has inked a deal to go from broadcast radio to satellite radio for five hundred million dollars to be paid over five years.[1] America's marketplace is not under moral constraints. It seems to simply obliterate them.

Six years after Columbine, our federal government—specifically the Department of Defense—is using our tax dollars to create violent military video games to use in training exercises. It is then allowing the industry to market and sell these same "games" to kids. Did we learn anything from Columbine? Apparently not.

In the immediate wake of the 2 Live Crew controversy, conservative columnist George Will wrote of "America's slide into the sewer."[2] That was fifteen years ago. It's clear to see that the sewage is flowing even more freely today. Watching prime-time television any night of the week proves the point. The entire world knows America as the exporter of "Hollywood" and its nonvalues. If all of America could buy a mirror, it could not look itself in the face.

Does God, then, have a right to judge America for what it has become? Of course He does. To say otherwise would be to deny that there is a God and that He is just. But God is also the author of mercy. Abraham knew that, or at least he sensed it. That is why he bargained for the righteous ten—if they were there—who were swimming in the sewage of Sodom.

Over the past decade or so, many Christians in America have hung on to the hope found in 2 Chronicles 7:14: "If my people, who are called by my name, will humble themselves and pray and seek my face and turn from their wicked ways, then will I hear from heaven and will forgive their sin and will heal their land."

There is a "remnant," a body of believers in God Almighty who live and work and worship and pray in the United States of America. They call upon God, some of them daily, to heal their land. God is God, so He surely hears these earnest prayers. But is God answering that prayer? Or has the judgment begun?

Polls of those leaving the voting booth in the November 2004 national election indicated that the number one issue on the minds of voters was not the war on terror, not the economy, but "moral issues." It would seem that a huge number of Americans at least have on their mind what millions of believers have been asking God to have on His mind.

That is encouraging, regardless of how one defines "moral issues." The very fact that the word *moral* is in the mix indicates that we as a nation, with all our divergent views and all our divergent "lifestyles," may not live, not quite yet anyway, in a latter-day Sodom.

So does God owe an apology to Sodom by virtue of His failure, so far, to judge America? No, and I don't believe Billy Graham thought God would ever issue an apology to Sodom, nor that He could ever owe one.

It was his way of issuing a warning, a warning that God, if He is truly God, cannot forever look away and pretend that sin is not sin. Sin has consequences. "The wages of sin is death" (Romans 6:23).

Rev. Graham's warning is not an indictment of God. It is instead an indictment of America. I concur with that indictment, and indeed things have gotten much worse since he first uttered his warning.

No one can dictate to God what He will judge and what He will destroy and what His timetable may or may not be. My favorite American patriotic anthem is "America the Beautiful." Some wish it would become our national anthem. Days after the terror strike of September 11, 2001, CBS news anchor Dan Rather sat next to that network's late-night host, David Letterman. Dan Rather had a lot on his heart. He recited from "America the Beautiful": "Thine alabaster cities gleam, undimmed by human tears." I watched as Rather began to sob. Now those words were no longer true. One of the strongest cities in our nation was bathed in tears that night, as was the entire nation.

What difference does it make to Americans of faith if its popular culture powerfully spreads the gospel that virtue is vice and vice is virtue? The difference is that some may not hear the still small voice of God above such a racket. The soul-numbing cultural cacophony coming out of America does not stop at our shores. A millstone will be tied around our nation's neck if we continue to cause little ones, here and abroad, to stumble, with the entertainment effluent that increasingly defines America to the world.

Why would anyone in a distant land believe a gospel brought by an American? Our secular gospel is so loud that it is drowning out the real gospel, both at home and abroad.

I have tried to "fight the good fight" against America's entertainment industry because I believe that my part of that fight is part of spreading the gospel of Jesus Christ. My part is no more important than any other, and I do not labor under any misconception that God needs me to bring about His plan and His ends. He can do that through any means He chooses.

But He has, I believe, graciously chosen to make me a part of His plan, and I believe just as surely that you, dear reader, are part of His plan as well. If you feel a tug to "fight the good fight" (1 Timothy 6:12), then give in to it. If you feel God calling you to do anything, especially if He's calling you to believe in Him, then for heaven's sake, do just that.

My life has been richer because He first called me to Him and then He sent me out to do something, despite my flaws. God let go of me to do what I have done, just as I let go of my son's bike so he could pedal around that block so many years ago. It has, so far, been a wonderful ride, despite the bumps.

The Lord and I both want the same for you.

APPENDICES

25 CULTURE WAR TIPS FROM THE TRENCHES

⚠️

If you want to be a culture warrior—even after reading this book—then I have some advice for you on how to do it. These tips are things I have learned along the way that, at least for me, have heightened the chances of success.

1. **Pray.** First and foremost, pray before you start a fight. You may be outraged by an example of culture rot, but you want to make sure that God is in whatever you do. This is especially true when you undertake to do battle "against the forces of spiritual wickedness" (Ephesians 6:12, NASB). This is spiritual warfare, so you want to make sure that not only is God on your side, but also that you're on His side. If it's really a worthy cause today, it will still be a worthy cause tomorrow. Pray, wait, and get a good night's sleep before you declare war.

2. **Make friends.** Find a friend whose judgment is sound and talk to that friend—a lot. Use that friend as a sounding board and heed his or her advice. I have about three of these friends who have kept me out of trouble. A friend can help you see a new perspective on a matter, especially when you become emotionally involved in an issue. True friends will tell you if the war you're about to fight is worth it or if you are really tilting at a culture war windmill.

3. **Talk to your spouse.** If you're married, tell your spouse what you intend to do, especially if it is something that has the potential of

exploding into something big. It's not fair to thrust your spouse into a fight he or she never intended to fight. Always ask yourself: *Would my spouse rather know about this* before *I do this or* after *I do this?* If there's any doubt at all, tell him or her first. If you are afraid that your spouse might squelch it, consider that to be a good indicator that you need to be transparent and up-front. Although it is often easier to get forgiveness than to get permission, permission is better. Much better. Believe me.

4. **Consider your employer.** Tell your boss if you are about to dive into the culture war. If you don't want him to know, that's also a red flag that you'll probably be in trouble at work if your fight becomes known to the public. Make sure you either have an understanding boss or no boss at all. I probably would not have been able to do much of what I have done if I were not a sole-practitioner lawyer.

5. **Remember that it's not about you.** Just because you come across something that offends you in the media, don't think it's enough to start a battle. Ask yourself if the majority of Americans would be offended if they knew about the issue. If you have a minority view on what is offensive or inappropriate or wrong, my advice would be to forget it. This is still a democracy, and that's a good thing, not a bad thing. Pick the fights in which democracy is on your side.

6. **Learn the law.** Whenever possible, when fighting a culture war battle, find a law or some legal standard that can be used to prove that what is being done is not only wrong, but also illegal. I cannot think of a single culture war battle in which I have been involved that did not include a legal standard that was being violated. Were there moral considerations involved? Absolutely. But by raising the legal standard, I was able to say with absolute certitude that this is society's standard, not mine.

7. **Pick fights you can win.** Every time you lose a battle, you give the other side a victory. Pick your spots. The great tennis player Jimmy Connors said he did not so much enjoy winning as he "hated to lose."

Culture warriors must develop that mind-set. Hate to lose. It's amazing how you can win with that attitude.

8. Be mean. What do I mean by "mean"? Simply this: Do everything in your power, legally, to defeat the other side. The time is long past for identifying that we are in a culture war. The other side has been waging it for quite some time. It is time to strike back, not with persuasion, but with weapons intended to win the fight.

9. Take the offensive. Nobody ever won an athletic competition or a war by being solely on the defensive. In football, you have to score points to win the game. For too long in this culture war, we have been trying to defend our own shrinking turf. It's time that we take it to the other side. We must hurt these people where they do their nonsense, instead of allowing them to hurt us where we live.

10. Use all your tools. Do not be afraid to use the tool of shame. Every person who is assaulting our culture has a reason to be ashamed, whether he or she realizes it or not. It may well be that by bringing an outrage to such a person's attention he or she will see it and turn away from it. You never know. At the very least, the public will be apprised that there is reason for shame. Awareness of bad publicity, which sometimes looks like shame, can be enough to turn the tide.

11. Expect the unexpected. You never know when the tide is going to turn. I have been involved in immense struggles and have come to the place where it seems that all is lost, that there is no possible chance of winning, only to see the battle won the next day. I really have found that it is darkest before the dawn so many, many times. Satan would discourage us on the brink of his defeat. We must keep hope, because God is always there.

12. Start at the top. If you are taking on a corporation for some outrage in which it is involved, find out the name of the head of the company. Write to that person directly. This raises the stakes because if the company does nothing, the blame rests solely on the person at the top rather than some underling who has no power to effect a change.

13. **Highlight corporate hypocrisy.** For example, any company that has a foundation for kids, and yet is marketing or selling pornography or other adult material to children, is suffering from corporate schizophrenia. Point out things like this.

14. **Document everything.** It always helps to videotape or photograph things that you know are inappropriate. This evidence can then be given to the media. Pictures really are worth a thousand words.

15. **Set a deadline.** Give the target of your legitimate wrath a deadline and stick to it. People don't like deadlines, which is why you need to use them. Don't ask a corporation or an entity or a person to stop doing something with no timetable. Give them one, and then tell them what you are going to do if they miss it.

16. **Use the media to your advantage.** The media are your friends, and they are your enemies. Their bias is against you. People in the media tend to be distrustful of people. They see culture warriors as threats to their freedom. But they are also driven to beat their competitors to the news punch. Sometimes that impulse trumps ideology. And besides, there *are* "normal" people in the media, too. Find those people and make friends with them.

17. **Trust no one.** Well, trust no one in the media at least. Their first loyalty is to themselves, to their news organizations, and to their biases—not necessarily in that order. Assume that anyone in the media is lying to you unless he or she proves otherwise—in actions as well as words.

18. **Love your enemies.** We need to stop our enemies from doing what they are doing, not just for the sake of their victims, but for their own sake as well. When you have that attitude, the temptation to hate gives way to love. I have found that the deeper the hatred of their sin, the more my love for them. It makes sense. If the sin in which they are

involved and with which they seek to infect others is as bad as we fear, then we must focus on that sin because it is eating away their souls. If we are Christians, we are the fortunate ones. We must always remember that and try to spread our good fortune of being children of the light.

19. **Don't be afraid to go it alone.** There is strength in numbers, and there is also peril. I have done much of what I have done on my own, not out of choice but out of necessity. Whenever I have had allies, I've found it to be a huge asset, and a comfort as well. But sometimes God calls us to walk the road alone. Jesus turned the world upside down with a small band of followers. And depending on the nature of the struggle, you may not have a single ally. Always look for help, but if it is not forthcoming, and you are certain God is in it, then do it. Sometimes the allies come after the battle begins, not before. David strode out onto the field to battle the Philistine Goliath alone.

20. **Try to fit in.** Whenever you can, don't make a point of sticking out in a crowd. If you are going to be a culture warrior, the more you can do to appear credible and well adapted to mainstream society, the better. Remember, you want to convince those in the middle that you are right. Don't create stumbling blocks for your message by appearing to be out of touch.

21. **Check the log in your own eye first.** Don't take a stand in the culture war if you have skeletons in your closet. In fact, you must make sure you have no closet at all. If you are going to take a stand against immorality, you must be beyond suspicion. Does that mean you can't be a sinner? No. We are all sinners, but be mindful that whatever public sins you have, even if you think they are hidden, they will most likely be found out.

22. **Pin your hopes on Christ, not other Christians.** If you are a Christian, don't count on your fellow believers to join you in your fight. It took me well over a year to figure out that the church is sometimes more a part of the problem than a part of the solution. Our culture has

infected the church, rather than the church acting as salt and light in the culture. In my battles, the most hurtful barbs have come from fellow believers, not from the pornographers. I would suggest that your taking a stance against culture rot makes your fellow—but possibly nominal—believers uncomfortable. They know you are right but would rather cut you down than admit their own moral blind spots.

23. **Have fun.** Nobody decreed that to be a culture warrior means that you can't have fun. However, in order to have fun, you have to enjoy a good fight. If you are a shrinking violet, don't start culture war fights. You have to be the kind of person who likes both a fair fight and an unfair fight. Maybe you have to be a little bit "off" to be the kind of person who finds joy in the battle, but what person who ever made a difference was not a little bit different?

24. **Take a break.** Battle fatigue is a reality. Jesus went to weddings and banquets, and appears to have actually enjoyed Himself during His public ministry. You need occasional breaks to keep your balance.

25. **Know your enemy and know your Leader.** Yes, there are fleshly representatives of that enemy, but the enemy in chief is Satan himself. He is brilliant and more clever than you. Beware of him and his methods. They are frightening, and they are real. That is why we are in great peril when we do this kind of ministry, and it is a ministry. It is spiritual warfare. Satan is trying to lead the precious souls in this world astray. This is life and death for him. We are in the way.

The flip side of that is that this is God's battle. We are privileged simply to be a part of it. Would I trade all the hurts and the wounds and the disasters that have come my way in exchange for the safety of not being a culture warrior in harm's way? No. No way. If I have no reason to be here, then there is no reason to be here.

The jewels we get in our crowns when we get to heaven may feel like thorns right now, but for Christians, the time will come when they'll be revealed as the precious rewards that they are.

TIME LINE OF SCHOOL SHOOTINGS

February 2, 1996
Moses Lake, Washington
Two students and one teacher killed, one other wounded, when fourteen-year-old Barry Loukaitis opened fire on his algebra class.

February 19, 1997
Bethel, Alaska
Principal and one student killed, two others wounded, by Evan Ramsey, sixteen.

October 1, 1997
Pearl, Mississippi
Two students killed and seven wounded by Luke Woodham, sixteen, who was also accused of killing his mother. He and his friends were said to be outcasts who worshipped Satan.

December 1, 1997
West Paducah, Kentucky
Three students killed, five wounded, by Michael Carneal, fourteen, as they participated in a prayer circle at Heath High School.

December 15, 1997
Stamps, Arkansas
Two students wounded. Colt Todd, fourteen, was hiding in the woods when he shot the students as they stood in the parking lot.

March 24, 1998
Jonesboro, Arkansas
Four students and one teacher killed, ten others wounded outside, as Westside Middle School emptied during a false fire alarm. Mitchell Johnson, thirteen, and Andrew Golden, eleven, shot at their classmates and teachers from the woods.

April 24, 1998

Edinboro, Pennsylvania

One teacher, John Gillette, killed, two students wounded, at a dance at James W. Parker Middle School. Andrew Wurst, fourteen, was charged.

May 19, 1998

Fayetteville, Tennessee

One student killed in the parking lot at Lincoln County High School three days before he was to graduate. The victim was dating the ex-girlfriend of his killer, eighteen-year-old honor student Jacob Davis.

May 21, 1998

Springfield, Oregon

Two students killed, twenty-two others wounded, in the cafeteria at Thurston High School by fifteen-year-old Kip Kinkel. Kinkel had been arrested and released a day earlier for bringing a gun to school. His parents were later found dead at their home.

June 15, 1998

Richmond, Virginia

One teacher and one guidance counselor wounded by a fourteen-year-old boy in the school hallway.

April 20, 1999

Littleton, Colorado

Fourteen students (including the killers) and one teacher killed, twenty-three others wounded, at Columbine High School in the nation's deadliest school shooting. Eric Harris, eighteen, and Dylan Klebold, seventeen, had plotted for a year to kill at least five hundred and blow up their school. At the end of their hour-long rampage, they turned the guns on themselves.

May 20, 1999

Conyers, Georgia

Six students injured at Heritage High School by Thomas Solomon, fifteen, who was reportedly depressed after breaking up with his girlfriend.

Nov. 19, 1999

Deming, New Mexico

Victor Cordova Jr., twelve, shot and killed Araceli Tena, thirteen, in the lobby of Deming Middle School.

Dec. 6, 1999
Fort Gibson, Oklahoma
Four students wounded as Seth Trickey, thirteen, opened fire with a 9mm semiautomatic handgun at Fort Gibson Middle School.

Feb. 29, 2000
Mount Morris Township, Michigan
Six-year-old Kayla Rolland shot dead at Buell Elementary School near Flint, Michigan. The assailant was identified as a six-year-old boy with a .32-caliber handgun.

March 10, 2000
Savannah, Georgia
Two students killed by Darrell Ingram, nineteen, while leaving a dance sponsored by Beach High School.

May 26, 2000
Lake Worth, Florida
One teacher, Barry Grunow, shot and killed at Lake Worth Middle School by Nate Brazill, thirteen, with .25-caliber semiautomatic pistol on the last day of classes.

Sept. 26, 2000
New Orleans, Louisiana
Two students wounded with the same gun during a fight at Woodson Middle School.

Jan. 17, 2001
Baltimore, Maryland
One student shot and killed in front of Lake Clifton Eastern High School.

March 5, 2001
Santee, California
Two killed, and thirteen wounded, by Charles Andrew Williams, fifteen, firing from a bathroom at Santana High School.

March 7, 2001
Williamsport, Pennsylvania
Elizabeth Catherine Bush, fourteen, wounded student Kimberly Marchese in the cafeteria of Bishop Neumann High School; she was depressed and frequently teased.

March 22, 2001
Granite Hills, California
One teacher and three students wounded by Jason Hoffman, eighteen, at Granite Hills High School. A policeman shot and wounded Hoffman.

March 30, 2001
Gary, Indiana
One student killed by Donald R. Burt, Jr., seventeen, who had been expelled from Lew Wallace High School.

November 12, 2001
Caro, Michigan
Chris Buschbacher, seventeen, took two hostages at the Caro Learning Center before killing himself.

January 15, 2002
New York, New York
A teenager wounded two students at Martin Luther King Jr. High School.

April 24, 2003
Red Lion, Pennsylvania
James Sheets, fourteen, killed principal Eugene Segro of Red Lion Area Junior High School before killing himself.

Sept. 24, 2003
Cold Spring, Minnesota
Two students are killed at Rocori High School by fifteen-year-old John Jason McLaughlin.

March 21, 2005
Red Lake, Minnesota
Jeff Weise, sixteen, killed grandfather and companion, then arrived at school where he killed a teacher, a security guard, five students, and finally himself, leaving a total of ten dead. [1]

LETTER TO HOWARD STERN

John B. Thompson, Attorney
1172 South Dixie Hwy., Suite 111
Coral Gables, Florida 33146
August 22, 2004

Dear Mr. Stern:

In two weeks I am going to address three thousand people who will be gathered in a large American city over Labor Day weekend to celebrate their faith in God. Knowing of my work against violent video games, the leaders of this event have asked me to come and address all of them regarding the American entertainment industry's assault on our children. They asked me my fee. I told them there would be no fee. I told them that being with fellow believers would be payment enough. I am not going there to be famous. I am going there to be blessed.

I want you to know that in my presentation I am going to ask all three thousand of these believers to pray for you, Howard Stern, along the following lines. Pray for Mr. Stern that he might repent and turn, of his own free will, from what he is doing to demean women, promote racial stereotypes, and assault children with pornography. We will as a group be asking God to show you, through His Holy Spirit, that what you are doing is hurtful not just to others but to your own immortal soul. As you recall, Clear Channel took you off their air in February 2004 because I sent to the company and to the FCC the following comments moments after [they were] aired on your show: "Ever bang any famous n—— chicks? What do they smell like? Watermelons?" In five seconds you were able to demean African American women to children. That is your daily trifecta.

In our prayer, we will also ask God to stop or silence you, against your will, if you do not come to your senses about the evil that you weekly [promote]. Our prayer, then, will be: Lord, show Howard Stern why he must stop. If he will not stop, then stop him Yourself.

Please know that not one of us who will be praying toward that end thinks we are in any fashion better than you. "All have sinned and fall short of the glory of God" (Romans 3:23). I have more in common, as a human being, with your nature, than I do with the nature of God. The difference between you and me appears to be that I am a sinner, I know it, and I want to do something about it. I don't call myself the "King" of anything. I am, like the apostle Paul, "chief among sinners."

My own fallen state does not stop me from being one beggar telling another beggar where to find bread. But prayer for and advice to my enemy does not prevent me from trying to stop my enemy from hurting innocents. I owe it to him, but I also owe something to them. I have fought what you do while at the same time praying for you. I could be you, and you could be me. There but for the grace of God go I.

Jesus said, "If anyone causes one of these little ones who believe in me to sin, it would be better for him to have a large millstone hung around his neck and to be drowned in the depths of the sea" (Matthew 18:6). Mr. Stern, you have tied a millstone around your own neck. It has made you famous. It has made you rich. It threatens to steal your soul. Every weekday you are mentally molesting minors for money. You are going to pay a wicked price unless you turn from it. There is always time to turn, until it is too late to turn.

You think me a fool upon reading these words, but you thought me a fool before this letter.

Which of the two of us is really the fool? You daily talk about sex as if it were dirty. That is a lie. You treat women on your programs as if they were mere objects. God gave us sex and it is beautiful, and Christian men are taught to lay down their lives for the beloved ones as Jesus laid down His life for the Church. But one does not have to be a Christian or even a person of any faith to know that men should treat women with utmost respect. You joked about your wife's miscarriage the next day on the radio. You are now divorced. Who is the fool?

God spoke the world into existence. He created the very radio frequencies over which you claim to be "King." He created you. You have been wonderfully gifted by Him with a sense of humor, a keen mind, and other abilities that are reflective of His image, whether you know it or not. You have not been a good steward of God's blessings. You have perverted what He gave you and turned it into something hurtful and selfish and criminal.

I was once like you. I had a foul mouth, and I made sport of people of faith. God reached into time and space and showed me that He loved me. If He loves me, with all my sin, then surely I can love you, and I do. I love you enough to try to stop you. It is the most loving thing I can do for you. There is no fame in that, only scorn. But His burden is light. He carried all that burden for me, and for you. Accept His gift. It is far better than His judgment that awaits.

Blessings,
Jack Thompson
Copies: Media

LETTER TO JACK THOMPSON

For every thousand hate e-mails I receive, including threats on my life, I get one of these which make all the others worth it. This keeps me going.

August 8, 2005

Mr. Thompson,
I just wanted to let you know that I appreciate what you are doing. I'm a gamer and have been a gamer since I could hold a controller in my hand. Though I debated with them when I was young, my parents were very strict about making sure that I only played games rated GA (Old Sega rating) or KA (Old ESRB rating). Now that I'm an adult, I see that they were right to be so strict regarding which games I should own. I currently own hundreds of dollars of games since it is my favorite pastime. All of them are rated E or T.

I just wanted you to know that my prayers are with you. I'm very much appalled by the direction of the gaming industry. It is due to the amount of violence and sexual themes that I do not own an XBox (I own just about every other game console). The Microsoft XBox is a game console that thrives on M-rated games. It frustrates me to see parents buy an XBox for their six-year-old. I wish more companies would look at the success of Nintendo to see that games can be fun and rated E or T. If you wish to see a "good guy" gaming company, look at Nintendo. I can't wait to get my hands on "Nintendogs" or "Mario Kart DS."

I have heard about your plans to protest the game "Bully." I personally was bullied since the third grade. I often came to school bloodied because I didn't listen to the cool music, my clothes were uncool, and I didn't fight back. Even the teachers bullied me with their words. They blamed me since it was always someone beating on me. They assumed that since I was the lowest common denominator in all these fights, I was the problem. I looked to God for hope, but often times, I wondered if it was my last day [alive]. I lived in terror of other children until I moved to [another state] when I was in the eighth grade.

When I heard about "Bully," I was angry. [From my experience], kids would imitate movies when they would beat me up. They would repeat characters' lines as they tormented me. I shudder when I imagine how much worse it is going to be for kids today who are bullied every day at school. Now bullies will get to train on their PS2 and XBox on how to make their victims' lives even worse. Please pray for these kids and help to get rid of such awful games.

I just hope that it is encouraging to know that there are gamers who are on your side.

Jason

A FINAL THOUGHT

In July 2005, I received a call from Senator Hillary Clinton, whose staffer asked me to prep her for a news conference about sexual material allegedly embedded in the hyperviolent video game from Take-Two/Rockstar *Grand Theft Auto: San Andreas*. I was happy to do so, as the targeting of kids by the video game industry is not a partisan issue.

After Senator Clinton's news conference, the Entertainment Software Ratings Board (ESRB) found that Take-Two/Rockstar (who are defendants in our Alabama wrongful death case) had in fact illegally put the hidden sex in the game and had lied about it. The U.S. House of Representatives voted 355-21 to ask the Federal Trade Commission to investigate the matter and possibly fine the game's makers for fraud.

On October 5, 2005, this same video game company was set to release *Bully*, a violent game in which the "hero" is a high school student who is bullied but who then becomes a bully "settling scores" against his classmates and teachers with physical violence.

In six and a half years we have gone from the knowledge that Columbine's Klebold and Harris were bullied and then rehearsed their revenge on the video game *Doom* to the video game industry's creation of a "Columbine simulator." In mid-July 2005 I met some Washington, D.C., kids in New York City for a protest outside Take-Two/Rockstar's corporate headquarters.

In early August 2005 I sued major retailers to stop the release of the game on the theory that it posed a public safety hazard to school children. The suit drew the attention of CNN's *Lou Dobbs Tonight* which aired a wonderful piece that expressed Mr. Dobbs's view that *Bully* is the latest example of pop culture gone mad. As this book goes to print, the fate of *Bully* is undecided.

Finally, one week after *Bully* is set to be released, Take-Two/Rockstar is set to release a hideously violent game called *The Warriors* based on the Paramount Pictures movie of the same name released in 1979. The movie was about gang warfare and spawned so much copycat gang violence that Paramount stopped advertising the movie and allowed theaters to back out of their contracts to exhibit it.

I expect *The Warriors* to lead to copycat gang violence this time around as well. "Popular culture" nowadays is increasingly popular, but it surely isn't culture.

ACKNOWLEDGMENTS

It took me eighteen years to live through the events recounted in this book. There are people who prepared me for those events as well as those who loved me through them. I want to thank them all, but space allows me to thank only the following. I express my eternal gratitude to:

My parents, John and Carolyn Thompson of Canton, Ohio, who loved me by teaching me many things, including the vast difference between being right and being popular, and my older sister, the sweetest woman I know.

My wife, Patricia Halvorson Thompson, whose incredible skills as a lawyer are surpassed only by her patience and grace toward me.

My pastor, Steve Brown, who is the most gifted preacher I have ever heard and who brought this hardened heart of mine to know the Lord Jesus Christ in 1976.

My son, John Daniel Peace Thompson, now thirteen, who has sat in too many TV studios watching Daddy be interviewed, always telling Daddy he did well even when he didn't.

My wife's family who have been ardent encouragers throughout all of this, treating me like one of their own.

My friend Mike Thompson, the brother I never had, who taught me what real perseverance is.

Lottie Hillard and Robin Reisert, two Christian counselors who taught me that any evil that targets a child must be destroyed, not persuaded.

All the Democrats and liberals with whom I have worked who have put children ahead of party and ideology.

The people of faith, some of whom I have met and some whom I have never met, who have prayed for me and asked God to deliver me out of harm's way. Their indispensable prayers have been, and continue to be, answered.

My new friends at Tyndale House Publishers, especially my talented and patient editor, Lisa Jackson, who translated this lawyer's words into plain English.

All my lawyers (you know a lawyer is in trouble when he needs one), especially Ray Reiser, who have labored to keep me out of trouble, or more often, to get me out of trouble.

All my enemies in the illicit nether regions of the entertainment industry and their allies in the legal community. The harm they intended for me God used for good.

Finally, I am thankful to Michael Powers in my fifth grade class. Everyone picked on him, including our teacher, until I stood up and asked them to stop. Michael thanked me. Michael's gratitude shaped me and thrilled me. Michael, wherever you are, thank you.

ENDNOTES

CHAPTER 1: TO THE GATES OF HELL

1. Liz Balmaseda, "Courtroom Crusader Kathy Fernandez Rundle Combines a Prosecutor's Clout with Social Activism," *The Miami Herald*, February 6, 1990.

CHAPTER 5: PROTRACTED CONFLICT

1. The current Florida statute (1003.46 Health education; instruction in acquired immune deficiency syndrome) includes the following:

   (1) Each district school board may provide instruction in acquired immune deficiency syndrome education as a specific area of health education. Such instruction may include, but is not limited to, the known modes of transmission, signs and symptoms, risk factors associated with acquired immune deficiency syndrome, and means used to control the spread of acquired immune deficiency syndrome and its prevention.

   (2) Throughout instruction in acquired immune deficiency syndrome, sexually transmitted diseases, or health education, when such instruction and course material contains instruction in human sexuality, a school shall:

   (a) Teach abstinence from sexual activity outside of marriage as the expected standard for all school-age students while teaching the benefits of monogamous heterosexual marriage.

   (b) Emphasize that abstinence from sexual activity is a certain way to avoid out-of-wedlock pregnancy, sexually transmitted diseases, including acquired immune deficiency syndrome, and other associated health problems.

(c) Teach that each student has the power to control personal behavior and encourage students to base actions on reasoning, self-esteem, and respect for others.

(d) Provide instruction and material that is appropriate for the grade and age of the student.

CHAPTER 6: LOVE YOUR ENEMIES

1. *The Untouchables*, Paramount Pictures, 1987. See http://www.imbd.com/title/tt0094226/quotes for this and other memorable quotes from the movie.

CHAPTER 7: IS THIS LAWYER INSANE?

1. Commission on Presidential Debates: September 25, 1988. Presidential Debate Transcript at http://www.debates.org/pages/trans88a.html.

CHAPTER 8: THE 2 LIVE CREW

1. This statue states:847:012 Prohibition of sale or other distribution of harmful materials to persons under 18 years of age; penalty. (1) As used in this section, "knowingly" means having the general knowledge of, reason to know, or a belief or ground for belief which warrants further inspection or inquiry of both: (a) The character and content of any material described herein which is reasonably susceptible of examination by the defendant, and (b) The age of the minor; however, an honest mistake shall constitute an excuse from liability hereunder if the defendant made a reasonable bona fide attempt to ascertain the true age of such minor. (2) It is unlawful for any person knowingly to sell, rent, or loan for monetary consideration to a minor: (a) Any picture, photography, drawing, sculpture, motion picture film, videocassette, or similar visual representation or image of a person or portion of the human body which depicts nudity or sexual content, sexual excitement, sexual battery, bestiality, or sadomasochistic abuse and which is harmful to minors, or (b) Any book, pamphlet, magazine, printed matter however reproduced, or sound recording which contains any matter defined in s. 847.001, explicit and detailed verbal descriptions or narrative accounts of sexual excitement, or sexual conduct and which is harmful to minors. (3) Any person violating any provision of this section is guilty of a felony of the third degree, punishable as provided in s. 775.082, s. 775.083, or 2. 775.084. [Bold type added by author for emphasis]. The 2005 Florida Statutes on Obscenity can be found at http://www.leg.state.fl.us/Statutes/index.cfm?App_mode=Display_Statute&URL=Ch08347 last accessed August 22, 2005.

2. Http://www.ontheissues.org has archived debates tracking where past and present presidential candidates stand on the issues.

CHAPTER 9: AS OBSCENE AS A COURT WANTS IT TO BE

1. Patrick Buchanan, *Where the Right Went Wrong*, New York: Thomas Dunne Books, 2004, quoted on back of book jacket.

2. George Will, "America's Slide Into the Sewer," *Newsweek*, July 30, 1990.

CHAPTER 10: COLONEL CAN-DO

1. Ice-T, "Cop Killer," on the album *Body Count*, Sire/London/Rhino, 1992. See http://www.darklyrics.com/b/bodycount.html last accessed August 2005.

2. Gerald Levin, "Why We Won't Withdraw 'Cop Killer,'" *Wall Street Journal*, June 24, 1992.

3. Jack Thompson, "My Day with Charlton Heston," *Washington Times*, August 16, 2002.

4. The following summary teaser ". . . a faction of Time Warner's board, led by Henry Luce III, and opera singer Beverly Sills, has entered into what amounts to open warfare against Levin's "free speech" policies, which aren't all that free: Time Warner said it supported artistic expression during the "Cop Killer" controversy, then dumped Ice-T at the first opportunity . . ." was accessed at http://www.nationarchive.com/Summaries/v260i0025_02.htm August 19, 2005 referring to an article in *The Nation*, volume 260, issue 0025, June 26, 1995.

CHAPTER 12:PADUCAH

1. Senate Commerce Committee Hearing Testimony, "Labels and Lyrics: Do Parental Advisory Stickers Inform Consumers and Parents? held on June 16, 1998. See http://www.massmic.com/testpell.html.

2. Ibid.

3. The Entertainment Software Ratings Board (ESRB) currently uses seven different ratings which are printed on virtually every video game on store shelves. The ratings are: EC: Early Childhood (Content may be suitable for ages three and older. Contains no material that parents would find inappropriate.); E: Everyone (Content may be suitable for persons ages six and older. May contain minimal cartoon, fantasy, or mild violence and/or infrequent use of mild language.); E10+: Everyone 10+ (Content may be suitable for ages ten and older. May contain more cartoon, fantasy, or mild violence, mild language, and/or suggestive themes.); T: Teen (Content may be suitable for person ages thirteen and older. May contain violent content, mild or strong language, and/or suggestive themes.); M: Mature 17+ (Content may be suitable for persons ages seventeen and older. May contain mature sexual themes and more intense violence or language.); AO: Adults Only 18+ (Content suitable only for adults. May include graphic depictions of sex and/or violence. Not intended for persons under the age of eighteen.); RP: Rating Pending (Used in advertising games that are yet to be released. This means that the game isn't finished, hasn't been officially rated yet, or both. Often game fans start discussing games long before they arrive on the market.) For more information on ESRB ratings and content descriptors see http://www.esrb.org/esrbratings_guide.asp.

CHAPTER 13: *60 MINUTES* AND MORE

1. Transcripts of Eric Harris and Dylan Klebold's, "Basement Tapes" (as well as

multiple links) can be found at http://columbine.free2host.net/quotes.html. Please note: The transcripts contain graphic language. Also see a reference to "Arlene" and *Doom* in Nancy Gibbs and Timothy Roche, "The Columbine Tapes," *Time*, December 20, 1999.

CHAPTER 14: IS IT RIGHT VERSUS LEFT OR RIGHT VERSUS WRONG?

1. Federal Trade Commission, "FTC Releases Report on the Marketing of Violent Entertainment to Children," see http://www.ftc.gov/opa/2000/09/youthviol.htm.
2. Peggy Noonan, "The Culture of Death," *Wall Street Journal*, April 22, 1999.
3. Excerpted from transcript of the presidential candidates debate, Des Moines, Iowa, December 13, 1999 last accessed August 26, 2005 and found at http://www.gwu.edu/action/primdeb/primdeb1213t.html.

CHAPTER 15: STERN STUFF

1. Jennifer C. Kerr, "FCC Fines CBS $550,000 for Janet Jackson Super Bowl Show," *The Detroit News*, September 22, 2004. Last accessed August 22, 2005, at http://www.detnews.com/2004/business/0409/22/business-281635.htm
2. Barry A. Jeckell, "CBS Apologizes, FCC Investigating Jackson's Halftime Exposure," *Billboard*, February 2, 2004. Last accessed August 30, 2005, at http://www.billboard.com/bb/daily/article_display.jsp?vnu_content_id=2081443.
3. Cosmo Macero, Jr., *Boston Herald* columnist, "Cos Blog: March 1, 2004." Accessed August 30, 2005, at http://www.cosmomacero.com/2004_03_01_cosmomacero_archive.html
4. Eric Fisher and Jennifer Harper, "FCC to Probe Super Bowl Show," *The Washington Times*, February 3, 2004, at http://washingtontimes.com/national/20040203-120720-1502r.htm last accessed August 30, 2005.
5. Jonathan Foreman, "The Howard Stern Show," *National Review*, April 7, 1997 found on http://www.looksmarttrends.com/p/articles/mi_m1282/is_n6_v49/ai_19298066 last accessed August 30, 2005.
6. CBSNews.com, "Radio Chain Bumps Howard Stern," February 26, 2004, found at http://www.cbsnews.com/stories/2004/02/26/entertainment/main602462.shtml last accessed August 30, 2005.
7. The transcript of the Notice of Apparent Liability (NAL) issued against Clear Channel Broadcasting Licenses, Inc., Citicasters Licenses, L.P., Capstar TX Limited Partnership on April 8, 2004, by the Enforcement Bureau of the Federal Communications Commission was accessed August 30, 2005, at http://www.fcc.gov/eb/broadcast/NAL.html.

CHAPTER 16: STERN'S BACK

1. Heard the week of August 16, 2004—the first week *The Howard Stern Show* was back on the air on WQAM-AM in South Florida.

CHAPTER 17: SWEET HOME ALABAMA

1. Johnny Kampis, "Life Is a 'Video Game,'" *Tuscaloosa News*, December 2, 2004.
2. NBC Television, *Law & Order: SVU*, "Game," aired February 8, 2005. Synopsis found at
   http://www.nbc.com/Law_&_Order:_Special_Victims_Unit/episode_guide/130.html

CHAPTER 18: BACK TO SCHOOL

1. In a review by Matt Keller, *PALGN: PC Gaming*, July 25, 2005 found at
   http://palgn.com.au/article.php?id=2650 last accessed August 22, 2005.
2. *Frontline* interview with Deborah Yurgulen-Todd, "Inside the Teenage Brain," in
   online version at
   http://www.pbs.org/wgbh/pages/frontline/shows/teenbrain/interviews/todd.html
3. Based on a 1999 Harvard study at McLean Pediatric Hospital/University of
   Massachusetts.
4. Report of Gallup's online poll of 519 adolescents found at
   http://www.mediafamily.org/enews/9_23_2003.shtml. Also see Reuters, "Video
   Games Linked to Aggression in Boys," August 22, 2005, accessed at
   http://www.nytmes.com/reuters/tech-media-videogames.html
5. This study was conducted by the Delta-Schoolcraft school district based in Escanaba,
   Michigan. The pilot study was in one school in the fall of 2004. The school initiated
   a curriculum which culminated in a ten-day TV/video game turnoff which resulted
   in an 80 percent reduction in violence in that school after the "detox" or cold-turkey
   period. In the spring 2005 semester, most of the district schools participated in the
   program. The majority received a statistically significant reduction in violence and
   bullying, ranging anywhere from 30 to more than 50 percent. Five schools that put
   the program in place before the state standardized tests received a 14 percent
   increase in math scores and a 12 percent increase in writing scores compared to the
   remaining seven schools without the program. This was the first district-wide
   application of the Stanford University "SMART" Curriculum, which was
   demonstrated to be effective at reducing violence in a double-blind, controlled
   experiment conducted by Stanford Medical School.
6. "Joint Statement on the Impact of Entertainment Violence on Children,"
   Congressional Public Health Summit, July 26, 2000, found August 29, 2005 at
   http://www.aap.org/advocacy/releases/jstmtevc.htm.

CHAPTER 19: SCAN

1. Malcolm Gladwell, *Blink*, New York: Little, Brown and Company, 2005.
2. Transcript of *Roper v. Simmons* found at http://straylight.law.cornell.edu/supct/html
3. Elizabeth Powell, "Studying Functional Differences in the Adolescent Brain May
   Prove Evidence that the Nervous System Is Responsible for Behavior," found at
   http://serendip.brynmawr.edu/bb/neuro/neuro04/web1/epowell.html accessed on
   August 23, 2005.

CHAPTER 20: DOES GOD OWE SODOM AN APOLOGY?

1. Dominic Basulto, "Stern Finally Gets Sirius," Tech Central Station, October 18, 2004 last accessed on August 22, 2005, at http://www.techcentralstation.com/101804G.html. See also Howard Kurtz and Frank Ahrens, "Sirius Lands a Big Dog: Howard Stern," *Washington Post*, October 7, 2004 found at http://www.washingtonpost.com/wp-dyn/articles/A10953-2004Oct6.html last accessed on August 29, 2005.

2. George Will, "America's Slide Into the Sewer," *Newsweek*, July 30, 1990.

APPENDICES

1. Timeline of school shootings accessed August 15, 2005, at http://www.infoplease.com/ipa/A0777958.html.